Charlotte Grimshaw is the author of seven critically acclaimed novels and two outstanding collections of linked short stories. As a reviewer in the *New Zealand Listener* noted: 'A swarming energy pervades every page she writes . . . her descriptive writing has always been of the highest order. Most of it would work just as well as poetry.'

She has been awarded the Buddle Findlay Sargeson Fellowship and is a winner of the BNZ Katherine Mansfield Award. Her story collection *Opportunity* was shortlisted for the Frank O'Connor International Short Story Award, and won New Zealand's premier Montana Award for Fiction, along with the Montana Medal for Fiction or Poetry. She was also Montana BPANZ Reviewer of the Year. Her story collection *Singularity* was shortlisted for the Frank O'Connor International prize and the Asia Pacific section of the Commonwealth Writers' Prize. Her novel, *The Night Book*, was a finalist in the New Zealand Post Awards. Her novel *Mazarine* was longlisted for the 2019 Ockham New Zealand Book Awards. She has won a Qantas Media Award for her columns, and was the 2018 and 2019 Voyager Media Awards Reviewer of the Year. Her bestselling novels *The Night Book* and *Soon* have been made into the TV miniseries, *The Bad Seed*.

The Mirror Book

a memoir

Charlotte Grimshaw

VINTAGE

VINTAGE

UK | USA | Canada | Ireland | Australia
India | New Zealand | South Africa | China

Vintage is an imprint of the Penguin Random House group of companies, whose addresses can be found at global.penguinrandomhouse.com.

First published by Penguin Random House New Zealand, 2021

10 9 8 7 6 5 4 3 2 1

Design by Katrina Duncan © Penguin Random House New Zealand
Cover photograph by Marti Friedlander (1993, detail), courtesy of the Gerrard and Marti Friedlander Charitable Trust
Author photograph by Jane Ussher
Prepress by Image Centre Group
Printed and bound in Australia by Griffin Press, an Accredited ISO AS/NZS 14001 Environmental Management Systems Printer

A catalogue record for this book is available from the National Library of New Zealand.

ISBN 978-0-14-377600-0
eISBN 978-0-14-377601-7

penguin.co.nz

Perhaps the best way to write is to do so as if one were already dead,
afraid of no one's reactions, answerable to no one's views.

— Nadine Gordimer

This is a memoir about a personal crisis that generated a wider family dispute. I've spent decades writing fiction, but when I was jolted off-course and wanted to discover what had gone wrong, I went looking for the true story. Almost immediately I ran into disagreements about memories, people, events — about 'reality', no less.

Disputes happen in families; they're part of life. They don't define a relationship; they don't define a family. Even in the most bitter arguments there's the bond, the shared experience and the love. Perhaps one party is wrong, or somewhat wrong, or everyone is wrong. Rifts can heal, arguments can be forgotten. In all of this though, I learned one undeniable fact: telling your story is existentially important. This is what I'm interested in recording, the destructive effect of silence, and the restorative power of narrative.

'Truth' is something else. Truth is for the reader to judge and consider, to decide, or perhaps to conclude: 'Families are complex — how can one ever really know?'

Why write this account now? I've thought about it, and my answer is that it must be more honourable to give my genuine opinion of the facts at a time when those who want to dispute it can do so.

I'm temperamentally an optimist, and I've always had a sense of hope. In this book I describe my excitement and pleasure hurrying to meet my parents in London when I hadn't seen them for a year. In this respect, nothing has changed. I haven't changed. I am still devoted to them, still only a few streets away, and as I've always told them, if they need anything, day or night, I am on my way.

ONE

When a writer is born into a family, the family is finished.
— Czeslaw Milosz

When the writer who was born into the family (and finished it) goes on to have his own family, does he keep up his truth-telling ways? Is he as cold-eyed a critic of his own handiwork?

What happens when a writer is born into the family of the writer? What does *that* do to the writer's family, to the stories the writer's family tells itself?

Does it mean the fiction of the family is finished?

I was born into a writer's family of five, my father the writer C.K. (Karl) Stead, my mother Kay, and three children: my older brother Oliver, I in the middle and my younger sister Margaret.

We called our territory 'the gully'. Our house was a modest white weatherboard bungalow built inside the curve of Tohunga Crescent, an inner-city Auckland street sloping down through overgrown sections and wooden houses to Hobson Bay — the bay, with its slow tides, its mudflats and dreamy mangroves. The Crescent was a dead end, with no through-traffic, beginning at the top near Brighton Road, where some of the houses were built on soft, erosion-prone clay cliffs and had sections that were shrinking, threatening to send whole houses off the edge, and gradually sloping in a half-circle down to the bay, where the last properties sat right at sea level, prone to tides that crept higher and higher across lawns and paths, towards front doors.

Number 37, halfway down the Crescent and just below the sharpest bend, had two gardens, front and back. In the back was the shed where Karl wrote, a plum tree that produced a large crop every year, and a lawn that had a pleasing feature: if you went to the edge of it, at a point below the stone wall, you would find you could roll up the turf, exposing a network of roots and writhing worms. Behind ours and through a giant, sagging hedge was the garden belonging to our neighbours, the Bonnys.

Parnell is a crowded, hilly suburb that used to be full of shabby rentals and railway workers' cottages, and is now gentrified. Our wider territory was Auckland, Tāmaki Makaurau, place of a thousand lovers, the sprawling city built on an isthmus between two harbours, the Waitematā and the Manukau. From the bottom of Tohunga Crescent you could look across to the Waitematā Harbour and the top of Rangitoto Island, its volcanic rim shouldering up over the horizon. We always said in Auckland you could see Rangitoto 'from everywhere'; its shape was imprinted in our minds.

Spreading out from the city centre with its collection of office blocks and modest skyscrapers, Auckland was in my childhood (and still is) mostly low-rise, a shanty town, a haphazard jumble of wooden houses, overgrown gardens and meandering streets built around the volcanic cones whose names resonate throughout Karl's poem 'Scoria':

Maungawhau, Maungakiekie, Owairaka. A city rain-lashed, scoured by tearing wind, or shimmering and still under a haze of sun, or blazing with photographic clarity under a metallic-blue autumn sky, or sunk in the steamy lethargy of summer humidity; a Pacific city, the City of Sails, an island city, the conditions so changeable it's always said, 'If you don't like the weather in Auckland, wait ten minutes.'

In Tohunga Crescent, down at the edge of the mudflat and just outside his house, Mr Balldick had tethered a large white goat that would knock you down if you didn't avoid it, and, nearby, Old Balldick had dug a shallow pit in the mud, where ducks swam when the tide filled it. Old Balldick's beautiful stand of toetoe plumes stood pure white against the sky until the drought-hit summer I was five, when a friend and I, at a loose end, set it on fire and it went up like a bomb, the crackling fronds shooting into the air.

When the fire brigade arrived and one of the kids in the gully named us as culprits, there was a brief court case at our front gate. A fireman in a silver coat and helmet found us guilty and lectured us as we hung our heads and wept. The lesson wore off quickly, though: we went right on playing with matches. We messed around with fire all the time; it was a substance to experiment with, like sand, dirt and water. We had just enough wit not to burn down the house. (I asked Kay about this; she raised an ancient memory of her cousins burning down the hen house at her family farm at Omokoroa.) I have a picture taken by the photographer Marti Friedlander when I was around two years old. If you look closely you can see in my grubby paw a box of matches.

All the houses within the Crescent had gardens, and the curve of the gully created a large area across which we roamed with no respect for territorial boundaries. There weren't many fences, but if there were, we climbed over them. We had our routes and our trails that extended through the sections, around the bay and across the properties to neighbouring streets that also sloped down to the bay. And there was the bay itself, at low tide an expanse of mud and mangrove, and at high tide a brimming stretch of water, crossed by a concrete storm-water pipe (called by everyone the sewer pipe or the Pipe) that spanned the whole bay, re-joining the land at Ōrākei, on which we could walk, play and even bike. Often we walked far out onto the mudflats to catch the eels that lay under rocks waiting for the tide to come in.

As children we had space and, when we weren't at school, complete freedom of movement. We lived in a temperate climate, we were unsupervised, we were expected to go out for the day and amuse ourselves, and so home was a place to return to, often reluctantly, to stop in at overnight, to pass through out of necessity. The older we got, the further we ranged and roamed.

Karl was a writer, a poet, novelist, literary critic and academic, and so writers came and went from our house. The poet Allen Curnow lived directly across from us on the Crescent. I remember, as a small child, meeting James K. Baxter (a lordly old hippie who sat on the floor in the upstairs room I regarded as my space; I hated him immediately, he and I glared at each other), and squirming under the mordant, beady eye of Dame Edna's alter ego, Barry Humphries. The poet Sam Hunt arrived in the gully one day, driving an old ambulance. Perhaps he had his famous dog Minstrel with him; I can't recall. I still have books and toys given to me by Frank Sargeson (especially Little Richard books and a croquet set) and warm memories of the shy, quavering, tentative Janet Frame. We visited Janet Frame's house in the South Island once, and when she opened the door she said to me, 'You're the one who always called Katherine Mansfield Kathromancefield, all one word.' She was sensitive about noise, and had piled all the furniture in her modest house around the walls, to keep out unwelcome sound. She lived in a small town; the street outside was empty, completely silent.

Recently, I re-read a short story by Frank Sargeson called 'An International Occasion', written when I was three. Set in Mrs Hinchinghorn's boarding house, it features an irascible Swede named Karl, a woman called Lottie, and Coral, Lottie's tiny 'Maori-dark' child.

After a dinner furiously cooked by Karl (he frog-marches a guest from the kitchen, lest he cause the cake in the oven to sink), Karl and Lottie retire to the bedroom, leaving Coral in the care of Lionel, the lodger who has a predilection for underage girls. One of the occupants is so outraged by this that he sets the house on fire. The story ends with tenants fleeing through the smoke, the old paedophile dragging the screaming, crying Coral by the hand.

The first time I read the story I was puzzled and slightly chilled by it. I forgot about it for years. Then one day, inexplicably, in the middle of writing, I went to the bookshelf and found it. I wondered what to make of it, with its eerily resonant characters, Karl (like my father Karl, fierce, of Swedish descent and comically tyrannical about food), the mother Lottie (my name) and her child who is (as my mother and I are) 'Maori-dark'.

I consulted *The Letters of Frank Sargeson*. He mentions the story as containing 'a kind of Last Supper followed by a kind of Crucifixion', and says that 'Lionel' was modelled on a drifter nicknamed Ponsonby Jack.

I tried to get a fix on the haze of my childhood. Were my recollections real, or had I read them in a book?

This is the strangeness of a whole life lived in fiction. It was a story by a writer friend of my writer father, some of whose characteristics are echoed in the plot. I had grown up and become a writer myself, dedicating myself to writing fiction, and one day, while writing a short story, something I was inventing had prompted me to walk to the shelf, pull out the book and go straight to this story.

What had prompted me? Which part of my mind?

'An International Occasion' is the product of hundreds of artistic choices. Writers don't live in a vacuum and are usually lawless about material; fragments of life will always be there. As the writer Janet Malcolm put it, 'This is what it is the business of the artist to do. Art is theft, art is armed robbery, art is not pleasing your mother.'

The story's allegiance is to its own internal artistic logic. If you look for reality in it, you won't succeed. And yet there it is, fixed forever, ineluctably, with its disturbingly recognisable strands, its feints and hints, its sly, slippery, elusive darkness.

For me, the question will always be there. Why those elements, why those choices?

I'd been inventing and writing stories since I was a child. When I decided to try something different, to write a true account of my life, I ran into a wall of fiction.

This was how the year began. I had been married for two decades. I was the mother of three children. I'd established a career as a writer, columnist and reviewer, and so far hadn't run short of new ideas for fiction. I was a dutiful daughter to my parents, who lived nearby, and who often called on me to look after the old house while they were away overseas. Although I'd been living in London when my first two children were small, Kay often minded our youngest child, Leo, after I and my husband Paul returned to Auckland, and looked after our three children if we needed. Outwardly we were a functional and stable extended family.

I had been loyal to my father all my life and had publicly praised and defended him when called upon. I'd always toed the line, more or less. He was still in Tohunga Crescent, still one of the country's most celebrated writers, a novelist, critic, poet and combative public intellectual who, the UK *Sunday Times* noted, 'looms like a cultural monument' in New Zealand.

Since I'd chosen, after starting a career in law, to change course and follow him into writing, I was often asked about our literary family. I always gave a standard public response, variations on *Lovely childhood, a house full of books*.

This was how it was, at the beginning of the year. And then it all fell apart.

In the course of one shocking, unexpected week my marriage seemed to have ended, and I found myself alone without a single close friend to call on. I was forced to confront the structure of my life, and for the first time I realised how strange, rigidly narrow and constricting it was. I'd spent a life avoiding people, focusing solely on the family without making any other associations, and now, outside it, I had no support at all.

At first, dealing with the immediate crisis I floundered, blundered on, tried to get through the day. But after that period of bewilderment, I started to wonder. There was something unexplained about my life, as if I'd accepted a story on blind faith, without inquiring. It felt like a crisis of faith, that I was lapsing. But lapsing from what?

There was another oddity that added to my sense of unexplained mystery: just after my marriage crisis, my mother stopped speaking to me. No more coffees, no emails, no birthday phone call, no enquiry when I mentioned a health scare and surgery.

I got a call one day from Karl, who said, 'I'll put Kay on; you and she can have a coffee.' They were about to fly out to London, and needed to talk to me about taking care of their house.

There was a silence and then the noise of the phone hitting the floor, as if he'd put it in her hand and she'd dropped it.

He came back on and said he would meet me instead, which was unusual; he didn't like cafés. When we met, I asked, 'What's going on?' He shrugged, looked evasive and said it would pass. But it didn't. The silent treatment was one of Kay's tricks or tactics; she was open about the fact that she'd once given her sister the silent treatment for four years. It was a minor, petty detail, but the timing, just as I was groping my way out of a calamity, was so notable it made questioning unavoidable. It seemed to be a clue, or a signal. There couldn't be any more blind faith.

Finally, after much witless frowning and pondering (and glazed staring and tearful drinking), I formed this solemn conclusion: there was something wrong with me. With the state of my social connections.

So, what to do about that?

My mind kept drifting back: back to Tohunga Crescent. Could my problems have begun in the past? Whatever it was that had caused my mind to grow into an unusual shape — one that was resistant to change and so restricting — must surely have happened long ago. It seemed logical: this state of affairs could only be explained by looking back.

My search for answers to this question — how did I end up so alone? — was not about self-pity. The drive was journalistic. It was a mystery. It began to be about writing, too. Writing was what I did and I wasn't much good at anything else; I did it compulsively, and so it was inevitable I would try to record this disastrous turn, either in novels or short stories or essays. Most of all, I was trying to save myself. It had been brutally demonstrated to me what it meant to feel completely abandoned. If I could learn to change, perhaps I could find my way to belonging.

Looking for clues in the past: this was where I started running into trouble. Trouble with my literary family, who were resistant to my questions.

'If you want to understand psychology read the Russian novels.' A psychologist told me this. I thought about it. Successful novels, the ones that work and endure, have to be informed by psychological accuracy. A squeamish refusal to confront messy human truths is not going to result in complex fiction. This then was part of the mystery: how had I emerged from a literary family — a family that should theoretically have embraced, *relished*, the rich details of human life — with the sense that my own narrative history was poorly defined, shallowly rendered, strangely bowdlerised and obscured?

The chronological details were clear, but the emotional elements, truths about the family dynamic, 'how it was, how it felt, what we were like' were not only unclear but also, it seemed, the more I tried to find out and discuss and explore, off-limits. Forbidden.

Paul and I eventually reunited, but everything had changed. Like some slow, defensive creature, I'd spent years building layers of protection around myself: marriage, children, work, a whole new self.

Now they had been ripped away, leaving me as raw and exposed as I'd been at the end of my young adulthood.

Everything had unravelled, the security was gone, and I was so wildly unnerved that the ensuing conflict threatened to wreck the marriage all over again. Any hint of a new threat, any reminder of Paul's sudden defection, sent me into desolation and pain. When conflict arose, I felt I was reaching out and catching nothing. To have the sense of being completely alone, as if spinning in space, was an intensely terrible and bleak experience.

So, the past. Previously, whenever asked, I'd sketched my experience of the literary family in a way that was positive and superficial, without consulting my memory. I'd spent my young life watching interactions, noticing what was hidden, what was subtext. But I'd sublimated and generalised the information, transforming it into fiction, acceptably disguised and stylised.

The family's response to experiences had always been: It's material. Go and write a story about it.

But there were designated roles in the family, and one didn't criticise, or step outside the official boundaries. It wasn't contemplated that one would *change*.

There was the rigidity of roles and there was a problem you could call generational, a clash between my parents' code, which was dominated by front and face, and the current fashion for 'openness', for talking about ourselves, for sharing, and casting off shame.

Now, firmly discouraged from looking back, I started searching my memories in earnest. The past is a foreign country. They do things differently there. What was it like?

The questioning gained its own momentum. It felt urgent and vital; I was trying to save myself. I had started an uprising in my own mind, and I wanted to write about it. I got preoccupied with the idea of a family living according to a repressive narrative that denies individuals their own truth.

Perhaps it wasn't surprising that at this time I also grew fascinated with Donald Trump: wannabe autocrat, patriarch, pathological demagogue who sees people as objects, who ruthlessly exiles anyone who stops flattering him, who rejects women who look too old, too real or too powerful. Who can't tolerate dissent, and rules through splitting, conflict and division.

We'd entered the era of 'fake news', of 'post truth', and I wanted to question the record. Within the literary family, I'd done my duty and I'd been very good. I was a practised operator; I knew how to play the right notes, to be agreeable, dutiful and kind. There was nothing wrong, per se, with any of that, but now there was this sense I couldn't get rid of — of lapsing.

It was strange, to find what would and wouldn't be tolerated. If I expressed my true self it wasn't welcome, nor was it even really seen. The traffic was all one-way.

There were other mysteries. It had been understood that compared to my mother and sister I was paralysed by social uncertainty, and that this would always be the case. And it was jokily acknowledged by my sister and me that our mother had no feeling for me at all. I remember Margaret pausing in some conversation and saying, matter-of-factly, 'If Mum had to choose, it'd be you she'd throw off a cliff.' We both nodded and moved on, barely thinking about it. It was a fact like the weather, unarguable.

Margaret also said, accurately I thought, referring to a significant point in our childhood, 'Everything had turned to shit, and I was her baby.'

It was those banal, mundane life events that changed everything for me. My marriage blew up, I found myself alone, and in the aftermath I lost some family support. And suddenly, for the first time, I wanted more: I wanted to understand.

I entered territory unthinkable in my literary family. I consulted a psychiatrist and then a clinical psychologist. And I went to the literature — not fiction, not the Russian novels, but books and articles on psychology.

This was what struck me: the infinite variety of human behaviour, and its sameness. That a disorder will produce recognisable modes of thinking and action. That a mental illness manifests with symptoms as identifiable as those of a physical disorder. That mind and body are one, and all is reaction.

That we are all animals, displaying our animal behaviour. We are unpredictable, but so much more predictable than we think.

As Trump was being diagnosed a narcissist and everyone was becoming familiar with terms like gaslighting (Trump is gaslighting the American people!), I was poring over the ways narcissism manifests itself.

My understanding of the texts was variable and imperfect, but I'd got hooked on the material and on trying to understand. It was a revelation, a fascinating ride into human complexity.

Kay had always specifically warned me off counsellors (they were frauds, sinister creeps), and she and Karl took a fairly dim view of psychiatry. When she heard I'd seen a psychologist she referred grimly to 'Freud'. They'll be talking *all that Freud*. Their friend Janet Frame had spent years in mental institutions, and had just avoided being lobotomised, and they had in mind the infamous cases of satanic ritual allegations, dubious recovered memory cases, all that.

At a dinner at Tohunga Crescent, the subject came up, when one of Kay and Karl's friends, the poet Kevin Ireland, said he'd had such a terrible childhood he'd been happy ever since. The only way was up. I found this entirely persuasive; Kevin was a cheerful guy, and great company. He was dismissive, though, of those who consult psychiatrists.

He said, 'They seize on this stuff about it being their parents' fault because they want an excuse for their fucked-up lives.'

Fault, excuse.

This was, I thought (to myself), underrating psychology as a science (it's all babble and mumbo jumbo) and was also the crux of the generational clash. I'd got interested in finding out what was wrong with me, to try to cure it and also, if anything had been 'caused by my parents', to understand it and not pass it on in my own family.

It seemed likely that a person's life was affected by upbringing, by environment. But surely 'blame and fault' were as irrelevant as 'excuse'. I thought it was a given that if you'd been, as per Philip Larkin, fucked up by your mum and dad, your mum and dad had in turn been fucked up by theirs. It seemed to me the code of blame and shame my parents' generation operated on prevented understanding and perpetuated problems. If anything went wrong they had to suppress it, move on, pretend it didn't happen — and go on messing things up.

For Kay and Karl, because of the Sixties, there was a narrative about children turning on their parents — actually turning on them — not out of anything to do with the dynamic between them, but out of rebellion. They'd hated their parents' conservatism and ignorance, and now their own kids would probably turn on them, and what could they do? It was inevitable. I found this rather a grim view of family.

I was interested in free will.

There's a story in my collection *Opportunity* called 'Free Will', about the degree of control we really have. It seemed to me there wasn't much room for free will — but there *was* room.

I thought the way to disrupt the baleful maxim in Auden's poem 'September 1, 1939', that those on the receiving end of evil do evil in return, was to acknowledge the evil, understand it and do something different. There seemed to me something oddly powerless about my parents' acceptance of the state of things: genes, fate, the unalterable. Things were the way they were. What could you do except, if necessary, lie?

It was clear, though, we didn't go in for 'sharing.' We didn't do any kind of introspection, or looking behind the façade. We polished the façade; if it looked tarnished we buffed it up a little more.

I was aware of, I felt, the feminist outrage at Trump, whose presidency was the spectacle of misogyny that supercharged the Me Too movement. Kay had always rejected feminism (the wimmin, she derisively called them). I'd been somewhat influenced by my family's take, but was increasingly less so. Now I felt mostly opposed to their stance.

As the writer Suzanne Moore noted in *The Guardian*, this was a time when old male French intellectuals were complaining about climate campaigner Greta Thunberg because she wasn't 'sexy' enough. When I forwarded him Suzanne Moore's column, Karl, unimpressed, sent me a bristling email that said something to the effect of: 'Let's be serious intellectuals, not fashionable whingers on behalf of "my gender".'

Enough of that, I thought.

Had I grown up in a sexist environment? Was this linked to my lack of confidence and social connection? It seemed to me comically evident: Karl sure hated a bossy woman.

But if I'd grown up in a 'sexist environment', I had to re-examine my own record. Misogyny, you could speculate, might be caused by early experience: being fucked up — Larkin again — by your mum and dad. Was there a hint of misogyny in my own writing? Was I a person who, because of experience, had regarded women as opaque and impenetrable, terrifyingly bitchy and way too fond of shopping?

Had I written sceptically on some women's issues because of this? This was the terror and the comedy of interrogating the past: it wasn't about blaming someone else for my fucked-up life, it was about reassembling something out of a mental structure that had been hit by an earthquake, much of it in ruins, the rest teetering on the brink of collapse.

At that dinner at Tohunga Crescent when psychiatry was panned, I had another (again private) thought: was it too presumptuous, too outrageous a proposition (yes it was) that if Karl and Kay had given themselves a break from front and face, if they'd relaxed their uncompromising insistence on a rigid narrative, they could have been easier on themselves, more humane towards everyone including themselves, and allowed toxic shame to evaporate into the air?

I was changing and I felt the force of my literary family's reaction: their dismay, incomprehension, occasional anger. I had become alien, charmless and, worst of all, a feminist. My quest to find out what was wrong with me could be cast as brutal within the family. I'd become some grim inquisitor, bent on exposing sensitive secrets and causing hurt. They accused me of humourlessness, of being in thrall to bogus shrinks. They urged me to come to my senses.

Karl lamented, 'Where is the girl who had such a clear sense of reality and its boundaries and such a marvellous sense of humour — replaced by this scolding (as it seems to me) fantasist?'

It was no use replying that I hadn't gone anywhere. It was just that I'd broken loose. I'd got fixed on the idea of finding out.

But I would come back to that rhetorical question of his. *Where is the girl who . . . ?* It was the sentence that roused up the writer in me, and made me think that no matter where it led me, or what trouble I got into, I would formulate some kind of response.

This was the father I'd sometimes told when growing up, *'You are my favourite person in the world.'* From the time I was very young, we understood each other's jokes. We played verbal games. I made him laugh; we made each other laugh. When I read his poetry, I could hear a tone in it I identified as an iron quality, marvellous and uniquely his. I loved his long poems, 'Scoria', 'Quesada'. The language excited me, as did his vivid evocation of light and landscape and weather. I loved the wit of his Catullus poems.

I adored his sense of humour, his take on reality (always bracing, cogent, original, rigorous) and his fantasies, the stories he made up, the stories we invented together.

But now. Now I wanted to talk about our real lives, to stop repeating the accepted lines and ask a few questions, this was too much. It was too much reality and light.

Everything changed. We got into disputes.

He issued denials, usually by email. The memories I had weren't real. He kept using the word 'scolding'. Elsewhere he accused me of 'always using the same birdcall'. He called me 'unworthy'. He wrote smooth, patronising emails that might have been directed at the world (if so, his archived letters would form a record) and also at whoever I'd been consulting. He affected 'puzzlement'. He wrote more in sorrow than in anger; he denied my perceptions were real.

Just as I could hear the iron quality in his poems, now I could hear the new tone in emails that were conveyed with a sideways glance, a commentary intended for a wider audience.

Where is the girl who had such a clear sense of reality and its boundaries . . . ?

Was it likely, I asked him, that I would suddenly become a 'fantasist'? I recalled Trump's Orwellian instruction to the American people: 'Just remember, what you're seeing and what you're reading is not real.'

At times there would be a flash of steel, cold anger. He wrote that everything in the family's past had been perfect, or nearly so, and my memories were wrong.

The more I began to question, the more I was bewildered by the obfuscations this provoked.

He turned up at my door on my birthday with a present for me and the words 'Kay sends her love'. Kay was a few streets away, in good health, and had not communicated in any way, but a day later, when I remarked in passing, 'She doesn't speak to me; for example, she never said a word to me on my birthday', he told me, 'That's not true. She speaks to you *all the time*.'

After I mentioned to Kay, while dropping them as requested at the airport, that I'd had a needle biopsy for a suspicious lump in my neck and that this was frightening, I didn't hear from her about it again, and never had an exchange with her about the subsequent surgery. I offered this as evidence of her silent treatment, and Karl said, 'That's not true. She speaks to you *all the time*.'

One day he sent me a passage from his third volume of autobiography that referred in passing to a woman with whom he'd had an affair. I'd met her, and the affair was common knowledge in the family at the time. I mentioned it, and he said, 'I didn't have an affair with her.' When I disputed this, he insisted, 'You're wrong. You get these things wrong *all the time*.'

(I checked this one with Kay, who burst out spontaneously, 'What? *Of course* he had an affair with her!')

It was baffling. None of it seemed necessary. It had an effect; not that I doubted my perception, but I was exhausted and undermined. It was demoralising. My memory would be denied, and I would be given to understand that I was being destructive. If I insisted on a particular fact the tone would change; now my behaviour was causing concern.

It was possible I'd gone mad.

When Karl was made New Zealand Poet Laureate, I wrote a diary piece in *The Spinoff* about the family trip to a marae, part of the official celebration. The account was warm and affectionate, but it mentioned my new thinking.

> *Family rules. I'd been re-reading Volume Five of Karl Ove Knausgaard's* My Struggle. *Savage family truths were the new black — I'd been finding that aspect of Knausgaard's saga exhilarating. All families must have their own ways of keeping the peace. I thought about the rules in my whānau of origin, the way some things were*

> *deemed unsayable: nothing too terrible, no really ghastly skeletons, just small truths and pathologies that were firmly shut down* in the interests of harmony *if one tried to discuss them. But did in the interests of harmony really mean in the interests of* soothing someone's ego? *I used to respect the no-go areas, like a loyal party member. These days, I felt like going there. Talking is important, especially if it helps people. Not talking is destructive, if it denies need. And who decided what we could and couldn't talk about, when it came to our very own lives?*

During the marae ceremony, Oliver performed a loud Māori chant. I didn't altogether like its histrionic volume and intensity, and mentioned this to Margaret. She had reacted negatively when I'd confided I was trying to help myself by seeing a psychologist; perhaps she foresaw disloyalty to our family.

Now she told me, 'It wasn't a chant, it was a beautiful song. The only reason you don't know that is because you have a tin ear.'

This really struck me. I'm not musical, as our brother is. But I don't have a tin ear, and can easily distinguish a loud, flat shout from a beautiful song — as can my sister. It seemed she had latched on, as if by instinct, to the current mode: a firm assertion that what I had perceived was *not real*. I didn't hold this against her particularly; it seemed almost unthinking. I'd been just as quick myself with required responses, prior to my 'lapse'.

The more outrageous the denial — the sky is not blue — the more undermining it was. It induced a feeling of helplessness.

These family oddities are minor personal mysteries, but I started to wonder why I'd met such a determined resistance. If there was an accepted family story, why was this so, and why was it 'enforced'?

Was there a clue in any of this to my current difficulties?

It was an irony that when Karl wrote me emails about Kay, denying that my memories and perceptions were real, the only person apart from me who would pick up the false notes would be her.

He urged me to show his emails to whatever psychologist I'd been seeing. 'If you're courageous you'll show them . . .', he wrote in one particularly patronising and (as it seemed to me) fantastically disingenuous message.

I replied angrily, 'You have no idea how courageous I've had to be.'

He flew into a rage and used the word 'violins' to describe the way I talked about my children.

'Telling your story is existentially important.'

In his autobiography, *You Have a Lot to Lose*, Karl wrote of our family, Kay and Karl and three kids:

> *There was a minimum of piety among us, tears but not too many, shouting but not too much, some songs, some recitations from memory, and endless jokes.*

I wanted to ask about this. Why was a minimum of piety important? What were the pieties ruled out in favour of endless jokes? How much would be too much shouting, how many tears would be too many?

How did we, such an intense little group of people, manage to stay perfectly within this set of parameters?

How did we manage to be so well behaved, so controlled?

In order to understand, I consulted a psychologist who made a statement that would spell trouble, if only I'd known it at the time.

She said: 'Telling your story is existentially important.'

Implicit in this was the understanding that the story it was existentially important to tell needed to be true. Not a fictional story, but the real one. What actually happened, what it was really like.

So why question Karl's description of our family? There's nothing wrong with it. It says: We were a lovely family, everything was just right, within the right boundaries. Not too many, not too much. We each tell our own stories. That's his.

But if, for each of us, telling our story is existentially important, I wanted to tell my own.

One problem was, where they intersected — which wasn't often since he didn't write much about the family — our versions somewhat clashed.

But there was something else too, if you looked at the implication of what he'd written. It ruled out 'excess'. Not too many, not too much. It ruled out heaviness: there could only be songs and endless jokes. There could be a minimum of piety. Pieties are associated with a moral code, with obligations, responsibilities, duties of care.

What family operates without excess, without mess, without spilling over the borders? What family is too cool for pieties?

He's remembering us as children. Were we really those cool little customers, willing to march forever on a diet of endless jokes, songs, the bracing intellectual rigour of no pieties?

Was there a point at which the disapproval of piety (Meaning what? No sentimentality, no false reverence. Only honesty, wittiness, toughness) became a piety in itself, one that repressed and outlawed the normal human need for love, kindness, caring, safety?

And what happens when a group of individuals who are temperamentally intense, emotional, energetic, tending (some of them) to histrionics, capable of strong feeling, insecurity, rage, love and hate, come up against this almost frantically controlling force (furiously intense itself) that insists on *not too many, not too much?*

You don't get the harmonious little band of travellers he describes. You get chaos. You get clashes. You get needs denied. You get the messy reality of family life — and much more.

But then there was this.

In *You Have a Lot to Lose*, Karl wrote revealingly of the inner peace that came with writing a good poem:

> *I recognised that there was probably something neurotic about this. One wanted to control the world and make it more orderly and beautiful than reality could ever be, so one created a world of one's own, and controlled that.*

If a poet, a father, wanted to describe his family in a way that idealised them, if he made the story more controlled and beautiful than reality, would it be a bad thing, an act of betrayal, to contradict him?

If he made the family into a poem, would it be monstrous to tear the poem up?

Or was he inviting contradiction by controlling the material, altering the reality, rendering us as fiction?

If I told my own story, would I hurt the people I loved? Or would they stay safe within their own reality, comfortably sure I was crazy, and making it all up?

This was the family tragedy: if we couldn't see each other, we were lost. If we couldn't share a common reality, we were lost.

I wanted to tell the real story so what did I do? I went to the default style of the family; I turned my preoccupations into fiction. I was still gathering ideas; I didn't have the nerve to write a true story down. I started writing my novel *Mazarine* when Donald Trump's relationship with Russia wasn't yet big news. It must have been in the air, though, in the collective consciousness. In London, acting on some odd impulse, I went to West Hampstead Station where a man had died falling in front of a train. The man, it turned out, was a barrister who'd at one time acted for Julian Assange. That day, I knew I had the subject of my novel.

Fake news was about to be the story of the time, and to me it seemed personally relevant. Stories were out of fashion; we were all about the truth. But how real is selfie literature? We were publishing our 'real' lives on Facebook and Instagram, but we were curating, editorialising (only flattering photos, please.) We were 'talking openly' on Twitter, but who doesn't self-edit when the whole world can read the words?

In the era of autobiography, we were already slyly adept at false narrative. Our concept of privacy eroded, we'd honed our skills at airbrushing. Unchained from conventional notions of veracity and invention, we were primed for the era of Trump. It wasn't fiction versus truth anymore, it was my version of reality versus yours. Trump's message was straight from the Soviet playbook inherited by Putin: the 'mainstream' media is false; the only source of truth is Trump. Soon we'd be assailed by the phenomenon he pretended to rail against: disinformation.

I decided to write a novel about a family that was secretly dysfunctional and controlled by false narrative. I was seized with the idea of truth-seeking, but, true to form, paradoxically (and never one to follow literary fashion) I was turning my ideas into a plot-driven story.

I was travelling and Trump was everywhere, sexist, aggressive and so narcissistic he could remark, while musing weirdly over her 'voluptuous' figure, 'If Ivanka weren't my daughter, perhaps I'd be dating her.' I watched him flanked by his compliant, plastic women and felt a force growing in my mind.

I'd written pieces about Karl Ove Knausgaard and Elena Ferrante, whose books I admired, and about novelists' abandonment of plot in favour of selfie fiction.

Wanting to write obliquely about the Time, I invented a family ruled by a subtle tyranny, whose false narrative preserved the status quo. In this group, you were either an acolyte or you were fired. To live in this way meant that you, your true self, wasn't permitted to exist.

Mazarine was all about not being allowed to be selfie. About false narrative. Loss of the self. The fragmented self. Authoritarian rule.

I watched CNN footage of weird, repressive, authoritarian men: Trump, Putin, Xi Jinping, Kim Jong-un. The posturing. The bizarre hairstyles, the violence and cruelty.

I found an old paperback: *People of the Lie* by psychiatrist M. Scott Peck. I skated over his Christianity, but he had some interesting ideas. In one essay he drew a line of narcissism, from lack of empathy in families (with hair-raising examples of covert parental cruelty) all the way to atrocity on a grand scale.

Writing plot-driven fiction, writing *Mazarine*, I was reaching for the universal; I wanted to mirror the Time. A global experience: ruled by a narcissist, gaslighted when we protested, bamboozled by false narrative and confused by fake news.

I thought, if fiction is the lie through which we tell the truth, then fiction could trump real lies. All the time I was travelling, I was following the line of my story, trying to define my true self.

The further away I went, I hoped, the closer I was getting to home.

I decided the principal characters of *Mazarine* would be women, even though I knew this could turn off male readers and reviewers. It's the story of a woman whose upbringing has rendered her socially paralysed, and who only belatedly learns to communicate with women by falling in love with one.

It seemed consistent to me that a novel about a woman's quest to understand herself and her dysfunctional family could also involve a search for meaning in the era of Trump.

Mazarine's action widens to include the covert Russian interference in the 2016 US elections that brought Trump to power.

I was interested in the idea that Trump's narcissism had infected his followers, translating itself into nationalism, which you could describe as a collective manifestation of his own pathology.

In a review of Karl Ove Knausgaard's *The End*, which includes his essay on Hitler, I expanded on the idea. I wrote:

> *Here is Knausgaard on Hitler's uncanny ability to mesmerise the German people:*
>
> > That his appeal should be so vast . . . seems unfathomable to us today; we read the arguments and the perils are plain to us, the idiocy, the sheer contempt for fellow human beings, yet it was not by arguments he won over the people, but by the very abyss that ran through his soul, or by what it generated within him, for what he thereby expressed, his inner chaos and his yearning for that chaos to stop, were curiously congruent with society's inner chaos and its yearning for that chaos to stop.
>
> *You could say that Knausgaard is delving into Hitler's pathology here, territory that inevitably, in 2018, brings Donald Trump to mind. The essay has a quality of universality: it leads you to extrapolate to the present. Using its ideas as a starting point you could speculate now, for argument's sake, that the Fuhrer's was the same pathological narcissism as has been diagnosed in Trump (see* The Dangerous Case of Donald Trump, *in which 27 psychiatrists and mental health professionals diagnose the current President): an inability to empathise, a need to externalise inner chaos and to live by divide and rule, a compulsion to categorise certain types as 'other', in Hitler's case the Jews, in Trump's case immigrants and the migrant caravan.*

Further extrapolating, and keeping in mind Trump's recent assertion, 'I am a nationalist', you could argue that by externalising his inner chaos, the narcissistic demagogue manages to infect the whole nation with his own pathology, that the resulting collective narcissism can be called nationalism, and that nationalism, following the same course as individual narcissism, seeks out an 'other' to subjugate, to denigrate, and ultimately, potentially, to kill . . .

An editor who read some chapters of *Mazarine* described it as a 'women's book'. I assumed he meant too domestic, insufficiently large in its scope. I wondered how it could be a 'women's book', yet concern itself with Russian election meddling. But perhaps, to be fair, he didn't want to read about autocracy or tyranny or corruption in microcosm, in the minutiae of personal relationships. He didn't want to be bothering with the representative when literary fashion and the market demanded something else: the big canvas — or what critic James Wood amusingly calls Hysterical Realism.

Of the big, contemporary novel, Wood wrote in *Serious Noticing*:

It has become customary to read seven-hundred-page novels, to spend hours within a fictional world, without experiencing anything really affecting or beautiful.

Wood identified the problem with the contemporary 'big ambitious novel':

An excess of story-telling has become the contemporary way of shrouding, in majesty, a lack; it is the Sun King principle. That lack is the human.

I agreed with Wood on this. *That lack is the human.*

A sprawling literary novel on the State of the World, a De Lillo or a late Rushdie, say, was always brilliantly entertaining, but you wouldn't rush to read it twice. It seemed to me that psychology was the link between the portrait on Jane Austen's 'little bit (two inches) of ivory' and the big picture, that the infinitely subtle interplay of human relationships was the basis for everything, from love and hate to politics and mass movements, that a story of a small group of humans wasn't necessarily trivial (a women's book) if it was psychologically accurate; in fact it could better represent the world than a big-canvas novel that went in for all kinds of pyrotechnics but neglected character and lacked the human.

I was working and outwardly all was well, but I needed help and I had a proposal for my literary family: let's talk. Let's have a Truth and Reconciliation Commission. I had an idea, The New Frankness. Naïvely, I thought they would help me find out what had gone wrong with me, so I could better connect with the world. But the answer came back: No thanks! Stick to fiction, please!

When I tried to discuss the past, we got locked into a trap, a kind of reflex black-and-white thinking. If they insisted everything had been perfect, I would respond with denial. No, it wasn't!

Of course, black-and-white thinking (a psychological phenomenon I'd read up on) got us nowhere. In our exchanges, their insistence on airbrushing (we were *one hundred per cent* the *best* family, the most *perfect* family) earned them a wave of resistance, a rude bucket of shit over the picture, making the image no clearer. In fact, nothing is black and white, no story is uncomplicated, and there was a great deal of good in the story along with the bad.

Subtleties got lost in the back and forth.

Arguments about what was and wasn't 'real' left me feeling demoralised and guilty, yet at the same time I wasn't going back to my old role.

In a rare email exchange with Kay, I wrote, 'Our lives matter. They matter.' I meant the lives of her children. I thought about this. Strange to make that plea to a mother.

I wanted to write about all of it: the black-and-white thinking, the suppression, the resistance, the subtleties. The issues of the Time, and of my time.

I'd been trained to be the writer who was now disturbing the family peace. It's material, my parents would say. Go and write a story about it. Art before all, would be Karl's response when criticised for using autobiographical material in one of his own novels.

These were the questions I was trying to understand. Why was my literary family resisting my attempts to help myself, save myself even, by solving puzzles that affected me?

Why had I spent a whole adult life avoiding close contact with women? Why were my perceptions denied, and why did my family call my memories fantasies?

I read in an online journal article on trauma and personality disorders by Professor Peter Fonagy and others:

> *[An] adverse event becomes traumatic in its aftermath when it is accompanied by a sense that one is not accompanied — that one's mental experience is not shared and the 'mind is alone.' Trauma obtains from a primitive, adaptive human terror of isolation.*

I experienced that primitive terror of isolation after my marriage seemed to break down. And this was the revelation that undid everything: I recognised the feeling. I remembered it. It wasn't new. I had experienced the terror before *when I was growing up*.

This was the beginning of my years of questioning.

I was at home working on a novel when the phone rang. A voice, whispering.

'Do you know your husband's carrying on with another woman?'

I listened. A dog barking in the distance, the skittering of birds on the iron roof. A pause, a beat of time. I didn't understand. Carrying on?

'Who is this?' I asked. My voice sounded thin and high, faintly outraged.

There was a gulp, perhaps the rattle of ice in a glass.

'The bastards,' she said, vague, fading in and out; drunk or mad, I thought.

Eventually she gave a name I didn't recognise, and after much sighing elaborated: she was the wife of one of my husband's colleagues, some Gav or Kev or Keith. She rambled on, conveying, or trying to it seemed, solidarity. So unfair. We women have to. The wife's always the last to.

She stopped mid-sentence, letting out a hiccup of alarm, as if someone, perhaps Kev or Keith, was about to catch her drinking in the day. She put down the phone and I listened to the sound of the suburbs. A car droning up Portland Road, the whine of a hedge trimmer, the noisy dog next door hurling himself at the gate as the postman went by.

I went out for a run. The information was strange, distant, disconnected. I ran a 5-kilometre circuit of the neighbourhood, noting the ordinariness of the scene. Cars drove, leaves shivered in the breeze, the rain clouds banked themselves across the sky. Back home I showered, changed, flexed my fingers and emailed Paul, using the woman's quaint formulation: Are you carrying on with another woman?

The answer came back, surprisingly dramatic for him: I've done a bad thing.

I stared at the screen. A bad thing. Somewhere near, sensation was approaching, but I felt nothing.

Sudden squall of rain against the window. A seagull letting out a series of melancholy screams. The dog's paws, clicking as he paces on the deck below my window.

He came home and didn't deny it. He confirmed it, not looking at me. I was outside myself, stuck at a distance while some other, the wronged wife, went about the business of reacting. This self that shouted at him, threw things, watched him walking away down the stairs, clawed at by wild disbelief. Was it me?

A couple of times that week he came back; there were more rows. I threw him out, never wanting to see him again, hoping and assuming he would return. I hurled three coffee mugs, reckless about the damage they could cause. He sat without moving as the cups smashed on the wall and I was stunned by his cool stillness, the nerve of it, as if he'd wound himself to such a pitch of bravado he was impervious.

After a few days of turmoil and crisis, he texted: he was leaving me. At moments I would marvel over this fact, the exotic outrageousness of it: after 20 years of marriage I was dumped *by text*. He stopped communicating, so I didn't know where he was, nor when he would surface, which he did at unexpected moments, asking to see our youngest, Leo. Our other two kids were old enough to be avoiding him, showing their disapproval.

I emailed him, remonstrating, sending the message to his work address. I stopped short of storming into his office, making a scene — or hunting down and shouting at his girlfriend. Some instinct told me that attacking her would only make things worse, push them together — their bond strengthening as they bandaged each other's claw marks and scratches, et cetera.

Karl said because of my marriage crisis he and Kay would not go to Europe as usual, but instead would stay in Auckland for a time to help me out. I was deeply grateful, touched by his kindness.

On the side of a muddy football pitch Paul and I watched Leo play with his team. After the game Paul walked away from me across the field. The grief was so strong it bent me sideways.

I learned that his girlfriend was glamorous, and younger. I recalled myself at that age; she would be ruthless and self-centred; for me she would have no mercy. I'd once had a crush on an older married man, and I'd never even considered his wife except as an obstacle. This pitiless force had entered and I felt the nearness of the cold universe, all that was haphazard, morally neutral. I'd thought myself loved, valued and safe. The security I'd gathered around myself had been torn away.

I thought: we are all animals.

It was hard to take it in; he really had left. We'd had three children together, we'd been each other's sole companion and friend for over 20 years, and in all that time we'd spent no more than short periods apart when I'd gone to London to publish a book. We never went away without each other, not for a weekend or even a night. There'd been no warning signs, no increase in fights, no spending more time with friends than together. We were it, the unit, us and the kids. He'd vanished so abruptly I was left in shock, as if at a sudden death, and the shock was combined with something deeper and worse: existential despair. I realised how alone I was.

I took stock. I had male friends I got on well with. There were friends Paul and I spent time with, couples. But there was a terrible gap: I had no close women friends with whom to share this catastrophe. I hadn't had a woman friend since high school, had avoided women and had never allowed one to get close. This hadn't seemed a problem before. Now I confronted my loneliness, and I saw it was a disaster. I'd seen the comfort and pleasure my sister got from her women friends, and wondered why she'd been able to have that while I'd made a spartan virtue of forgoing it. I'd avoided women so consistently I didn't know how to find friends. Women spoke a foreign language. I could neither read their signals nor feel certain I was using the right words.

In the first few days after he left I kept the house in order, looked after the children, and tried to keep working, but in the weekends, when free time stretched ahead and I had no friends to distract me or to confide in, I was gripped with a secret impulse so powerful I had to obey it: Paul was lost, and so I had to find him.

As soon as Leo was safely busy with friends or sports I went out looking, walking the city streets all day, a strange, irrational search. It was instinctive, primitive, impossible to resist. (It was a very secret craziness; I would never have told the kids what I was doing.) I had no idea what I would do if I found him, and I never did. Auckland is a big city, and I had no clue in what part of it he might be. After a few days, I stopped doing it.

One morning I took Leo to the café where I'd usually gone with Paul.

With the kids Paul had always been endlessly patient, kind, solid, a real security figure, and his sudden departure was a blow. Leo was uncooperative and we argued. Everything seemed ruined and broken, and I was hit with sadness. I walked out, Leo following.

I felt something collapsing inside me. For the first time I thought I might not survive emotionally. I'd spent my whole adult life not confiding, shoring myself up against the world, living a solitary inner life, sharing with Paul only what I judged to be suitable for him to know. I'd been like a closed regime, uncompromisingly walled off, never seeking any outside contact except with family. Now it was all falling down.

That night I watched footage on TV of a tsunami crossing a landscape, the camera view from a helicopter following the churning wave as it crossed the plain, obliterating cars, trees, houses, highways. A vision of destruction, the black water, the drowning world.

He'd dumped me by text, and he announced his return by text. I was shopping in Newmarket when I received his message.

Looking at the words on my phone I felt nothing. Emotion was somewhere beyond, waiting to connect. As I walked home, I was completely calm. During our reunion I felt nothing. I look at photos of the time after he came back. In my face I see tranquility, peace, relief — the face of a woman who's been rejected and condemned, and who is now reprieved. My face is smooth, expressionless. My whole body is relaxed.

But there was a force inside me, an overpowering and destructive black wave. It lurked like a virus until it was unleashed, surging out, a distinct and terrible pain. I'd seen his capacity to betray me, and I'd understood what it was to be completely alone.

To feel that you're reaching out into the void and catching hold of nothing is a terrifying, annihilating experience. Now, if I encountered even a hint of the memory of it, I couldn't be reassured. Any reminder would set me off and I would be back there, spinning in my own solitude, adrift, stricken with it. I couldn't accept his repeated promises that the crisis was over, that he'd made a horrible mistake, that he would never do it again. The thing that had entered couldn't be exorcised; it was a force so uncontrollable, it threatened to wreck our marriage all over again.

When I was a child my mother would shut her bedroom door on me, locking me out, and I would feel the same existential despair. I felt there was nothing holding me to the Earth, nothing between me and the cold universe. Now the abyss had opened up again.

This was the way I saw it: before I met Paul, I had an old self that had functioned poorly. I had killed off that self in my early twenties during a time of intense crisis, when I was alone and distressed.

The self who'd met Paul, had three children and started a happy life as a writer was my new self. The new self forged ahead, looked after the children well, was organised, hard-working and efficient, and never talked about the old self.

Old self-new self was a kind of magical thinking that had its own representative truth. Now this mental organisation had broken down, and I was struggling to put the pieces back.

Those afternoons when he'd left. High scream of a distant gull. The dog's paws clicking as he paces. The space that has entered and can't be filled. The abyss.

After he'd come back and in the middle of all our turmoil, I got the idea of going to visit Margaret, who lived in London. Even though everything was fragile and fraught, I wouldn't cling, I would leave. I would show him: I too could just go off. He would be thrown in with the kids, have to deal with them, get back to being a good father.

I flew away, feeling as if I was leaving Earth, everything I'd known and loved vanishing behind me.

Walking alone around the foreign city, I remembered a year I'd come by myself to stay with Margaret in her flat at Maida Vale. I was five months' pregnant with Leo, there to publish a novel with Little, Brown UK. We spent New Year's Eve up on Primrose Hill watching the fireworks with Margaret's friends, and the following morning when everyone was in bed hungover, I, who had not been drinking, got up early and took the eerily empty Tube to Russell Square. Not far from there was Mecklenburgh Square where I'd lived as a child.

The streets were dirty, freezing and deserted, and I had a feeling of dismay at the bleak scene. My revulsion was so extreme I knew it had to do with being pregnant. All my reactions were out of proportion;

I couldn't bear the spit and dog shit and rubbish on the pavements, the dark and cold, the frightening silence and emptiness. I was alone at the end of the world.

Now, years later, it was warm and mild in London and the city looked beautiful. I emailed and texted Paul breezy messages that conveyed, I hoped, *Having a good time without you*. He messaged back, on his best behaviour, his news full of the children, his not doing anything wrong.

Margaret and I and her children drove to their little beach hut outside Whitstable, on the Thames estuary. She was editing a manuscript for work, and I took the children walking out along the sea wall. In the distance we could see the towers of a nuclear power plant. The estuary was fringed with waving tussock grass and the wind blew over the flat land.

We drove through the narrow lanes to a village pub for lunch, and when we stopped at an intersection I could hear electricity humming in the overhead wires. I felt how overlaid Nature was here, with centuries of occupation, grids of history and connection. Nothing was wild.

I was buoyant, cheerful. Margaret worked, I walked with the children, listening to the wind, the electric current singing in the wires. We drove in to the village and had dinner in a busy café. The children ate fishcakes, we drank wine.

In the evening, I watched Margaret brushing her daughter Bella's hair, and I couldn't bear it. It was getting dark outside, a single lamp was on and I could see them reflected in the window, Margaret leaning over the small blonde head, gently untangling the strands. Beyond them was the dark stretch of the Thames estuary, a light blinking far away across the water.

I told Margaret I would have to go back to London.

She drove me to the station, and it was only when I was on the train watching the countryside flying by that I relaxed. I saw it again, Margaret brushing Bella's hair. I was 12,000 miles away from my children, from the family that had been broken and lost and maybe regained, and I'd realised the only way to get through it was alone.

Back at Margaret's empty house in Queen's Park, I spent some peaceful days. I sat in the sunny garden, sewing a button back on my jacket. I watched movies. I walked alone through the city. I stood on Westminster Bridge and looked down at the fast, brown water. I walked through areas where Paul and I had lived, Mecklenburgh Square, Hunter Street, past the big apartment in Ridgmount Gardens that we'd rented from the editor of the *South China Morning Post*. Something inside me was straightening out.

Paul rang. It was evening. I'd just watched the BBC news, reports of an eruption in Iceland, flights being cancelled because of volcanic ash.

'An Icelandic volcano lies between us,' I said.

I can't remember what he said in reply. Maybe, *Come home*.

Leo and I were in the bathroom of our house at Upland Road. He was three years old, and we were preparing to go to his afternoon kindergarten, where he would spend two and a half hours while I worked at home on my novel.

'When are we going? When?' he asked.

'Soon,' I told him.

'What's soon?'

I stared out the high window, over the suburb.

'What's soon?'

'Soon is a fierce dwarf who lives under the house.'

He raised his eyes.

A year after that throwaway remark of mine, *Soon is a fierce dwarf who lives under the house*, Soon was still with us. He would live with us until Leo was 10 years old.

For seven years I told the story of Soon. I never wrote any of it down; it was an exclusively oral narrative. All details of plot and character existed in my head, and, increasingly, in Leo's. Soon's world expanded to include multiple protagonists, but the heroes were Soon and his brother Starfish, who lived in an imaginary land where they embarked on journeys, solved mysteries, fought battles and survived adventures.

On the walk to school, on winter mornings, in summer rain, in waiting rooms, on car journeys, I would brace myself for the effort. Leo's appetite for the story was insatiable and he wore me out with his constant request: Make Soon talk.

It was his urging that made the story expand. He never tired of it, and it became a discipline for me. I had to invent continually; I had to stay on form to satisfy the demands of my small audience.

The plot grew large, complex, meta. Eventually it emerged that the story itself was controlled by a tyrannical overseer, Mrs Grimshaw, assisted by her ambitious son, The Son, who constantly pushed for a greater role. After a few years Leo started to contribute here and there. The plot elements and characters he came up with were original, witty, and exactly in keeping with the overall tone.

After no more than a few months I'd produced a large cast; after a few years, Leo started to say that if Soon and Starfish were ever made into books, he would have to share the rights with me. He was thinking: the movie, the merchandise.

We've occasionally said to each other that I should write the stories. I imagine embarking on it, recalling the best threads: The Tales of Soon and Starfish.

I used fragments in my novel *Soon*, when I described a relationship between a fictional mother and her young son, the mother using the stories to reflect, obliquely and ironically, the machinations of the adult world around them. But I'd never written down a children's story; writing adult fiction was my greater interest and absorbed all my time.

It was only after Leo was much older that I thought with any attention, analytically, about the personalities of Soon and Starfish, whom I'd invented and gone on developing without any conscious planning.

Leo was an acute, discerning listener, who, if the story was weak, would convey his disapproval with a slackening of attention, some nuanced gesture or expression that showed me the thread had loosened.

The demand for new material was gruelling, yet it must have kept me mentally fit. I remember toiling up the hill to school on a cold winter morning, a headache throbbing in my temples, grinding out some complex new episode that pleased me and made me want to weep with tiredness, Leo walking beside me, letting me know he was listening, that he got it. He always got it — he was exhaustingly sharp.

From the beginning, the point of Soon and Starfish was the difference between them. Starfish was honest, good-hearted, conscientious and hard-working. He tried to learn the language of other animals, he was kind and had a law-abiding, empathetic, uncynical nature. As I was leaving Leo at school I would often say, with tongue-in-cheek and irony, but also with seriousness: 'Work hard. Be good. Be Starfish!'

But Soon was the star. He had a complicated mix of traits that I strove continually to get right for the personality I had in mind.

Soon was only three inches tall. He was poignant because of his size, or, to put it another way, his size rendered comic his more dark and menacing attributes. As well as being very small, he was inept, ineffectual, accident-prone, and usually needing to be bailed out by Starfish.

He was tiny but his ego was large. He was furious and grandiose. He went in for grand gestures, sweeping rhetoric. He was dishonest, foul-mouthed and shifty. Whenever possible, he cheated. He was a liar, an exaggerator and, unless restrained by Starfish, capable of all kinds of crimes. He was a covert abuser and torturer, always ready to deliver a secret kick, but only to creatures smaller than himself. He took credit for things he hadn't done. He was jealous, competitive and sensationally malicious.

When given the choice, Soon *always* took the low road.

Starfish was shocked by Soon's behaviour, earnestly trying to correct it whenever he could. At the same time, he was carried along by Soon's energy and black comic qualities, his anarchic nature, his capacity for adventure, his iconoclasm and his wickedness. Soon would proceed, behaving very badly, while Starfish trailed behind, demurring and wringing his hands. Starfish was more intelligent than Soon, who was completely uneducated and fairly stupid, although possessed of low cunning.

They stuck together, for the whole seven years.

In the tales of Soon and Starfish I drew on recollections of the gully. Scenes and incidents came to me in flashes of childhood memory, often intense, vivid and wonderful in various ways: images of Nature and weather, atmosphere and colour. They arose in my mind as discrete experiences, and it was only when I started trying to construct a line of narrative beyond making up the Soon stories that I began knitting them together and trying to attach meaning to them — and perhaps at first my account will reflect this. Memories that arrived randomly later seemed to signify more when I went back to them, to form patterns that would shape a meaningful story.

So, first, some of those experiences that came to me as I turned out stories for Leo . . .

As a child, I had freedom to roam in wild and marvellous places. I had ranged around Tohunga Crescent and Hobson Bay since I was a toddler. The landscape of mudflats and mangroves, the pōhutukawa overhanging the clay banks and the caves around the bay were our territory. We and the children of the gully walked out onto the mudflats to catch eels, we built rafts and sailed them across the estuary when the tide was high, we made huts in the bush by the shore.

I loved watching the slow water creeping in over the estuarine flats, waiting for the tide to rise so we could raft out into the middle of the bay, paddle back in under the low trees, wade in the hot, shallow water in summer, or pick our way through the cold tussock on wet winter days under the low white sky.

Alone out on the flats one afternoon I got stuck thigh-deep in the mud and was rescued after my panicked shouts alerted a woman in a house at the bottom of the street.

During my teenage years I crossed several kilometres of the Pipe every morning on my way to school.

Tropical storms came from the Pacific Islands, usually lasting three days, bringing torrential rain and purple flashes of sheet lightning. Summer began with humidity under a heavy white sky and turned to hot, blue days in the new year; in autumn the light changed and grew hard, bright and clear. The blue sky stretched taut over us like an iron bowl, sounds were muted in the thin air, the light was painfully bright and colours strengthened; a tūī against the sky was blacker than black, and the gulls, rising ahead of us as we crossed the Pipe, screaming their high cries, had round and red-ringed eyes, vivid red beaks, feathers that were pure white.

The poet Allen Curnow wrote about pōhutukawa trees like the ones that grew at the bay (although this poem, 'Spectacular Blossom', pre-dates his life at Tohunga Crescent):

Mock up again summer, the sooty altars
Between the sweltering tides and the tin gardens,
All the colours of the stained bow windows.
Quick, she'll be dead on time, the single
Actress shuffling red petals to this music,
Percussive light! So many suns she harbours
And keeps them jigging, her puppet suns,
All over the dead hot calm impure
Blood moon tide of the breathless bay.

Allen Curnow walked his dog up Tohunga Crescent every day, and he often swam in the bay at high tide. When he'd finished a new poem, he would cross the road and put it in our letterbox for Karl to read.

Every day we walked to and from Parnell Primary School, which back then was 60 per cent Māori/Pasifika and 40 per cent European/Pākehā. Before it changed and the rental houses were sold off, the suburb was full of Pasifika families, and on Sundays walking up Tohunga Crescent we listened to the beautiful singing coming from the houses on the corner of Lee Street, where Cook Island families gathered to sing hymns.

I loved the Polynesian flavour of the school, especially the singing and drumming. The Niuean and Tongan and Cook Island boys set up wooden chairs to use as drums, bashing out rhythms to accompany their dancing. We practised drumming at home, imitating the complicated sequences. We learned Māori songs, as all schoolkids did, and practised Māori poi twirling and stick games. The Island boys wore their hair long in traditional style, until it was cut short in a coming-of-age ceremony. The classrooms smelled of the coconut oil the kids rubbed into their hair. There were big families who had a kid in just about every class, the Latus, the Faleukas, the Lafafagus, the Falanatulis . . .

I was five when Karl was awarded the Katherine Mansfield Fellowship. The grant gave him a year living and working in Menton, France, and we travelled to the other side of the world on a Greek passenger ship, the *Ellinis*. There were the weeks at sea, the beauty and calm of the tropics, days when we were confined below decks because of a violent storm, the ceremony when we crossed the Equator and a crew member dressed as Neptune came up over the side of the ship to mark the occasion. We sailed through the Panama Canal, and I saw a man being beaten by three others on the edge of the waterway.

At some point in the voyage a person died and was buried at sea, sewn into a sack and dropped down a chute into the water. We sailed into New York, past the Statue of Liberty, on a freezing February day. The hit song playing everywhere was Don McLean's 'American Pie', which I loved for its surreal, atmospheric lyrics.

The Northern Hemisphere cold seemed stunning, frightening. We walked around the winter city, wandered through MOMA and the Guggenheim, visited Macy's and went up the Empire State

Building. There's a photo of me at the top of the skyscraper wearing red mittens, terrified.

We sailed on, to France. From Paris we took an overnight train south, and when we reached Menton in the morning I was enraptured by the golden light at the station at Garavan. The scene was so luminously beautiful I felt I could fall onto the railway tracks. I was gripped at times by intense euphoria as a child; I was a sucker for beauty, of landscape, weather, light and sky.

Karl was to work on his edited collection of Katherine Mansfield's letters and journals. He had the room at the Villa Isola Bella to work in, and a flat was found for us, but we were soon evicted by the landlady who accused us children of spying on her through a crack in the wall. Karl found a better place, a spacious apartment in a mansion block by the olive grove at the Port of Garavan. Oliver and I spent our free time wandering among the olive trees hunting for lizards, or heading down to the marina to look at the yachts, and to count the exotic sports cars heading for the corniche on their way to Monte Carlo. In summer we swam every day and Karl bought us an inflatable canoe that we paddled out to the stone breakwater.

We went to school in an old house just across the railway line and down the alleyway from our flat. The walls were pitted with wartime bullet holes. There were two classrooms and a shaded courtyard that served as the playground. The toilets were in a wooden outbuilding, little cubicles with a round hole in the concrete and footprints to stand on, on either side. I soon understood when spoken to in French, and developed a perfect French accent, which I lost and never regained after we left Menton.

The photographer Marti Friedlander came to stay with us at Garavan, and took endless shots, ordering us into position, insisting we look natural in her trademark tyrannical style, which invariably caused shyness and paralysis. 'What are you doing, darling? Why are you wriggling like that? What's that funny look for? Come *on*!'

Eventually, standing next to her, I dropped a heavy pétanque ball on her foot. In the uproar that followed I insisted it had been an accident, nothing to do with her constant harangue, and the adults seemed more or less to believe me.

In the summer Karl bought tents and camping gear and we drove across Europe, camping at Lake Como, Venice, Lake Garda. A few months later we went to Tuscany, Pisa and Florence, stopping at Rapallo on the way back in honour of Ezra Pound.

At Pisa, a man tried to steal Margaret's stroller while Kay's back was turned. She'd been amusing Margaret, waiting for us to come down from the leaning tower, and she had to chase the thief and wrench it back. At the top of the tower I was terrified by the slippery floors and the lack of guardrails, and by the huge metal bell Oliver and I sat under to pose for a photo.

As we were driving away on the autostrada, the stroller came loose and flew off the roof-rack, and Karl had to pull over and run a long way back to retrieve it. Two policemen who'd found it rebuked him at length in Italian before handing it over.

In the camping grounds, Kay cooked on little gas bottles, although sometimes for a treat we'd try to find clean clothes and go to a restaurant, a challenge because we were so shabby.

There were fights and dramas on these trips. I remember a moment in the camping ground at the Pont du Gard. Kay and Karl were arguing in the tent, at it hammer and tongs, while torrential rain bucketed down. As I gazed out through the zips listening to the fight, I watched a large shit floating down the centre of the muddy path. So apt, I thought. I was five, and already a collector of scenes and symbols.

My memories of our European trips are filled with dreamy and idyllic images, the beautiful camping grounds, the freedom, the summer weather, the smell of the canvas, the road, Kay and Karl's openness to adventure, their daring and resilience, their willingness to lug three children across multiple countries.

There's also the memory of overpowering anxiety. When things went wrong, as they often do on trips, there was maximum agitation and drama.

Some time around 2005, Paul and I hired a car in Nice, intending to drive from there to Tuscany to meet up with Margaret. In the rental-car yard we were led to a small, boxlike vehicle, laughably too small for our luggage and three children, but our objections were met with a French shrug of indifference and we had to make do, cramming it all in, squashing three children in the back, setting off into the teeming streets, feeling the overloaded wheels scraping on the rims.

We were only 10 minutes into our drive when there was a terrifying bang. We swerved and to our horror found ourselves on the wrong side of the road. Faced with oncoming traffic, I shouted incoherently. Amid blasts of indignant horns and abuse we wove to the side of the road and stopped.

I was so unnerved I had to get out and light a stealthy cigarette behind the open boot while Paul inspected the damage. He'd driven the car into a low wall, trashing the back wheel. It was a write-off. It was obvious, I told him later, he wasn't happy with the tiny car, so he'd briskly wrecked it. (Presented with Paul's *fait accompli*, the rental car man stopped shrugging and gave us a new car — and it was much bigger.) Now, as we conferred over the mangled metal, I glanced into the car and saw something that astonished me. All three of our kids were laughing.

If this had been me as a child, and the parents leaning over the damage had been Karl and Kay, I would have been rigid with terror and anxiety. Here were our three, relaxed, blithely amused, waiting for us to sort it out.

'Look,' I said to Paul, marvelling (and gratified), but he wasn't surprised. He didn't have the memory of family tension rising, of hysteria, frantic nerves, hypersensitivity.

To this day, I have a faint aversion to Italy. I have to be persuaded not to avoid it. I think that in my childhood, as we shuttled around the coast between Italy and France, Italy was trickier, it was rougher, the language less familiar and so it represents for me anxiety, breakdowns, tension, parental freak-outs, screaming matches on the side of the howling autostrada . . .

'What's going to happen now?'

Karl had bought a decrepit old Bedford van for £120. We'd set off, loaded up with tents and luggage and gear; the intention this time was to drive back from Menton to London via Spain. We were on our way to Barcelona when something fundamental went wrong with the van.

I was standing up looking over the seats; Margaret was playing with her doll in the back and Oliver was reading. None of us had seatbelts.

Karl began swearing and hauling on the wheel, which seemed to have stopped responding. Meanwhile the van had started to lurch and bounce, tossing gear and luggage around in the back, sending

Margaret pitching forward and throwing Oliver to the floor, where a box of laundry detergent came loose from a shelf and upended itself into his mouth.

The bouncing and lurching lasted long enough for me to shout, 'What's going to happen now?'

We went on hurtling forward, Karl wrenching the locked steering wheel, until we veered off the road, the world tipped sideways, and we crashed into a ditch. Kay was thrown into the windscreen. When she struggled up and turned, we all screamed. She had a bad cut at the edge of her eye and had lost the tip (only the very tip — she was lucky) of her nose. There was a lot of blood, much childish wailing. Oliver was frantically trying to clear his mouth of laundry soap. Luckily, we'd been going quite slowly. And another piece of luck: if the wheel had locked earlier we could have been driving on a mountain highway, through an alpine pass with sheer cliffs below. We all imagined the van's sickening plunge into thin air.

Kind French motorists stopped to help. We'd bounced onto on the wrong side of the road (but avoided a head-on collision — more luck) and they spent time pointing out to Karl, the Anglo driver, that he should have been driving on the right. An ambulance showed up eventually. A medic tipped up my head and looked at my eyes. In my memory the ambulance was an old Citroën station wagon and Kay's stretcher was slotted into the boot, while we kids crouched around her.

We were transported to hospital, where Kay was admitted and her injuries stitched. It was a French hospital, very good, she reported, with a generous amount of red wine served at meals.

In 2009 I wrote a short story called 'The Olive Grove', for my collection *Singularity*. The story is told from the point of view of a child, Emily, and I included an incident we'd seen in Menton: young North African men being beaten up and arrested by police.

Emily has met a young policeman in the olive grove. She likes him very much, and thinks of herself as his friend. But as she and her family watch the incident in the town, she realises her friend is among the policemen violently beating up the young North African men.

It's a story about masks, disguises, about a child who suddenly perceives that adults have different selves. I used intense childhood memories, remembered observations of the adults around me, ambiguities, contradictions, hidden emotions and tensions.

Emily has noticed a man in the town. He's a street performer who covers himself in gold paint. His name is Golden Guy, and she knows instinctively he's not golden at all, he's evil.

I included the memory of a night terror caused by fever, when I hallucinated a witch in the cupboard in my bedroom. The witch was a fully realised, three-dimensional apparition that did not fade even when the light was turned on, and Kay, summoned by my cries of terror, waved her hand through it saying, 'Look, nothing there.'

This only made the witch more terrifying. She laughed and whispered, 'See? No one can help you. No one else knows I'm here.'

The witch in the cupboard stayed vividly in my memory. Perhaps she represented ambivalence. A dark figure split off from the warm, positive representations of the adults who lived in the flat in Garavan, who lived in 'The Olive Grove.' The parents in the story were golden, idealised, as they are in all the interlinked stories in *Singularity* where Emily and her parents appear.

After Menton, we moved to London. At night, from our apartment in the Nuffield flats in Prince Albert Road, we could hear the call of the exotic animals from London Zoo. I went to Primrose Hill School, and pined for the beauty of Menton. As far as I was concerned London was claustrophobic, except for the parks and the canal. After a short time in the big city I had a craving for any form of Nature.

There was always that yearning in London — for space, the out of doors, animals, wilderness. It seemed intensely thrilling to visit Richmond Park and watch the deer. A few years later, when Karl was on sabbatical and we lived in Mecklenburgh Square, the square garden seemed a magical place, full of its own rich atmosphere. I felt for the Mecklenburgh garden in the way one feels a *craze*. I loved it even more than the olive grove in Menton, because of its contrast with the surrounding area, especially the nearby Brunswick Centre, which was back then (before it was rehabilitated and became quite posh) a bleak and squalid concrete maze.

London at that time seemed so harsh and unaesthetic that we took to visiting McDonald's, a novelty back then, for its bright American cleanliness and cheeriness. The British attitude to food was grim, and I remember the strangeness of the diet after living in the South of France.

As a child, my version of essential needs was along the lines of Cicero's: a garden and a library. For me, the happiness of childhood was physical freedom, the landscape, the bush, animals, the sea — and books. Our house full of books did include a wonderful collection of children's literature. As for gardens, I preferred a very large habitat, preferably one with no borders, no walls.

In the long vacations, back in New Zealand, the family left Auckland for Karekare in the Waitākeres, out on the west coast. Karl and Kay had built a bach in the bush on Lone Kauri Road, and we spent weeks there during summer holidays. I took to sleeping outside in a tent, where I was woken every morning by tūī squabbling in the trees.

Karekare was a wild, beautiful place. The bach was built on a hillside with a view down the valley, surrounded by dense bush in all directions. It was a little wooden house with a corrugated-iron roof, a sitting room, two tiny bedrooms, a large covered verandah and an outside toilet.

There was always the knowledge that if we went too far off any track, even fairly close to the house, we'd quickly get disorientated and lost. I strayed off a path a few times, losing my sense of direction. The bush was so thick you couldn't get a clear view out of it, and the only way to escape — like getting stuck on the mudflats — was by standing still and shouting.

The sounds of the bush in summer: the song of the grey warbler, the elaborate warbling and chuckling of tūī, the cicadas whose sawing grew louder as summer went on, rising to such a pitch in the hot afternoons that my mind transformed the buzz into a visible force in the air, a shimmering wall of sound. In the bush we were followed by tiny fantails, flitting around us as we stirred up insects; above us kererū, native pigeons, creaked by on slow wings, and kingfishers were a quick flash of blue against the green. At night the cries of morepork, the native owl, and closer, the sinister guttural snarl of possums as they scrabbled in the trees.

At the bottom of Lone Kauri Road was Karekare Beach (the beach in the movie *The Piano*), a vast glittering expanse of black sand and dunes ending in lines of rolling surf that roared ceaselessly, the sound echoing against the cliffs. I was exhilarated by the hard light, the sky and the big surf.

I loved swimming there, so much that I would eventually join the lifesaving club at 15 and qualify as a lifeguard, which involved hours of training, even practice jumping out of the rescue helicopter far out beyond the breakers, and swimming back in to shore. After the experiences I had as a child, perhaps it was fitting I would want to arm myself against drowning.

We'd walked down on a hot afternoon to swim. The air was rippling with heatwaves that made mirages appear like puddles of mercury shimmering over the black sand. There had been a summer storm and the sea was wild, whipped into massive swells by the offshore wind, and it happened to be dead low tide, the point when the surf is rolling over shallow water and, near the shore, the waves are breaking on hard sand. I had no fear at all of wild surf and launched straight in, but after a few minutes I noticed lifeguards running down the beach, people gathering. Karl had been picked up by a huge breaker, turned upside down by it and dashed on his head onto the hard sand.

He was hit, he later told us, by a searing pain down his arm, and staggered towards the beach thinking he'd broken his shoulder. He collapsed in the shallows and when the lifeguards got to him he was in agony and couldn't get up. They called the rescue helicopter, which soon came thrashing furiously down onto the beach, blasting sand in all directions. They strapped Karl onto the outside of it and choppered him away to Middlemore Hospital in South Auckland, where it would be discovered he was suffering transferred pain from a fractured vertebra in his neck.

One of the surfies had summoned me to stand on his board so it wouldn't blow away when the helicopter landed. I stood there, dutifully balancing, shading my eyes as Karl lifted off, disappearing into the white mid-summer glare.

After he'd gone there was a moment of stillness, as if the waves and the wind had stopped. Kay came surging towards me, her face creased with agitation, and we seemed to enter one of those dreams where you struggle to run in deep mud: with wailing little Margaret in tow we had to toil across the vast, hot expanse of black beach, then trudge back to the bach, up the winding gravel road through the bush.

Kay kept saying, 'Why did they have to *take him away* like that? He would have been *fine*.'

We piled into the car for the hair-raising ride along the sliding gravel of Lone Kauri Road, through the bush and on to South Auckland as Kay, rising to the emergency, gripped the steering wheel and tried to do what she was very, very bad at: driving, especially driving fast. I remember our screams as she smashed at speed over the judder bars in the hospital grounds.

In the ward they'd packed sandbags around Karl to keep his neck immobile. He was in shock and uncomfortable, but he'd been lucky. If the break had been any worse he would have been paralysed, and most likely would have drowned. In the end, all he suffered was nerve damage that withered the muscles in his arm, and he had to lift weights to build them back up.

None of this put us off swimming in the surf, although we'd learned the lesson about avoiding dead low tide. Karekare was a dynamic environment, a landscape always in wild motion: the boiling surf, the wind, the dancing glare off the black sand. The sand itself was a hazard in summer; its blackness absorbed heat, and if you got caught on a stretch of it without shoes you could suffer terrible burns.

There are these lines from Karl's poem, 'Quesada' that capture the sense of ceaseless movement:

The waves drive forward against an offshore wind
That turns their crests to banners.
They shiver in the heat haze silver and white
Shaken against sunlight above the crack of broken rollers
Driving up the hill of sand again and again defeated.

The weather, the atmospherics: at night during a storm, lying in a bunk while the wind roared through the bush and the rain thundered on the iron roof — huge rain, deluges that sustained the rainforest and filled our rainwater tank and left the bush steaming and dripping and rustling with water, and swelled the stream below the bach, so that when we crashed down through the bush and followed the stream to the beach, about a 2-kilometre distance down through tangled vegetation, flax and native trees, mānuka and kānaka, kauri and rimu, the pools were brimming and the fast water raced over stones and the native eels rose when we flicked the surface, poking their horned snouts out of the water. There was one giant eel we summoned with our flicking; he was more than a metre long and thicker than my arm. We fed him breadcrumbs.

Following the stream all the way down Lone Kauri Road towards the beach we'd reach the Opal Pool, a round swimming hole with steep rock sides, so deep you couldn't see the bottom, and shockingly cold all year round. Beyond the Opal Pool the Karekare waterfall flowed down from the hills, crashing into a shallow pool where we waded out, slipping on the mossy rocks, to stand as close as we could to the falling water.

Those long Karekare summers, I had a friend, Rachel Holt, whose parents had a bach high up on the Piha Road, and some days we'd take the Horoeka track from the Karekare Valley up to her place. It was a steep track through dense bush and we'd go up it fast. We walked everywhere, covering miles. The Holts' bach was built on an acre of bush and pine forest. The previous owner had built a network of fishponds. There were goldfish and, hidden among the lily pads, native frogs. Hunting for the frogs was an enchanting pastime. They were delicate and beautiful, marked like the local native geckos in vivid greens, flecks of gold, tawny brown.

Like us, the Holts had a long-drop toilet, a wooden outhouse built over a pungent hole in the ground, but theirs had the added feature of giant cave wētā that would creep up out of the hole and send you shrieking off the seat when their long antennae brushed your backside.

Staying over aged about nine, I remember Rachel and I getting up early and walking through the bush and pines to the back of the section where mature trees stood at the edge of the Karekare Valley. We climbed high into one of the trees. It was a hot morning and we could see all the way down the dense bush slopes of the valley, the sun striking off the shimmering leaves, the heat rippling in the air. The birds were loud around us, and from far away there was the distant roar of surf.

The air was absolutely clear, the light hard, bright, sharp. We were so high above the valley we felt as if we were flying. It was a moment of euphoria, joy.

This is the kind of memory that stands out to me as intense and marvellous, that helped shape my imagination and made me feel vital and alive as a child, that I used when I made up stories for Leo, and later formed part of the true story I tried to construct. This is another:

The Waitākeres are a vast rainforest and coastal wilderness, and they're only an hour's drive away from the centre of Auckland. This was an advantage for Karl, who liked to leave us at intervals during the long vacation. He would take the only car, driving back to town to conduct his affairs.

While Karl was away in town, Kay led expeditions. With little Margaret gamely in tow, we would head out into the bush.

'Just put one foot in front of the other,' Kay would say on the way home, when Margie grew hysterical with tiredness and refused to go on.

On the wild coast along from Karekare, in the stretch of black sand desert that leads to Whatipū, loggers had cut a tunnel through a rock bluff. It was built for a small railway line that used to transport logs from the Pararaha Gorge. According to one of Oliver's maps, a track called the Tunnel Track would take us from one of the hilltop trails down to the black sand desert, emerging right on top of the tunnel. From there, we could walk back around the coast to Karekare Beach.

We set off, and after a long time on the bush tracks through the hilltops beyond Zion Ridge, we found the entrance to the Tunnel Track at the edge of a nīkau palm and pūriri glade. Its sign was faded and cracked and had partly fallen over. The path was narrow, overgrown and steep, and grew steeper, although this was expected, since it was supposed to wind down through the bush to the tunnel far below at sea level.

We kept going, one foot in front of the other. The difficulty increased until it turned into a climb; half the time we were sliding on our haunches, braking with our heels, clambering around rocks, hanging onto branches to keep our balance. I had my eye on the sea, which was still a long way below, and I was starting to sense a problem. I wondered if we'd taken a wrong turn, always possible, since the tracks were narrow, primitive little trails, sometimes with confusing detours and forks.

Margaret was behind me and above her Kay stumbled and dislodged a big rock. We were on a steep slope and the rock rolled down and hit Margaret in the chest. She couldn't get it off, it was lodged there. She cried out, sliding, teetering as we clawed our way to her. After we'd pushed the rock off and guided her to a point where she could rest against a tree, there was a ragged shout below us. It conveyed such fright we froze.

Oliver, who was further down, had come to a stop at the edge of a cliff. Below him was a hundred feet of air, and below that was our destination: the top of the tunnel.

Now we could see what had happened. There'd been a landslide, carving out the hillside, and the track had fallen away. Oliver was bracing himself by hanging onto a tree, right on the crumbling edge. If he'd been a bit hastier, he would have skidded into thin air.

We were exhausted, at the bottom of a terrifyingly slippery and difficult track, with a crying four-year-old in tow, and a sheer drop below us. I've dreamed about it ever since, with variations; in the nightmare I'm always trapped on a slippery slope above a great height, sliding towards the edge.

There was a moment of despair and panic. We steadied ourselves as best we could and listened to Margaret's high-pitched wailing.

We all heard it at once: the regular thud of the rescue helicopter. It came buzzing over us on its usual patrol along the coast, looking out for swimmers in trouble in the surf. We waved and shouted — and on it flew, buzzing away out of sight, against the black cliffs.

Kay rested her face against a tree trunk, her hand gripping Margaret's arm. She was sweating.

In the end I said, 'Well, we're just going to have to turn around and climb back up again.'

It took twice as long and was much harder going up, now we knew what was below us. One slip could send us sliding down and down, and over the hundred-foot drop. When we finally got to the top, Kay lay down on the ground and closed her eyes. We sat beside her in silence, waiting. Expeditions were part of her genius with kids, the way she threw herself into the project, the camaraderie, the drama, the lack of adult caution, too, which meant anything could happen. This one had nearly got away on her.

That night after we'd struggled all the way back along the Zion Ridge and finally reached the bach, Kay said she'd been panicking and it was my words that had saved the day: 'Well, we're just going to have to turn around and climb back up again.'

I was filled with happiness. We had survived, I had helped. I treasured her praise.

'I won't be made to feel a heel!'

Kay said this often. She made it sound as if there were people out there just waiting to make her feel guilty, and she was ready for them.

One holiday when we were staying at Karekare, she and Karl allowed me, Oliver and a family friend to tramp alone into the Pararaha Gorge. Margaret, who was four, stayed home with them. This expedition turned out to be a day-long hike through a gorge signposted 'for experienced trampers only', with no proper track, which ended in a remote coastal walk around surf-lashed rocks that could only be safely negotiated at low tide. Oliver was ten, I was seven, the friend was five.

Karl described the Pararaha Gorge in a novel, *The End of the Century at the End of the World*. He wrote, 'Once you'd entered the gorge, there was no going back.'

This was the case: once we'd got a certain way in, the track disappeared, and we spent the next hours trying to find it, following false trails and sheep tracks that petered out halfway up cliffs. We realised we were lost, and that by now we couldn't go back even if we wanted to, because the bluffs and waterfalls we'd climbed around were too hard, especially for a five-year-old, to scale.

We had to deal with the dangerous, fast-flowing white-water river, steep cliffs and dense bush for the whole day until we were found. It was only after a long period of trying to find a track and following trails that led us to dangerous places and dead ends that we understood we should just follow the river itself. I remember intense fear and despair, the hours of terrified crying as we tried to find our way, and the objectively correct understanding that we could die. We got stuck on steep bluffs, we struggled with the five-year-old trying to climb around waterfalls, we had to swim, climb and fight our way through the stark, unforgiving landscape.

In 2009 I wrote about it in a short story 'Pararaha', which I included in *Singularity*.

I described the vast, wild, exhilaratingly beautiful setting that I loved, despite the terror of that day:

> *They reached the top and there before them was the huge curve of the coast, stretching many kilometres south, all the way to Whatipu, and to the north towards Karekare, a desert of black sand and dunes and scrub rippling with heatwaves, and, far across it, fringed with surf, the wild sea. Emily turned and turned; it seemed to her that the whole landscape was full of bright, violent motion. The fluffy toe toe waved in the wind like spears borne by a marching army, the surf ceaselessly tumbled and roared, the light played on the sand, casting a powerful, shimmering glare. Where the black desert met the land there were enormous grey cliffs that sent the sound booming off them.*

In this story, as in 'The Olive Grove', the parents are golden and blameless; they're distracted, they just haven't quite noticed what the children are setting off to do.

Many years after I wrote the story, as an experiment, instead of describing the Pararaha episode in the house style of the literary family, *jokes, a minimum of piety* (in order that no one would feel a heel), I tried to talk about how frightening it had been. Kay was dismissive.

She told me I should think differently about the past.

For me to describe the day as traumatic, as not funny, suggested another foray into 'scolding'.

Refusing to examine the notion that three young children had spent a whole day thinking they were going to die, Kay described the Pararaha experience as 'a triumph'.

I suppose, like the episode on the Tunnel Track, it was a triumph because we had survived.

Childhood involved an enormous amount of roaming around. (Where you been? Oh, nowhere. Roaming around.) If I was at a loose end, I would walk right out west, miles away from home and back again. I burned with constant, restless energy, and without exercise I would go up the wall.

One summer I was sent to stay with my cousin Leila at her brother's house in Tologa Bay. I used the experience to write a story called 'Gratitude', and it won a prize in the *Sunday Star-Times* competition, which drew my aunt and uncle's attention to it. They congratulated me on the prize, but were hurt by the story when it was published in the paper.

It wasn't entirely flattering about the set-up I'd been sent to stay in.

A detail I'd remembered, and had incorporated into 'Gratitude', was a habit of Leila's I'd noticed when I stayed with her. When my back was turned, she would nip in and do some service, straightening my bed, or folding my clothes. Then she would launch into a diatribe about how lazy I was. She had to do everything for me, she would say, and I should be grateful for how much she did. It was no use protesting that I would have got around to it if she'd waited five minutes.

I was fairly immune to her reprimands and I knew none of this was spontaneous. I knew she was imitating her mother, Kay's sister. Her mother's most frequent refrain was that Leila should be *grateful* — for everything, but especially for her mother.

My aunt would say to Leila, 'Imagine if you had Sarah's mother. Imagine if you had Jane's mother. You should be so *grateful*.'

(It would send Leila into a daydream: 'Imagine if I did have Sarah's mother. *If only . . .*')

This was the set-up I used in 'Gratitude': my adult cousin, Leila's brother, was working as a cray fisherman in Tologa Bay. My impression was that his then-wife kept calm by smoking richly pungent roll-your-owns of whatever type. Their house was a ramshackle wooden bungalow set among paddocks on a rural road out of town, near the river. They had two small children.

When my aunt and uncle dropped me and Leila off there, we were told we'd be sleeping in an old car in the garden. I was eight and Leila was about ten years old.

So began long, dazed days of freedom, ranging around the countryside, being served strange meals by the glazed mother of the toddlers in the evening, nights in the old car, waking in the garden — dawn breaking through the windscreen — winding down the window to check the weather and wondering if we could sneak into the house to grab some food and use the bathroom before anyone was awake.

The evening meal was a challenge. It was the only time we went inside the house, apart from occasionally nipping in to use the lavatory. Can my memory be right that the walls were unlined, that the floor below the dining table had a crack through which I could see the dirt beneath? In my memory the interior was messy, pungent. In my mind's eye the toddlers were naked, dirty, tousle-haired.

I was shy and silent, aware of Leila monitoring me for ingratitude. I recall grappling with a rock-hard kūmara that shot off my plate across the room. With a dreamy smile the toddlers' mother picked it up off the floor and put it back on my plate. I was aware I was unwashed, that I smelled. My hands were caked in dirt, my fingernails were black. I was secretly sure I had worms.

At night I was scared to get out of the car in the rain to pee behind a bush.

There was a bath in the garden, in an enclosure surrounded by wooden stakes, to which my adult cousin would withdraw after dinner. The night-time garden: steam rising over the bushes. The soft smell of incense drifting from the house. Rain pattering on the windscreen.

To pass the time in the car, Leila shoved a tape into a small stereo and played songs from the musical *Jesus Christ Superstar*. I squinted over a book in the faint glow from the interior light. The vinyl squeaked and crackled under our sleeping bags. The seats were cranked back as far as they would go, but they weren't flat and I kept bruising myself on the handbrake. I could smell the crammed ashtray. One night I dreamed we'd got hold of the keys and driven the old bomb through the hedge and out of the garden, droning away up the road . . .

I think, back then, I knew all this was material, that I would *go away and make a story of it*. When Leila accused me of ingratitude I had a sense not of injustice but irony — and comedy, too. I laughed over the scene in the garden, the old car with tinny music coming from its windows, the bath beyond the bushes where my cousin grandly and humourlessly lurked, the wafts of steam and smoke. The way we'd *wind up* the car windows when it was time to go to sleep, and then, all domestic-like, *wind them down* in the morning. I laughed even as I writhed with discomfort and nerves and fear.

One day, unsupervised and at a loose end as always, we ranged down to the river, which was broad, deep and fast-flowing. We untied Leila's brother's dinghy and pushed off, intending just to mess around near the bank. But we hadn't reckoned on the current, and were quickly swept right out into the middle, far from the river's edge.

It was impossible to fight it. We were being swept down to the estuary, and would soon end up at the ocean on the outgoing tide. The water got rougher as the current strengthened, the dinghy rocking wildly in the chop. Leila was swearing and hauling on the oars. We realised the rough surf at the river-mouth would capsize the boat and we were going to drown. She was frantic, and I was frozen with fear. She shouted at me to help, but there was nothing I could do. I could hear the sea roaring.

There was a curve in the river, and near the bank an area of calm water, the current swirling past and around it. Leila rowed for the bend. Here we could escape the current, rowing close enough in to grab the branches of a clump of mangroves. We pulled ourselves to where we could stand, waist-deep. We struggled through mud, floundering in it, Leila pulling the boat. It took a long time to get to dry land.

We had travelled miles downstream, and unless we confessed to having taken it, there was no way to return the boat to its mooring, so we left it wedged between some bushes.

All the way back, along miles of riverbank, Leila cursed and berated me. I was an idiot, I'd been no help, I was a drip, a crybaby, we'd lost the dinghy, the boat was worth a lot of money, they'd kill us if they found out. In her fright and anxiety, she unleashed a tirade that was unending. It seemed to take hours to get back, and all the way she didn't let up and I listened and cried. In some detached part of my mind I was awestruck by the vehemence of her rant. It was intense. It was savage.

In the garden we draped our wet clothes over the bonnet and got into the car. I cried silently. No one was around. Through the speckled windscreen I watched a chicken scratching around the back door. I relived the fear out on the river, the helplessness, the certainty we were going to drown.

That evening as I chased another kūmara around the plate, Leila shot me death stares, warning me not to tell.

Neither of us ever did.

My cousin only found out who'd stolen his boat many years later, when the family read the story 'Gratitude' and were hurt by some of the details.

Only: Leila liked it.

Karl and Kay liked it. As far as it related to my aunt and her ways, there was an amused, indulgent sense for them of *if the shoe fits*.

There was another long, dazed spell I spent with Leila, when I was sent to stay at her parents' rural property outside Hamilton. I used an incident from it in my novel *Mazarine*.

My aunt and uncle's house was built on the hill and had a view down to Lake Rotokauri. When I arrived, I was told that Leila and I wouldn't be living in the house, but in a tent down at the edge of the lake, about half a kilometre or so away. We would have great fun by ourselves a long way from the house, and for this we would be so grateful!

Again, we were two small girls alone in a wide, empty landscape. More long, dreamy days of roaming around, the tape deck playing songs from *Jesus Christ Superstar*. (To which Leila had added the maudlin collected songs of Neil Diamond.)

As always, I would find my sleeping bag tidied and my clothes folded, and receive Leila's long reprimand for my laziness and lack of gratitude. We cooked meals in tins on an open fire. We played cards and Monopoly in the tent, leaving the board to range out into the paddocks, coming back to the game, wandering off again.

We lost sense of time and routine. We argued, fought, laughed, read, lay in silence in the grass watching the sky, listening to the wind in the raupō. We stalked through the tall reeds, looking for frogs and fish. We had the use of a dinghy, and rowed it around the lake, taking turns with the oars. There was only the sun and the sky, the light moving across the paddocks, the birds flying in the evening. The darkening sky, the stars, the cold moon.

At night the Waikato fog came down and we shivered in our sleeping bags. If I got up the courage to go outside to pee, I would point the torch at the ground, looking for cow shit in the long grass, coming back scraping my feet to clean them before getting back in my sleeping bag.

We began to be aware of a stranger, a big boy. At first, he was only crossing the top paddock, heading from the hay barn to the road, as if he'd been sent there on an errand. He was thin, with lank black hair and a lazy eye. I thought he was watching us from the hay barn.

One evening he stood on top of a stile, looking at us, shading his eyes. He didn't react when Leila waved at him, so she gave him the finger. We ducked down in the reeds. I protested, why did she do that? It was stupid, now he'd be angry.

An hour later, when we'd just pulled the boat in, I looked up to find him standing in front of us.

He pointed at the boat. 'I'm taking it,' he said, and picked up the anchor chain.

Leila stood up to him. 'It's not yours.'

They fought over the metal anchor in a tug of war. I bobbed around ineffectually; it was a kids' fight until he let go and the metal spike struck Leila's forehead just above her eye.

I remember running, Leila running and screaming, blood pouring out of her head. We were both sobbing when we finally reached the house, about the big boy and the fight and the blood.

When she'd cleaned off the blood and patched up the wound with a plaster, Leila's mother paused, smiled. 'There! Now, come and have a sandwich before you go.'

Go? We stared.

'Go where?'

'Back down to the lake, of course. You're loving it down there!'

I saw Leila falter, and then rally. Of course we would go back to the tent. We would *love* to sleep beside the black water, with the clacking of the reeds, the water glittering under the moon, the fog curling over the paddocks. The big boy still out there.

My aunt had another line: she knew you would love to do what she wanted you to do. You would love it.

Gratitude.

In the end I did love my adventures with Leila. The stalled dreamy days, the absolute freedom, the sudden dramas and alarms, the terror.

But I loved them only while looking in the rearview mirror, when they had become material, and I could make a story out of them. I didn't love them at the time. Back then, walking down through the paddocks to the lake in the fading light, I was terrified.

At the time, I was all ingrate.

It's material, go and make a story of it.

In 'Gratitude', writing about my aunt's family, I used the material freely. *If the shoe fits.* But when I used details of my own family, did I make it my task to write stories that tidied up and controlled reality, made it beautiful?

> *One wanted to control the world and make it more orderly and beautiful than reality could ever be, so one created a world of one's own, and controlled that.*

As in 'Pararaha.' The description of the parents in that story carefully minimises, controls and makes comprehensible a mystery, that they waved off a five- and seven- and ten-year-old on a day-long tramp through a vast wilderness of dense bush, into a white-water gorge, with no clear path, ending at surf-lashed rocks.

They didn't realise. They were distracted. But still. And yet. It wasn't as if the circumstances were *subtly* or *possibly* problematic.

The circumstances: in order to reach the track that led to the gorge, we first had to walk a few kilometres up the unsealed road through the bush. The end of the Pararaha Gorge, where the river meets the sea and where we finally emerged, is many kilometres around the coast from Karekare Beach and, at that time, part of the coastline of rocks and dangerously wild surf (which has now altered through time and erosion) which was navigable only at low tide. The Waitākeres is a wilderness of typical New Zealand bush: tangled, thick and impenetrable. Any mistake on any track, even a short one (if a seven- and ten-year-old mislaid a five-year-old, say) could lead to a person being the human equivalent of a needle lost in a haystack.

Just one single parental inquiry about any one of these elements of our walk would have opened the door to a vast wilderness of doubts . . .

Did Kay send us off down the Pararaha after we'd had our adventure on the Tunnel Track? This I don't know; I can't remember.

Writing this it's clear how much the fear of drowning features. In the Pararaha Gorge, all three of us could have drowned. There were wild rapids, steep bluffs above the water, waterfalls and deep pools. Parts of the river were jammed with dangerous floating kauri logs. At various points we had to climb, wade and even swim.

On the river at Tolaga Bay with Leila, I had thought I was going to drown.

At the age of two, a family story went, I was floating in an inflatable ring in the sea when Karl noticed something: I was upside down. The ring had flipped, my legs were in the air and I was drowning. His sprint down the beach saved me.

One summer, at Rotokauri, I got trapped under a boat in my cousins' swimming pool. I don't know how I got out of that one, I just remember being told I nearly drowned.

When Oliver was 18 months old, he jumped off a wharf into a fast-moving tidal estuary before Kay could stop him. Karl's sprint along the bank, where he knelt down and scooped Oliver out as he floated swiftly by underwater heading for the open sea, only just saved him.

Is nearly drowning just a standard part of a typical New Zealand childhood? I search my memory, and I can't find any story of either of my parents nearly drowning, nor of them being in physical danger as children. There are Kay's stories of being neglected at the farm in Omokoroa, but no discrete incidents, none of nearly drowning, or being lost.

After Oliver and I got out of the Pararaha, we never discussed with our parents the fact that we'd spent hours struggling, terrified and believing we were going to die. It was enough that we'd survived. The fear, the memory of it, would evaporate. There would be no sense of lingering doubt (aged seven) about what might turn out next to be unsafe. We would switch easily from thinking we were going to die to a sense of security and confidence. Why was this? Because we'd survived.

It was material. I would go away and write about it. The facts would be shaped, controlled, turned into a composition. I didn't anticipate I would return and tell the stories again, as if I was back in the wilderness of the Pararaha, still lost, trying to find my way to open ground.

The French novelist Henry de Montherlant said, 'Happiness writes white.'

In 'The Olive Grove', ambivalent figures are pushed outside the family: the witch in the cupboard, the secretly violent policeman, Golden Guy.

Had I made it my task to shape the material in such a way that my parents knew I was grateful? In order that no one would feel a heel?

This was the singularity. I didn't want to explore the mysterious reality, I wanted to write them white.

Leila and I were the daughters of two sisters. We were two years apart; our mothers were two years apart. We were girls together, at Tolaga Bay, at Rotokauri. Leila was hardy, strong, resourceful, clever. She had curly hair and always wore boys' clothes. I was physically smaller, anxious, shy. She was two years older, but I often beat her at word games, puzzles and cards. I was at least as quick, and often more cunning. I was always watching. I knew she was unhappy, and that when she berated me she was acting out what her mother did to her. I remember listening to her crying in the night.

Aged five in Menton I'd watched the adults, and observed that some have a mask, and I wrote about that in 'The Olive Grove'. When I was a child, staying at Rotokauri, I wondered if my aunt had a mask. She was a schoolteacher, famous for her warmth, an extrovert who was kind and generous to the young people she taught.

She had her lines. You'd love to go back down to the lake. You must be so grateful. Imagine if you didn't have me as a mother. I imagined that when her mask came off with Leila it would involve the kind of savage tirade Leila unleashed on me that day on the riverbank after we'd lost the boat.

Leila and I were different, but we had things in common. We punished ourselves for our crimes: ingratitude, being tomboyish, noticing too much. For not pleasing our mothers. Leila's mother felt her daughter wasn't feminine enough; she tried to persuade her to wear dresses, and failed.

We both had some form of face blindness. Neither of us could visualise faces, even of people close to us. Sometimes, Leila told me, she didn't even recognise herself in the mirror.

We were girls and then we grew up, and we both performed a trick. We disappeared.

I became a new self, and Leila did too, but, unlike me, she didn't keep her transformation hidden. She pushed it to the outside and became a different person. She stepped out of being ungrateful Leila, the unwanted daughter, and simply walked away.

I'd published three novels when I received an email from the writer Fiona Kidman asking if I'd like to contribute to a short story collection she was editing. I'd never published a short story before, and so I set to work. I wrote two, and called them both 'Opportunity'. They were really about opportunism. They seemed almost to write themselves, and I had very little idea what part of my mind they were coming from. I wrote more stories, linking them through plot and character, and they eventually turned into two collections, *Opportunity* and its sequel, *Singularity*. Those collections turned into further linked fiction, the novels *The Night Book*, *Soon* and *Starlight Peninsula*.

Opportunity won the Montana award for fiction and the Montana medal for book of the year, and *Opportunity* and *Singularity* were both shortlisted, in different years, for the Frank O'Connor International Prize, which meant I got to travel to Cork in Ireland for the Frank O'Connor festival twice. I remember Karl saying of the *Opportunity* stories, 'Well, you've struck a rich vein there.'

In one *Singularity* story, 'The Yard Broom', I'd written about a girl who pushes a broom up and down a yard when she's feeling distressed. I didn't know where I'd got the idea, until I was passing through London on my way to the Frank O'Connor festival in Cork with *Singularity,* and I visited Mecklenburgh Square, where we'd lived when I was a child.

Walking around the square I suddenly remembered where the broom had come from . . .

Karl was on sabbatical from Auckland University, and had taken a visiting research fellowship in the English Department at University College London. We had moved into a flat in Mecklenburgh Square, in a block owned by the London Goodenough Trust, which supplied accommodation for visiting academics and their families.

It was winter when we arrived, jet-lagged after the flight from New Zealand. The streets around the square were drab and freezing, the two-bedroom flat seemed dingy and too small, and we all sank into lethargy, exhaustion and depression. Eventually I suggested to Kay that we go in search of supplies, and she and I went out into the cold to look for a supermarket.

That night I woke and saw it was snowing. I'd hardly ever seen snow before, and I was thrilled by the delicate whirling white flakes. I was used to the huge rain thundering on the iron roof back home in Auckland, and the silence of the snow seemed mysterious, beautiful and atmospheric.

Margaret and I, then aged seven and ten, started at St Alban's School, a local state primary whose pupils came mostly from a nearby housing estate. They lived in tiny squalid flats, kids who were not only tough but pent-up, angry and violent. One or two seemed deranged, including an angelic-looking blond boy who produced an iron bar in the playground one lunchtime, threatening to use it, keeping the teachers who tried to disarm him at bay. The teachers were wary of the pupils, and of their parents.

My accent was alien and my clothes were wrong. I'd never taken much interest in clothes, except to favour a boyish look. I soon discovered this mattered to the urban kids I was now mixing with. Unlike the St Alban's girls, who wore what I regarded as high heels, I turned up in the standard Kiwi schoolchild's outfit of the time, including flat lace-up shoes, and I was identified as a weird frump who wore boys' clothes. Worse, my hair had been cut by Kay into a short Katherine Mansfield-style bob. I was hopelessly unstylish, and condemned to hang out with the 'Pakis' (as they were called), who had a rough time on the estate. During my time at the school the few Asian families were so demoralised by racist attacks (a favourite recreation of my classmates, fondly called 'Paki-bashing') that they moved away from the area.

(Many years later when I returned to London as an adult and looked around for a school for our son Conrad, the local demographic had completely changed. St Alban's had become a majority Asian school, with almost no white pupils.)

Every day in school I was hit, pushed around, jeered at, scorned. My appearance was loudly discussed, and I was the object of noisy hilarity.

At home in the flat tensions were high, as they always were in our family. We children fought, Karl's mood ranged from irritable to explosive, and Kay went in for melodrama, sulks, silences and outbreaks of furious shouting. Their relationship was volatile, and since there wasn't enough space in the flat for a family of five, we were all getting on each other's nerves.

Margaret and I had both developed psoriasis as children, and in London Margaret broke out so badly all over her body that she was referred to the Great Ormond Street Hospital for Children, where she once, to her horror, had to stand completely naked for inspection by a group of 12 junior doctors. I had psoriasis flares on and off, and was always conscious of it. I had the constant uneasy feeling my skin was on the brink of turning against me, betraying me. The condition was aggravated by the hard London water and the lack of natural light (it's cured by exposure to UV), and also, since it's an autoimmune condition, by stress.

There were many international children living in the flats, and in winter after school we congregated in the games room in the basement, a dingy space containing nothing but some large plastic barrels. I loved this space and, rather inexplicably, the barrels, and went there as often as I could. There were the Nkosi children from South Africa, whose parents were whispered to be 'collaborators' with the apartheid regime, because they were from Soweto yet living in London, and they owned a sleek new Mercedes. There were white South Africans, Ghanaians, Australians, Americans. There were beautiful Arab siblings called Amir, Amira and Amal, and a girl from New York who went on to become a movie actor.

One afternoon a girl from an African country, I don't remember which, pinned me against the wall and punched me in the head while repeating in a toneless voice 'We are the People. We are the People.'

That year in London, Karl and Kay booked tickets for *Götterdämmerung*, a performance that ran from 4.30pm until 11.30pm and involved a dinner break, meaning they were away for a long time. After that they were hooked, and went to all the performances of the Ring Cycle, which lasted many hours, and later to other operas, concerts and plays. They didn't bother with getting anyone to supervise us. During all these outings, they left us alone in the flat.

Oliver was an unbridled adolescent, newly obsessed with girls and sex. As the eldest he was theoretically in charge, but since, as far as I was concerned, he possessed neither sense nor empathy nor any notion of fairness, he wasn't up to the job.

Throughout our childhood, Oliver and I had spent a lot of time together. He was a hobbyist, brilliant at thinking up projects and expeditions. Along the way he teased me with the weapon he found most effective: noise. His favourite method of wind-up was to follow me around making infuriatingly loud, repetitive sounds, usually a mixture of tuneful singing and gibberish. This Guantanamo-style persecution drove me to rage and despair, and he was relentless with it. To this day, if I hear repetition in a song I react; I feel maddened and have to get away from it.

Now that he'd turned into a teenager he found worse ways of torturing me while our parents weren't home. I was being seriously bullied and shamed at school, and at home there was no respite.

When I complained about it, Kay reached for rhetoric, telling me intensely, in a cold, histrionic tone, 'Oliver would *never* lie. He would never tell a lie. *Ever.*'

I thought about this. Did she seriously think a boy would never, *ever* tell a lie? And was she saying *I* was lying? It was a very odd way of dealing with the problem, or not dealing with it. Could she not anticipate how he would behave when all parental controls were removed?

Shortly after I'd complained and she'd told me he would never lie, she packed me off to stay outside London with one of her friends. I felt I'd been sent away because I was a problem. When I returned she gave me a skipping rope. I recall the vague, oppressive sense that something was wrong with this, that the present was a kind of pay-off.

They left us food for the duration of the operas and plays, and one night they came home to find 'a mess'. We hadn't cleared the table after our meal, and the next morning they made a scene about it. I'd spent the whole evening being tormented; now I listened to them berating us.

I believed them: we were lazy and selfish. I believed everything my parents said, so much so that moments of doubt — like my sudden perception of Kay's irrationality about Oliver's lying — stand out.

It was morning and I faced school. And suddenly I couldn't face it. I made an announcement: I wasn't going. We argued, everyone grew angry, so I ran into the bathroom and locked the door.

Karl demanded I come out. He grew enraged, rattling the handle, shouting. In the past he'd said to me, 'Don't you *ever* say "no" to me. *Ever*.' My immediate response had been to say 'No'. Now I was doing it again.

After a while, to my intense relief, he walked along the hall and slammed the door. He would be storming off to work, I assumed.

Moments later I heard a scrape, a clank. I turned (reeled, spun) to see Karl's furious face at the window. He hooked his fingers under the sash and lifted it in one violent heave. Our flat was on the ground floor and he'd run, silently, nimbly, around the back of the building, clambered up the pipes and was now coming in the window, over the top of the cistern.

It's comical, the image of Karl shinnying up the pipes, leaping down onto his screaming prey — pure slapstick. Still, it was a bad moment.

Before sending me to school that day, Karl told me my behaviour was so bad they were going to send me back to New Zealand.

'But where will I go?' I asked.

He said, 'There'll be some place that will take you.'

Some institution, I took him to mean.

Oliver and I were fans of the Arthur Ransome series *Swallows and Amazons*. We had a running fantasy that we would own a yacht like the kids in the books. After school that day, alone and miserable and at a loose end, knowing it was rather lame but trying to cheer myself up, I made a yacht out of the couch cushions, using a broom for the mast.

Kay walked in and asked what I was doing. When I told her, she rolled her eyes.

The cold eye-roll did something to me. I dismantled the yacht, took the broom, walked out of the flat into the corridor and walked silently up and down, pushing the broom in front of me. I plodded slowly from the door of the flat to the end of the corridor. I kept going, mindlessly pushing the broom. I didn't know why I was doing it, except that it was an expression of defeat and distress. Perhaps the repetitive movement was soothing. I kept it up for a long time.

We weren't a normal family, were we? Kay said this to me in 2019. A rare concession. But what family is normal? What does 'normal' mean? She didn't elaborate and it wasn't a context in which I could ask her to.

For most of my life I believed we were a normal family, or at least that we were only unusual in ways that were positive, that made us interesting. When I was growing up I often felt distressed, inflamed with misery and anxiety. I could be driven wild with frustration at not being heard or understood, and, because I was articulate, Kay took to calling my outbursts 'raving'. She would say in a breathless, fearful voice, 'Look, she's raving again, Karl. She's mad.'

Kay often affected fear of people; in particular, me. Kay and Karl told me I had a 'dominant' personality. Kay was fragile and timid and I was strong, able to hurt her, so much so that she had to be shielded from me. In fact, she'd put this idea about, this needing protection from me, since I was about two years old.

There was a stock anecdote: when I was 18 months old a family friend had looked out a window and seen Kay in the park being repeatedly hit by me. My mother was just sitting there, not reacting.

The story was told to show how difficult I was, and how restrained she'd been. I accepted this evidence of my badness until I had my own toddlers, when I grew puzzled about it. None of my kids hit me repeatedly, ever. If they had, I would have judged them upset, and worked to put things right. I wondered what she'd been doing, or not doing, or saying.

I have a memory of myself aged 10, in the courtyard of the London Goodenough flats, facing my 10-year-old friend Melissa and repeating intensely, 'I won't be bullied by you. See? I won't be bullied by you.' I recall my friend's blank surprise, and my realisation that in this exchange I was channelling, weirdly and exactly, Kay's voice, and the thing she so often said to me. I had it perfectly, the peculiar rhetorical note, the icy coldness.

We'd been two little girls having some mild dispute, and suddenly this voice had burst out of me, as if I'd been possessed by an alien.

I can see Melissa capitulating, backing away . . .

I won't be bullied by you.

I'm not clear who Kay was talking to, whether it was me, or some other bully who lived in her mind.

Back in Tohunga Crescent, the house next to ours belonged to a man who owned a company that sold musical instruments. It was a square two-storeyed mansion with balconies, floor-to-ceiling windows and a flat roof. A mature kiwifruit vine with a thick trunk wound its way up the front face of the house, its leaves spreading across the plate glass.

The music man and his wife were known for spectacular drunken rows. One night she locked herself in their car and sat with her hand on the horn long enough for lights to go on around the gully, sending our household creeping to the windows to watch the music man dancing around the car, begging her to stop.

When they moved out, the couple rented the house to an American band. The Platters, the African American R&B vocal group famous for songs like 'The Great Pretender' and 'Only You', had gone on splitting and re-forming in different combinations until they turned up, with some unknown project in mind, renting the upmarket house of the music man in the gully of Tohunga Crescent.

We were immediately fans. The Platters were exotic, glamorous, urban, flamboyant. They were incredibly loud. We were dazzled by their jewellery and clothes, their unbelievable shoes. They were a riot of snakeskin and furs and gold. Who knows how disorientated they felt, holed up amid the trees and crowding vegetation, the sunshine and rain of a blustery spring, down at the bottom end of the world.

They radiated restless unease, fractiousness, electricity. The gully echoed with their talking, shouting, singing and fighting. We were thrilled and gratified to hear, for the first time in our lives, the word 'motherfucker'. The noisiest were Chick and Dick, who developed an issue as soon as they arrived. We would rush to the windows as another shouting match ramped up.

'You goddamn mother*fucker*.'

Chick's pithy reply '*Fuck* yo ass' would launch Dick into a tremendous, rich stream of invective.

It became clear their fights were over a woman, which caused Karl to remark at lunch one weekend, as shouts erupted over the fence, 'Dick's chick loves Chick's dick.'

This was the time when the space station Skylab had fallen out of its orbit and was spinning around the Earth, threatening to break up in the atmosphere and crash down in pieces. There were daily news updates and predictions about where it would come down, and how much damage it might do.

When Kay and Karl were out one weekend, Oliver and his friends got the idea to ring next door and warn The Platters that Skylab was about to fall on Auckland. Then they rained lemons down on The Platters' roof. There was tremendous noise as the lemons hit the skylight. Dick and Chick ascertained where this was coming from, raged over the fence, grabbed Oliver's friend, took him back to their house and (in a move afterwards agreed by the gully kids to be fantastically edgy and flamboyant) tied him to a chair.

Then everybody rang the police, Oliver in a panic to say his friend had been kidnapped and The Platters to complain that they were being harassed.

Once the police had untied the friend and placated The Platters, Karl had to drag Oliver next door to apologise to Dick and Chick, who opened the door looking aggrieved and formal in fur coats and hats, and listened in cold silence.

When The Platters moved on we were disappointed, but soon a couple moved in who would generate their own slow-burning drama in the gully. They were a man and a woman in their late twenties or early thirties. They drove a late-model sports car, and right after they moved in they started to be visited by a stream of visitors who also drove exotic cars.

We were keen for action and already covertly watching the new neighbours, wondering who they were, what they did, how they afforded their fancy car when they didn't seem to ever keep regular hours or go to work, or even get up in the morning. They were nocturnal, pale, glamorous, mysterious.

On an afternoon of thunderstorms, the sky swelling with black cloud, an afternoon of rainshine and stormlight, I arrived home from intermediate school to find Kay entertaining two men and a woman dressed in leather jackets and jeans.

They were from the police drug squad, and they wanted to use our house to surveille the couple next door, who were, it was suspected, part of an international drug-dealing syndicate. They were big-time, it was emphasised: hard drugs, a large-scale operation, serious money, the lot. They were tied to murders, even.

Our kitchen offered a perfect view. A lasiandra tree in front of the window would shield the team; they could hide and watch, logging and photographing everyone who arrived at the house. The upstairs sitting room was another good vantage point.

I listened, drifting away from the creaking leather jackets and the smell of aftershave to stare over at the house next door. The young woman walked across a room and switched on a light. The house was like a fish tank, the square frame, the glass front with its lattice of snaking green foliage, the flat steel roof, and inside, in the aquarium light, the couple in their bright clothes passing one another, silently talking.

Kay and Karl agreed to let the detectives in, mostly, they said, because two young members of our extended family (sisters aged 16 and 17) had got involved in the Mr Asia drug syndicate as it was called; one had become a heroin addict, the other a mule who'd run drugs from Thailand and only just avoided being jailed in the Bangkok Hilton. Drug dealers were bad, they felt, and so they agreed.

We quickly got used to the detectives. They came and went discreetly, photographing from the kitchen or from the room upstairs, both of which gave them a wide view of the house and much of its interior, thanks to the plate glass. The cops were friendly and easy-going and had their own aura of toughness and glamour, but we stepped up our own covert spying, and soon we were aware of divided loyalties. We liked the cops, but it was quite possible we liked the neighbours even more.

The detectives could be quite talkative, and sometimes gave a commentary. They said a lawyer who turned up often was a target himself, a crook and a money launderer. They pointed out the odd serious criminal or gangster or Australian hitman. Our family must have seemed so removed from that world, a university professor, his librarian wife and their kids, they were confident we were safely on their side. And we were, except that we paid so much attention to the couple next door we felt we were living with them, too; they were our secret story as well as close cohabitants, fellow members of the gully.

The watchers worked to an absurdly self-defeating schedule: they knocked off at midnight. A lot of action next door occurred after that. Cars arrived, the couple moved around the house, and the man had one notable routine after midnight: he went out to the balcony, got on the railing and climbed up the giant kiwifruit vine, onto the flat roof.

One day the police waited until the couple had gone out before putting a tail on them and getting into the house with searchers and drug dogs. They didn't find anything, but it didn't occur to them to get up on the roof. If the couple were keeping the drugs up there and climbing up the vine after midnight to retrieve them, none of the Steads at Tohunga Crescent ever told. Matters were left to take their own course. We were only required to be discreet and to say nothing, to keep the secret — all the secrets.

Karl used this drama in his novel *The Death of the Body*, in which he described the divided loyalties, the familiarity that can grow into fondness when you live alongside people. He invented extra connections and wove the real story of the Mr Asia syndicate through the narrative, and he turned it into a treatise on the mind/body problem.

His protagonist, the owner of the house the drug squad want to use, is a professor of philosophy whose wife has become a Sufi. She sits at home chanting 'I am not this body.'

The prof has a certain raciness about him. He drives a Porsche and, it turns out, has had a previous encounter with the glamorous young woman under surveillance next door.

It's one of Karl's best novels, an entertaining meditation on the mind/body conundrum, a satisfyingly complicated narrative puzzle with just the odd implausibility that doesn't work amid the ones that do. I was skeptical about the Porsche (a prof in a Porsche?) and never quite accepted that a woman met randomly on the other side of the world would turn up living in the house next door. Those are minor objections, though. There's such expertise in the telling of a complex, time-travelling story that goes beyond the linear, beyond the basics of beginning, middle and end.

The book is flavoured with Karl's preoccupations of the time, including his salty dealings with radical feminism, what he might have regarded as the 'excesses of political correctness'.

The professor, a bit of a success with women, is pursued at the university by a couple of grim 'dykes' from the Women's Collective bent on exposing him as a sexual harasser. He's had an affair with a student, and they're campaigning to get him fired. The professor is saved in the end by his wife and his mistress, who work out how to cover up the affair: 'Two women . . . have upset the social order; now two others . . . are going to restore it.'

Once saved, the professor is described as having (like a dog) come to heel: 'Yes, it's acceptance, and yes, it's wry. Is it also the death of the body? Who can say?'

The dog, in other words, is obedient but not entirely grateful. His body is not grateful.

The conventional women, the wife and girlfriend, restore the social order. Big of them! The ugly dykes retreat (it would be decades before the Me Too movement exploded all over the social order), thwarted by the wife who loves, the mistress who is 'in love'.

The prof survives, benefiting from feminine generosity (and conventionalism), but even with that he nurtures his own rebellion against the social order. His body is still alive. Deep down in his wild dog's heart he knows: you'll never keep him on the porch.

'You know so much about books. Do you write at all yourself?'

Kay got this question often. She would reply: 'No, I'm a *reader*.'

This was her role, Karl's first and best reader. Oddly though, at some stage when I was a child, I noticed she had trouble constructing a narrative with a beginning, a middle and an end. She did relate anecdotes, but her organisation was so shaky she would start in the middle, puzzling her listeners. She seemed to me to have an uncertain grasp of what was already known to her audience, as if she hadn't quite learned to gauge who was likely to be aware of certain facts and who wasn't.

An anecdote might start, with a knowing look, 'So, there was the *dog*', leaving people mystified — what dog? — and others jumping in to fill the gaps.

She had a strong sense of drama, tipping into melodrama, and would express a story with her whole body, as a performance: clutching hands, a special rhetorical voice, intensity.

Back when I was five and we were living in London, she said, she couldn't look at knives, for fear she might stab someone. This was when the marriage had been strained by Karl's affair and Kay had been, as she told me, so depressed she used to come home and put an orange cloth over the lamp, to create some warmth in the room.

She explained: 'I couldn't look at knives because once you've thought of something, you might do it.'

The barrier between the thing she imagined and reality sometimes seemed weak to her. If an action occurred to her, she felt she might do it; if she envisaged an event, it might happen. I accepted without question the blurring in her mind of the barrier between the imagined and the real; years later, when I started trying to understand the unusual ways her mind worked — *We weren't a normal family, were we?* — I wondered about the intensity of her belief.

When I wrote my collection *Opportunity*, I included a deadpan comic story called 'Daughters'. I invented a stepmother called Rania who was outrageously cold:

> *She liked to tell a story about how, when I was a young child, she'd suffered a bout of depression (she was 'highly strung') and had had to fight the urge to smother me. She told this story at dinner parties — while I was there. Her eyes went moist when she told it. Her nostrils flared and she smoothed her hair away from her bony face. The story moved her: how she had suffered. She said I had been an extremely difficult child.*

If anyone had asked me at the time of writing where Rania had come from, I would have shrugged and said 'out of my imagination'. Now, a long time later, I see the black comic outline of Kay, regaling her guests with stories of her suffering at my hands — in front of me.

I could put Rania down on the page, but I didn't consciously link her to my own life. I didn't think I was drawing from memory, or if I did, there was a barrier to my acknowledging it. But Kay got it. She must have, because I remember she described 'Daughters' to me as a 'story about a damaged child' — and I didn't clearly understand what she meant.

Kay once wrote to a judge in a murder case pleading for compassion for a woman who had strangled her teenage daughter. She got fixated on the case; she of all people understood, she grimly told me, how the poor woman had reached that point.

Her sympathy wasn't universal, it was usually an intense alliance with one against another. It was an equation: if there was a good guy, there had to be a bad guy, and she would take sides, strongly, on the basis of labels she'd bestowed.

As a grandmother, she decided one of my children was a 'conformist' and another was a 'golden rebel', and she seemed always to shape a narrative that confirmed this idea.

To a table full of extended family she said, of herself and the rebel, and pointing at the conformist: 'We spent a whole day in the garden digging a hole and making quicksand so *he* would fall in and disappear.'

I registered the word: disappear.

There was much jolly laughter, an atmosphere of approval: the way Kay threw herself into child-minding was so selfless, so engaged. I saw the grandchild who was meant to disappear look dazed amid the laughter, rise from the table and walk away for a moment, as if something had made him uneasy, but he didn't know what. This was how it was, these uncanny, subtle notes, a leitmotif you might just catch. It was hard to work out what you thought she was doing.

I found it strange that I was the only one registering what it must have felt like to be the one who was supposed to 'disappear.'

I puzzled over her labels, which seemed to me wholly inaccurate. It wouldn't have made any difference telling her they weren't based on proper observation of each child's authentic nature.

She'd felt bullied by her elder sisters, so perhaps, for her, elder children were repressive, and younger children were freedom-fighters. She seemed to prefer young relatives who were embattled, and was loved and admired by them. I've seen one give her the bowing-down-in-worship thing people do to winning sports teams (she suavely held up her hand to quell his enthusiasm), and heard another gush about her extraordinary general knowledge and literary sensibility.

There are these patterns in families, alliances, natural sympathies. The change was, I started to notice them. I wondered how it was, back in Tohunga Crescent. The 'conformist' got up from the table and walked away for a moment; that was the extent of it for him, a momentary chill. He didn't depend on his grandmother, or have a strong relationship with her. But what if she'd been his mother, and had made comments like that his whole life?

Kay once mused to me, as though drawing on a rich old memory, 'It's quite a power trip having a one-year-old child.'

She explained (it pained her, but one must face hard truths) that my young son (the conformist) unfortunately wasn't intelligent because he was argumentative. Children who were intelligent didn't argue, because they understood the adults' point of view.

I knew she was wrong (the child would soon prove to have an intellect that dwarfed hers and mine), but maternal authority creates such a mystifying haze that questioning didn't occur to me;

it wasn't until years later that I wondered if she had her areas of ambivalence, or if her personality was even (or actually extremely) complex.

There was the black comic quality, the sense of a mind richly fizzing with *Schadenfreude*. When Kay and Karl visited Janet Frame in the Maudsley Psychiatric Hospital in London, where she was being treated for mental illness, Frame wrote to Frank Sargeson that Kay looked like 'a little gypsy with a red and white spotted handkerchief on her head, and Karl's forehead is transparent . . . Oh the tragedy of little gypsies and poets . . .'

There's a sharpness in Frame's description; it's wry and affectionate and yet there's an edge, a consciousness perhaps of the level stare of the gypsy and the dreamy obliviousness of the poet. 'Little gypsy' presumably mostly refers to the handkerchief, but also to Kay's dark skin.

Karl and Kay and Janet were close friends and remained so until Janet's death. The only disruption to their friendship occurred early on and was caused by fiction, when Karl and Kay were hurt by a story Frame had written, 'The Triumph of Poetry', which seemed to contain malicious references to them.

In *You Have a Lot to Lose*, Karl wrote that Kay was convinced Janet was acting out of 'jealousy and thwarted love'. She felt the story was a 'kind of revenge.' Karl thought she'd written it out of 'a burning, child-like envy.'

In an exchange of letters, in which Karl was dignified and restrained about the cruel story, Frame called Kay 'novelettish', which was undoubtedly malicious but also seemed to aim at something specific. I could imagine that what she'd identified was a mordant quality in the eye of the little gypsy who'd appeared at her bedside, a sense that the visitor was not entirely to be trusted not to laugh.

Writing *Mazarine,* I made the daughter character adopted. In the story 'Daughters' I made Rania a stepmother. It was a retreat from facing a subject squarely. An adoptive mother or a stepmother: too easy. It's classic. A stepmother is almost expected to be 'wicked', since there's no blood tie. A stepmother's hostility is natural.

A mother is different; you are her and she is you. She can't be accused of anything without the accusation falling back on you. If she is 'unkind' in the Shakespearian sense, then you are unnatural and unkind, because she made you. It's unnatural and unkind to name the problem, or discuss it at all. It's a dilemma, and an interesting one for a writer — too interesting.

I think of Sylvia Plath's vehement, disgusted rejection of her mother in the poem 'Medusa', and the ambiguity of the poem's final line, 'There is nothing between us', which I read as simultaneously a repudiation (there is no relationship, no basis for us to be together) and an acknowledgement of stifling closeness (nothing lies between us; we could almost be one).

And I picture a photograph taken by Marti Friedlander, one of many she took of me and Kay. In it I am a baby, aged about three months. Whenever I've shown it, people have assumed it's not of me and Kay, but of me and my daughter Madeleine. We are that alike, it seems. These days, I sometimes hear my mother's intonation in my own voice.

I remember a small hotel room in Rome. Paul was kneeling by the bed, zipping up Madeleine's ski suit. Winter light was flooding through the window and pigeons were crowding on a ledge outside.

Conrad came towards me doing up the buttons on his coat, Paul said something and I laughed. There was a blue-and-gold-framed mirror on the wall, and I saw myself turn and make a particular hand gesture. I jumped up, startled. I thought: There's Kay.

There is nothing between us. There is nothing between us. You could look in a mirror and catch sight of her.

The tie between mother and child can be so close you could call violence towards a child a terrible form of self-harm. But we *are* separate individuals, with free choice and agency. In terms of behaviour, what lies between automatic cause and effect, between having evil done and doing it in return, is free will.

This was the basis for my interest in free will: I wanted to break out of learned behaviour.

There was space between me and Kay. There was something, not nothing, between us. This was the drive towards free will that for a long time wasn't conscious: I didn't want to act out negative experiences on my children.

Kay told us that when she was a child her parents took in a small girl who'd been temporarily abandoned. She recalled how much she'd loved pushing this smaller kid around. For once, she explained, she'd had someone *she* could bully. For once she wasn't on the receiving end. She had relished it, we were to understand, because in all fairness it was *about time* . . .

I remember Margaret saying, 'It was probably a trauma for her.' For the little girl, she meant.

This was what I grew up understanding: my mother was small, timid and powerless, and she had to stick up for herself. She told stories from her childhood, how she would contrive to get her domineering elder sister (Leila's mother) banished to the washhouse for alleged 'cruelty to Kay'. She recalled the scene, full of dark laughter: her small triumphant self at the table, her sister's furious face glaring through the laundry window.

When we argued, Kay would say to me, 'There's something bad in you. There's something bad in your self.'

If we argued Karl would come to her rescue, with his explosive rage.

Karl was famous for ferocity. As a public figure he was scathing, intellectually rigorous, fearless, forthright, rude. At home he was charming, full of laughter, playful and funny, and just as often blowing his top, losing his rag and boiling over.

He was intense.

Provoked at Tohunga Crescent — and he was easy to provoke — he would erupt in fury, chasing, shouting, smacking (although he never hit Kay, as far as I know). She spoke of his anger in hushed tones and often, in her melodramatic way, affected fear of him, said she couldn't possibly compete or stand up to him (he was so power-packed and brilliant) but she was full of reverence for his rage; it was sacred, evidence of his genius, also his rightness, intellectual clarity and justified irritation.

Far from being regarded as a loss of control, his anger was held to be righteous. He would explode, and then he'd be enraged that you'd made him angry. Because how dare you! That myth floated about: male rage was not 'hysteria', but the anger of 'females' was.

Meanwhile he described Kay to me in the same black-and-white terms she'd described Oliver: 'Kay's so honest it's almost a flaw. She just can't tell a lie.' He reinforced the line: I was the stronger personality and she needed shielding from me. She was soft and sensitive, whereas I was hard and tough.

They were a double act, and yet they were also at war with each other. I was a constant source of tension, because I'd always been so close to Karl. He and I played verbal games and had built up elaborate in-jokes; I could make him laugh, and my impression was we got on better than he did with my siblings, whom he tended to both over-discipline and ignore.

It was openly acknowledged as an ambiguous sort of family in-joke that by the time Margaret came along, Karl had got sick of having children. He was busy doing his own thing (as he recorded in his memoir, *You Have a Lot to Lose*, he was embroiled in an intense affair when Margaret was a baby) and consequently he tended to be vague around her, disengaged.

His affair caused arguments and distress. He was conflicted and disaffected, and Kay was distraught about it. The affair and the fighting over it went on and on. As he described in his autobiography, he swore he'd ended it but carried on with it, even while we were living in Menton, where he arranged for secret letters to be sent to him *poste restante*. The same drama was repeated over the years, with each new covert relationship he started.

Margaret was an easy-going, beautiful little fair-haired girl whom Kay could bond with because of the fact that she was ignored by Karl. She didn't get in the way of Kay's focus on Karl, didn't threaten her notion of her place. As Margaret had said, at that time *Everything had turned to shit, and I was her baby.*

Karl and I had our repertoire of jokes and games. I was good at my schoolwork, I was interested in writing, and he, having read some of my stories, had decided I had literary talent. He took an intense interest in me that increased as I grew older, and Kay reacted to that. I was caught between the two of them, and the tension in the house rose and rose.

Perhaps they had an unconventional idea of the special relationship between parent and child. I think they managed it well when we were children, when we were that family of travelling Steads (endless jokes, songs, a minimum of piety) in our marvellous journeys across Europe, our great family adventures, but as we grew into teenagers, perhaps the roles fell apart. They could easily deal with Oliver when he was a child, but when he became a young adult and got himself into trouble, they didn't know how to help.

They didn't realise he'd got interested in alcohol and other substances aged 16, and there wasn't any attention paid to this. They were oddly resistant to the idea of 'guidance', almost as if they shied away from it.

There was a general irreverence for the institutions that govern children. Schools required conformity, which was definitely a piety. You couldn't get Kay and Karl to take a school assembly seriously, or a parent-teacher meeting. They were too satirical. Schoolteachers, with their repressive and conventional ways, were often the object of ridicule. (And, it has to be said, the teachers often *were* awful and pretty funny.)

When there was family disharmony, Karl's response was either to react with rage or to evade. He valued order: the tidy, aesthetic house, the timetable and ceremony of meals, the clipped garden, the cleanliness and moderate living — no excess. Kay industriously tidied and cooked and kept her habits orderly. And yet somehow, in a secret way, emotionally, there was a layer of chaos that couldn't be admitted.

Before he left home, Oliver moved out to the shed in the back garden, which soon began to resemble the lair of a degenerate rock star.

In my memory, if alcohol was involved, my brother's personality took on a lurid quality. The nerd and hobbyist turned weird and flamboyant. He seemed to dematerialise and reappear transformed, to veer out of left field, which made the household as nerve-wracking as a fairground fun-house. You never knew when he'd pop up, bursting into your space with something jarring or puzzling or appalling. He would make grand pronouncements, sing at high volume, come out with obscene statements.

He wanted to be in a band, and became the local Cacophonix, driving the gully to insanity as he plucked and twanged his electric guitar. One neighbour, a doctor, would come raging over the fence to protest about the noise.

Oliver was always genuinely musical. He had a true ear and could belt out a beautiful song. He had piano lessons for years with his teacher, the writer and composer William Dart. He introduced me to a lot of music, but the band we really loved was The Clash. When they performed in Auckland, a friend and I managed to get backstage and meet them. We were driven by our devotion; no one else had thought of walking around the back of the venue and knocking on the stage door after the show. A dreadlocked roadie called Ray waved us on in.

Disconcertingly, heartbreakingly, I was taller than my heroes, Joe Strummer and Mick Jones. They were tiny, cool and exotic, and looked us over with a sort of wary tolerance. We knew we were clods, hayseeds, but we were thrilled to be near them.

When I was 15, I went with Oliver to the music festival Sweetwaters. He and his friends got me stoned on hash and left me alone, distressed and crying, among the tents in a dark paddock. I had never smoked hash before and was so badly affected I couldn't move. I was terrified.

Eventually I was picked up by a patrolling health worker on a quad bike and driven to the hospital tent. The next morning, I shakily discharged myself, farewelled the kindly paramedics, and staggered off to search for my brother, who hadn't thought to go looking for me. This was standard. No one, it seemed, had much of a duty to look after anyone else.

At Tohunga Crescent there were dinner parties for writers, academics and other friends of Kay and Karl: Janet Frame, Frank Sargeson, Barry Humphries, Maurice Duggan, Maurice Shadbolt, Allen and Jeny Curnow, Marti and Gerrard Friedlander, Fleur Adcock, Kevin Ireland, Marilyn Duckworth.

Kay was a talented, creative cook. She'd learned a bit from Frank Sargeson, and later from living in the South of France. Despite his reputation for ferocity and feuding, Karl was warmly sociable, and Kay was too. He was funny, charming, playful. After a few drinks he would balance the wine cork on his nose, make jokes, laugh.

They went out regularly with friends. Karl and Allen went on exchanging poems across the road. Karl loved the writer Elizabeth Knox and always described her as brilliant, even though he couldn't understand her preference for fantasy fiction.

Tohunga Crescent wasn't the kind of bohemian set-up many of their artist friends lived in. Kay and Karl kept fit by swimming and walking. He drove home legally from restaurants, breezed through police checkpoints. He didn't go in for long, boozy lunches or pub sessions, and always left a party before midnight, usually well before. He did get ferociously argumentative after drinking wine (don't we all) and relentlessly certain he was right (ditto), but he was moderate, no drunk.

Karl kept the garden trim, and the inside of the house was aesthetic and ship-shape, full of books, the walls crammed with works by New Zealand painters, Colin McCahon, Pat Hanly, Ralph Hotere, Peter Siddell, Don Binney, Louise Henderson, Toss Woollaston, Richard Killeen, Gretchen Albrecht and more. Looking back on that tidy, orderly scene at Tohunga: it was our family persona, our front and face. It was our emotional lives, our family interactions, that were harsh and chaotic. Behind the scenes, through the looking glass, there was the intensity, the anger, the Byzantine family dynamics, the histrionics, Karl's unstoppable infidelity.

As we grew up and left childhood behind, a strange carelessness about each individual's welfare seemed to expand and spread, invading everything.

'Do it again!'

Karl was the poet who could write in his terrific poem 'Quesada', about Jenny North, the student with whom he had a long affair:

Dulcinea, he'd like to show you
A path dropping through ancient trees that shelter
A pool so clear the small fish seem to hang
In sun-shafts over its shingle floor.
You weren't born when he said goodbye to that place.

He'd loved it as he has loved you
With a wild sweet self-consuming passion.
Last night he dreamed you were standing
Beside a dark unruly river.

The romantic poet, who liked to escape domesticity and who valued wildness and unruliness, was also the martinet who ordered me to vacuum my room and, when I'd finished, knelt down to inspect the carpet, picked up bits of dust, presented them to me with a grim flourish, pronounced my effort no good and ordered me to do it again. The whole pantomime caused me — seemed calculated to cause me — such rage I could barely express it.

It had been ever thus between us. One of my earliest memories is a fight with Karl. I must have been about two. He demanded I go to the door and wipe my shoes, which I'd already wiped on the doormat.

'Do it again,' he said.

It was his tone that was the spark that lit the fire in my tiny mind: I marched outside to the garden, found a patch of wet earth and worked my shoes into it until they were caked with mud. Then, wearing giant, heavy shoes of mud I threw open the door and squelched inside. I recall his face, the extraordinary series of squints and scowls, from incredulity to exploding incandescence . . .

'Pick your battles' a parenting guru might say. Karl picked every one.

I had a saving sense, though, that he was able to see me in a way that Kay didn't. After arguments with her I found soul-destroying, I could have a conversation with him and feel understood.

Always, he stressed I should work hard at school.

The most obvious clue to the disorder beneath the order at

Tohunga Crescent was the intensity and volume of the arguments that sometimes broke out between family members. There could be so much yelling that Karl would go around closing the windows. Sometimes he would erupt in fury and chase me out onto the street. I was capable of becoming wild with frustration. Kay would strike a theatrical, melodramatic note that was also intensely cold, and her tone would open me to that sense I'd had as a child, that there was nothing holding me to the Earth.

Karl kept on with open-handed smacking when he 'lost his rag'. This was standard for the time, nothing unusual. I remember a wry comment during the heated debate when the Labour Government finally banned the smacking of children: 'New Zealanders are passionate about smacking their kids.'

One day I pretended the smack had caused me to fall against a table. It hadn't, but I remember thinking this was something new. Trying some *tactics*. I experimented with exaggerating the effect of the blow, and once also with hitting him back. Eventually he may have sensed we'd entered a more complex and potentially very distasteful phase, and he stopped altogether. In that brief era, I had the feeling I'd become a participant.

I have no memory of my siblings having full-frontal battles with Karl. They were milder, perhaps more likely to slink away. I didn't have any fear of him at all, even when I'd wound him into a frenzy.

I've never accepted that hitting children isn't assault. Smacking anyone is domestic violence. It's counter-productive, unnecessary, it causes shame and humiliation. It's an introduction to the sick nuances of violence, the power play, the *tactics*.

Karl used to say he thought cold-blooded punishment was disgusting, getting kids to bend over or hold out a hand, and whacking 'more in sorrow than in anger'. Lashing out in fury on the other hand (within reason) was honest, spontaneous; it just happened — what were you going to do?

This is how I remember it. This is how I would take the material and tell the story.

There was the sense of family structure falling away, as if the 'minimum of piety' was a framework too fragile to withstand the fact that the children — the loveable, uncomplicated, mostly compliant little kids — were growing up.

Could it have been like this? A theory of the case.

When I turned 13 it seemed that, for Kay and Karl, I had become simply 'another woman' in the house. He joked and flirted, annoying Kay, and behaved as if we were not a family but a group of individuals: one man, three women (flatterers, rivals for his attention) and a son whom he tended to overlook. Oliver either refused to participate, or wasn't invited to the fan club.

All the language and behaviour changed; they stopped behaving like parents. He liked the idea I could write, and she, already stung, hurt and excluded by the disloyalty of his infidelities, grew so hostile towards me that daily life turned toxic.

Perhaps his ego had got tangled up in his regard for me; he was asserting it, putting Kay in the role of 'boring wife'. I was competent at school, set to get more educated than Kay. I was very bookish. It was said I had inherited his literary genes.

Aged 13, I was still a child, needing reassurance and security, but I was stuck in an atmosphere of intense adult warfare involving subtleties I didn't understand, and, along with that, blame from both of them for the stress (the 'chaos') it created.

I can see how this happened, how a man all fresh and bristling from his latest affair, flexing his frustrated machismo (because here he is, trapped at home) could create an atmosphere where his wife was 'the handbrake' and his daughter the one who, for example, 'made him laugh'. I can also see Kay couldn't manage the situation. She put him first and always would. And equally, in the end, he wouldn't put any of his children first. They would come second to the image, his and hers, the front and face.

Yet it was all undercover, overlaid with the rules of order that wouldn't admit, even in the face of glaring evidence, that we ever as a family went in for *too many* or *too much*.

We were tidily chaotic, respectably anarchic, stably unstable.

At some stage when I was a child I made up a story for Kay. I invented an imaginary boyfriend for her. He was smooth and very hot, and his name was Shibboleth. She and I didn't play games in the way Karl and I did, but Shibboleth was a running comic story. I felt for her. She always confided in me in detail about Karl's affairs and her rage over them, because I was willing to listen and sympathise. The Shibboleth story was a tacit expression of solidarity, an acknowledgement she needed more.

In the Eighties, second-wave feminism and 'political correctness' billowed up around us. Kay and Karl regarded radical feminists at the university as repressive and doctrinaire. 'The wimmin', Kay called them ironically. 'The feminists.' There were some unpleasant aspects and bad incidents, including the violent feminist attack on the playwright Mervyn Thompson, but in general a dose of feminism would have been good for our family, even if it was nothing more radical than Kay getting a university degree. She characterised her resistance to feminism, and later the Me Too movement, as 'rebellion' (meaning she was resisting the current intellectual fashion), but I wonder whether she would have been less resistant if she'd gone to university.

Karl didn't tolerate opposition well, so she had to operate obliquely. If she'd been able to confront him it would have been good for him, and we would have been better off. Instead he ruled, and the only person who directly challenged him was me.

At Tohunga Crescent, the insult Kay hurled at me most often was 'You're just like *him*.' Like Karl, she meant.

I can't specifically remember the insults I threw at her, but I know they would have been terrible. I do remember loudly wishing she'd die, and having no understanding that those words in themselves were violent.

Like him, I could tell a story. Like him, I could argue a point. But my ability to remain articulate under fire was described as harsh, tough and abnormal. It was also, in contradictory fashion, called raving and madness. To be told by your parents, with their all-powerful authority, that you are not wrong or unreasonable but 'mad' (i.e. insane) is deeply shaming.

I didn't tend to give in, but years of arguing with Karl and Kay took its toll. I ended up with a low level of confidence, so low that during a conversation I'd sometimes find myself checking data I should have taken for granted. I was talking to X, whom I didn't know well. Could I be *sure* it was X? My ability to distinguish faces was shaky. In that gap caused by lack of confidence I'd lose the thread, and grow more unsure. Sometimes I'd spend so much energy pretending to be listening that I lost focus on what was being said.

A partner at the law firm where I eventually found my first job told me, with a lilt of mockery, that I was the only law clerk who *apologised* when I hovered at the door of his office. I winced with shame as he imitated my deferential tiptoe and trembling hands, my musical *excuse mes*. It was a law firm; brashness and assertiveness were prized, and here I was, creeping around like a doormat who'd grown up in . . .

What had I grown up in? All those times I'd told the media: lovely childhood, a house full of books. Karl and I had got on brilliantly: we had the jokes, the shared literary sensibility, the conversations about literature . . .

Until my year of questioning, of lapse, I thought my upbringing had been mundane, my parents not unusual, it was just that there were a few things wrong with *me*. It took me a long time to free my mind, and, when I did, I found I was alone. The whole family — parents, sister, a cousin, various friends of my parents — reproached me for wondering, for writing, for cautiously trying to answer the question asked of one sibling by another in *Mazarine*:

> *Once I asked him experimentally, 'Do you ever wonder why we're so fucked up?' I'd had a few glasses of wine, and got carried away with the idea that he and I could help each other. His reply was eerie. 'But we're not fucked up at all, Frankie,' he said. 'I have* no idea *what you're talking about.'*

Karl was charming, intellectually fearless and witty. He could be warm and funny, and he could be as volatile and unrestrained as his stereotype of the female hysteric. If opposed in an argument he went all-in, he wanted verbally to dominate and overpower. He was a force of Nature. Opposing him was a lesson in total war. He had a radar for detecting weakness. Wavering, I learned, would produce a sudden focusing, a moving in, a patronising tone; were you going to cave, give in, apologise? Standing up to him required a very solid wall.

The prevailing family narrative, enforced by him and by Kay's reverence, excused his anger, honoured it as part of his forceful male brilliance, and so we dealt with it, year after year, and had to participate in defending and admiring it.

Kay worked in the university library, where she got on well with the students and academics, who loved her charm and helpfulness. But she feuded with the senior staff, whom she loathed. She regaled us with stories of their soulless, conformist behaviour. I marvelled at her bad luck: three bosses, and each, by some cruel twist of fate, more monstrous than the last.

There was a specific issue at play: the management, sticking to their rulebook, refused to promote her beyond a certain point because she didn't have a degree. Instead of studying for a Bachelor of Arts, which she could have done, she regarded it as an injustice that an exception couldn't be made for her. She was after all, extremely well-read. She felt she was someone who didn't need a degree. She wouldn't enrol for one, instead she complained to the Human Rights Commission. Her complaints were rejected but she didn't give up, and spent years in conflict with management. I wonder now why she never enrolled for a university course, part-time. She would easily have been able to do the work.

In 2017 I wrote in an article in the *Sunday Star-Times* that I'd 'grown up in a family so stressful I emerged from it chaotic'.

Karl denied it, and said that *I* had been the chaos.

Puzzling over it, I tried to recall more of Tohunga Crescent. Karl was such a disciplinarian about domestic matters, it sometimes seemed as if he was himself being harried and persecuted by a tyrant, some overlord of the Rules.

'You've started a new one.'

'What?'

'You've started a new one. But the old one's still *a quarter full*.'

'Oh god. Really?'

He would be holding up the jam jar as evidence. The odd thing was the intensity. How much it mattered.

If you threw up your hands and said, 'Yeah, but actually, so what?', or if you tried (truly outrageous) to ask why it mattered, you'd be off into an explosive confrontation.

He rigidly oversaw the food in the house. I suppose this could be a reflection of the era he grew up in, but I don't remember anyone else having such an intense fixation. To take fruit from the bowl without asking was a grave offence. If portions needed to be divided up he had to do it, and would fly into a rage if defied. He kept up this controlling behaviour around food as if it was an unstoppable compulsion, and would become tense if not allowed to supervise the doling out of food even in a gathering of adults.

All this eventually led me to drastic dieting. I starved myself for years until one day on the beach at Karekare, having changed into a swimsuit, I realised I'd taken it too far. I was making myself weak and ill. It was the most obvious equation: if one's father is highly controlling around food, and is also very interested in 'looks' and 'figures' and reveres people who can 'eat and eat and never gain weight' (as he could and I couldn't — I just got fat), one stops eating to opt out of all that.

I recall an argument in the Dordogne in France where we had met up on a family holiday, a drama lasting a whole afternoon, involving rage on his part and histrionics from Kay, when I had unwisely, sarkily, suggested that we 'children' (Margaret and I) could divide up some French pastries ourselves, without the need for his guiding oversight.

This argument took place when I was the mother of two children, and approximately 28 years old.

In the house when we were kids he laid down the law aggressively, while Kay was lax about order and rules. But as far as life outside the house went, there were no boundaries. If we were out of sight, we were out of mind.

At Tohunga Crescent, Karl made a high-jump set for us in the back garden, two properly measured poles on stands, a cross-bar made of bamboo and an old mattress to land on. This was an inspired and brilliant idea, a smash-hit entertainment, and I and the kids from the gully spent years practising on it, trying to break records, perfecting our Fosbury Flops and Western Rolls.

As I got older my hyperactive energy intensified, and after testing (taking things further and still further, waiting for a reaction) I discovered there were no boundaries to contain me. Kay didn't give me any useful instructions about sex, men or safety, and she imposed no control over where I went, at what hours, or who I was with. I was given no limits, no health instructions, no sense she was concerned about what I was doing. It was liberal parenting in its purest form.

When I was 13, I liked swimming at the public baths. One of the pool attendants was a man in his forties who started talking to me, flirting, writing me love letters and giving me photos of himself. We spent long, dreamy weekends by the pool. He told me about his beautiful South Island birthplace, promising to take me there. I reported to Kay, as usual. I showed her the love letters and photos, which I found comical; I wasn't in love myself. She didn't do anything about it. She wasn't alarmed.

When I was still 13, he pulled me into the First Aid room at the baths, announced we were to be married, and proceeded to behave, as he grandly put it, 'as my husband'. If I'd complained to the police he would have been charged with rape.

The episode may have contributed to my sense that I didn't have any rights. I wasn't off-limits or inviolable; just the opposite. I told no one at home, judging that a report would be regarded as off-putting, embarrassing, that the disapproval would land mostly on me.

At Tohunga Crescent there was a bracing atmosphere. We were all intellectual rigour and emotional prudishness. Karl insisted on his 'minimum of piety'. There was a general distaste for the sentimental or humourless. Irreverence was insisted upon. Humour was prized, which was a good thing, yet it tended to creep into oddly inappropriate situations.

Funerals, mysteriously, could sometimes send Kay into satirical overdrive. When her sister died, she didn't return from overseas even though she was due to return anyway in three days' time, but rang me wanting to have a laugh about how farcical she felt sure the funeral must have been. I was shocked — her own sister! — and refused to supply the expected string of jokes. Denied, she grew sullen and furious. I knew I was being humourless, a bore, and yet . . .

I remember both parents writhing at the new fashion for the word 'relationship'. Personal problems were not to be discussed. I recall Karl trying to force me to finish my meal while making jokes about anorexia. Anyone who suffered from it must be disgustingly neurotic. Jokey intolerance, robust mockery was the standard.

They had opposed the Vietnam War, and in 1981 we protested against the Springbok Tour as a family. They were liberal, committed Labour voters. And yet, during the Eighties, Karl was increasingly labelled in the media as a reactionary conservative. He regarded this as an injustice, and to a certain extent it was, the result of his arguments against the more radical assertions of second-wave feminism, like the notion that all men are rapists.

He was brave, willing to oppose current pieties, to make an intellectual stand against groupthink and mob rule. But his reputation as a conservative also reflected the aspects of his personality that were reactionary. He made statements about the drive to achieve equality for Māori that he later disavowed (he was never a racist, and he acknowledged he'd got things wrong there), but he didn't manoeuvre much or far on feminism.

What he did say to me and Margaret, though, consistently: you need an education, you need a career.

In 1981 the Springbok rugby tour divided the country. Half the population thought 'sport and politics shouldn't mix', and half wanted to protest against South Africa's apartheid regime by disrupting the games. It was my first experience of strong political feeling and commitment. We threw ourselves into it, going to every protest we could. There was a march every Wednesday, and a big one at each game in the weekend.

The Steads, in a spirit of rollicking camaraderie, piled into the family car, the battered old Morris, and drove to the match in Hamilton, where Karl was one of the group who managed to tear down the fence, storm onto the field and stop the game. The police marched out onto the field in full riot gear, the first time the country had seen local cops in helmets, carrying shields and long batons. The announcement was made; the game was cancelled. The stadium was packed with enraged and yelling fans, and the protestors who weren't arrested inside had to escape thousands of infuriated spectators. Many were violently beaten up.

Karl was arrested on the field and escorted to a paddy wagon. The images of the new beefed-up police riot squad were already drawing references to his 1971 novel *Smith's Dream*, in which New Zealand turns into a totalitarian state. In the cell at Hamilton police station he wrote on the wall, 'CK Stead, author of *Smith's Dream*, was here.'

Back in Auckland my friend Jayne (one of the last female friends

I had) and I made it our project to march in the front line every time. The demonstrations grew bigger and rougher, and the police response stronger, until the final game at Eden Park in Auckland turned into a genuine riot, with pitched battles, hurled bricks and hours of mayhem. The protestors had got organised, positioning a line of the biggest and heaviest men at the front wearing motorbike helmets and carrying shields.

The police had started surrounding stadiums with shipping containers and barbed wire to block the marchers. But a protestor got hold of a light plane and flew low over Eden Park, dropping flour bombs onto the field.

Kay was arrested during a protest in South Auckland, accused of having knocked off a policeman's helmet in a fracas. She was bravely trying to stop officers carrying off a young Niuean man who was being held around the neck, and who was shouting (like a forerunner of Black Lives Matter) that he couldn't breathe. She and Karl were charged with 'disorderly behaviour', defined in law as actions that would 'offend right-thinking members of society'. They defended themselves in court on the basis that as right-thinking members of society they were offended by the tour. They were both convicted and fined.

In September 1981, Frank Sargeson wrote to Janet Frame:

> *All the Stead family have been prosecuted and fined over the Springbucks — even down to the little girl — most improper!!!*

For a restless, sensation-seeking teenager, the Tour was a rich experience. At the time, half the country condemned the protestors as thugs, criminals and radicals. But we were on the right side of Judge Time.

When Nelson Mandela, still in prison, heard that New Zealand had erupted in huge protests against apartheid, he 'felt as if the sun had come out'.

There will always be the test question for New Zealanders of a certain age: What side were you on in the Springbok Tour?

Without rules I roamed freely. For Kay, I felt, the more hair-raising the tales I brought back from the night-time city, the better. As a young teenager I could hang out in central Auckland at three in the morning if I wanted to, and Kay would listen to my anecdotes of street life with apparent enjoyment. She always said she'd started turning me out of the house to play in the gully when I was two, and would just call occasionally from the back door to see if I was about.

Once I told her I'd got stuck out in the suburbs across town and had tried to sleep under a hedge, but found it too uncomfortable. She listened with interest.

This was Kay's stance, or at least this is how I interpreted it: she was on my side! If I wanted to do crazy things, she wasn't going to get in my way. If I wanted to risk my safety, push things to the limit, she was all for it. She would cheer me on. She would laugh and show me, with her keen enjoyment, that she'd be admiring if I went even further.

I was 14, walking across Hobson Bay to the gully with a friend. We'd been together for the afternoon, and now she was about to head home. All day I'd had the uneasy feeling I couldn't communicate with her properly, there was a kind of barrier between us. I remember thinking I was losing something. I couldn't get close, I couldn't get her to come close. I couldn't imagine her mind. That afternoon, walking across Hobson Bay, I had the sense I was disappearing.

This is a particular memory; the first moment I felt something altering in my brain. From that day the feeling of having lost the ability to communicate with my female peers increased. When I was a child, my close friends had been girls and I'd loved their company. Now I was cut off, and, because I was separated, I lost my ability to speak the language of women.

It was around this time I stopped speaking at school. Having been a willing and noisy participant, I clammed up in class and no longer talked to teachers. My silence became an oppressive force I couldn't overcome. When I moved to Selwyn College in the fifth form, battling the silence that had descended on me, my English teacher wrote in my report that I'd sat in class all term expressing 'dumb insolence'. If she'd known how I was struggling with the silence, how it stifled and inhibited me. I didn't fight my way out of it for years.

Eventually I got so unconfident and unpractised that after a conversation with a friend of hers I would ask Margaret, 'What did she mean by that comment? What was she actually saying? What's the best thing to say in reply?' It became an accepted fact in the family, a quirky detail: I was so socially uncertain, I looked to my younger sister to interpret an interaction.

I accepted this state of affairs. It was just the way I was. My silence and solitariness were the result of my personality. Margaret called me The Lone Wolf. It took my whole life falling apart — my marriage blow-up — for me finally to wonder what had gone wrong back then. I wasn't autistic. I'd started out sociable. What happened to me at the age of 14 that turned me so unsure and uneasy around women I spent decades avoiding them?

I can only sift through the material and try to make sense of it.

The material is the memory of conflict, the way it intensified as Karl started to annoy Kay by engaging with me, finding me witty, sharing private jokes, perhaps making her feel that an interloper had invaded the house.

What was my part in all this?

I can't recall, except that I looked up to Kay and wanted to please her. I found it easy to talk to her; in a conversation around a table my gaze would return to her, as if she alone was the principal listener. This was the case with Margaret, too; her gaze would slide back to Kay, telling her *first*. From my earliest memory it seemed a compelling quality of hers, the ability to draw out, to elicit the tone she wanted to hear — to be the one we always directed our thoughts to, and tried to please. We knew what kind of story she wanted, and we supplied it.

The material suggests this to me: back then, she wasn't torn. There was no contest. It was very simple. *If Mum had to choose, it'd be you she'd throw off a cliff.* Her whole life revolved around Karl, he was the sun who gave her light, and nothing could be allowed to interfere with that. I had no understanding back then, just a growing sense of disquiet, distress, insecurity, fear. Of disappearing.

With the material I try out this theory: while I was still completely dependent on both of them, my awareness of her hostility grew so strong I disappeared behind a wall to withstand it. She hid it, yet she also obliquely revealed it when, say, she would recommend a movie to me and it would turn out to be about a woman who loathed her daughter, and I would accept the perverse little shock; it was the way things were. I never clearly thought in terms of missing out, of a lack, yet it seeped into the way I saw myself.

Could it be that my trick was so effective, we were able to co-exist for years, as family, as extended family? Perhaps the key to the stability of our unstable family was this ability to 'control the reality', mentally to block off elements that were wrong.

It was all hidden, deniable, a problem that could be called a fantasy, something I'd made up, but that would eventually find its way, not into the 'family story', but into novels and short stories, into the fiction, Karl's and mine.

Going to the literature I read, the human animal has a reflex: avoiding situations that are a reminder of trauma.

Is rejection a trauma? During my year of consulting a psychologist, my listener would occasionally shock me by dropping her usual restraint and rapping out, in a burst of impatience, a forensic summing-up. One day, after listening to me rambling and puzzling, she drummed her fingers on her office desk and said: 'Here's a theory. He expressed his anger with her, using you. She did likewise. She was jealous of your intense rapport with your father. She didn't love you. For her, you were the scapegoat. She made herself the damsel and him the white knight . . .'

And then I was shaking my head, 'No, no. That's too . . .'

'Too what?'

'I don't know — too stark?'

'Life can be stark.'

'No, no, no . . .'

Disappearing wasn't part of Margaret's experience. The family story was that Karl tended to vagueness, wasn't really focused on her. She was the youngest, Kay's baby, who couldn't be associated with anything that had gone wrong.

Nor, with her fair hair and blue eyes, did Margaret remind Kay of the assumption often made: that Kay, with her jet-black hair, dark skin and characteristic features, was Māori.

After Karl made the character based on Kay in his autobiographical novel *All Visitors Ashore* a possibly/probably Māori woman called Patagonia de Thierry Aorewa, he had more than one encounter like this.

'Your wife's Māori.'

'Er, no. She's not actually. Her family are English and—'

'Come on! Yes, she is!'

Some weekday afternoons Kay and I would visit the Three Kings Supermarket while waiting for Oliver to finish his piano lesson with William Dart, and each time we'd be trailed around the aisles by an elderly Māori man who took a liking to Kay, automatically assuming she was Māori. He spent a lot of energy trying to persuade her to tell him her hapū and iwi.

He would say, kindly, 'Come on, Kay, just admit it!'

She tolerated him, and went on denying it. Her parents had been English and Irish. The racist jokes in her youth about her mother's 'pā-sneaking' (cheating with a Māori man) were untrue. The old man would shake his head.

'Be proud,' he would say. 'There's no shame.'

At the funeral for her sister, I looked at photos of Kay in childhood. Anyone would have said of her, without any doubt or hesitation, 'That is a beautiful Māori child.'

I was often taken for Māori myself. When my hair was cut short it tended to stand up in straight brown spikes like the spears of a sea urchin, and the Māori and Pasifika kids at school gave me the Māori name for sea urchin, 'Kina'.

At Tohunga, Oliver sometimes caused chaos. Pandemonium could break out at family events, from ordinary dinners to birthdays to Christmases. By the time I was a teenager, everyone seemed to have turned into a lawless entity; everyone was an individual and not a family member. When I think of my teenage years I recall continuous conflict, wild behaviour, a sense of insecurity and mayhem.

On a weekend when Kay and Karl were out of town, my siblings and I had a party at Tohunga Crescent, and one of the drunken crowd threw a brick through the neighbour's window. The neighbour called the police, who turned up en masse and broke up the party. The kid who'd thrown the brick managed to evade the police by hiding upstairs behind a curtain.

The neighbour was an elderly woman who could have been injured or killed by the projectile. When Kay and Karl got back they were angry and told us off, and apologised to the neighbour, but the recriminations died down fairly quickly.

I didn't have a proper appreciation of the wrong, no sufficient empathy for the woman. Now, I am struck by this.

Soon Kay was telling the Tohunga Crescent wild-party anecdote as a funny story, focusing on the detail about the offender evading the police by hiding upstairs behind the curtain. (She probably left out the terrible detail of the brick.) She seemed to have little feeling for the elderly woman, who'd been a neighbour for years, and who'd been subjected to an act of depressing violence.

It took me some time to unlearn this uncanny lack of empathy, this blindness. When we were lawless teenagers ranging around the suburbs, my friends and I tested our nerve and daring by wrecking phone booths and spray-painting walls. I remember calmly watching a car burning after someone had lit a bin bag and shoved it under the chassis. Soon it was completely gutted. We carried out acts of vandalism and minor theft on a regular basis. Defacing and small-scale arson were common entertainments.

Someone's car! This is the grim reality of the material here: I had the civic sense and empathy of a person raised by wolves.

When I became a parent myself, I had my wild youth firmly in mind. I suppressed details of my crimes, and tried to ban Kay from telling my children 'funny stories' about them. I pushed education, as Karl had done; I tried to smooth the path with the schools, to encourage the kids to empathise, including with their teachers. I wanted to lead by example.

This revisionist suppression of my early wickedness led to friction with Kay and Karl, who probably found it fraudulent and hypocritical, and didn't appreciate the motive: I wanted to protect my kids. There began to be hints that I'd turned humourless, conformist. Also, 'bourgeois'. Neither seemed to understand how destructive all the trouble and chaos had been. At Tohunga Crescent, while the parents were non-conformists intellectually, the children had gone troppo, and the end result was serious damage.

Back when I was a teenager, Kay appeared amused and entertained by my accounts of disorder, vandalism and arrest. I would mimic for her what the police would say, in bored tones, when someone was getting busted, 'Right. Get in the car!'

She repeated it, laughing, imitating the world-weary tone, 'Get in the car!'

Aged around 15 I strolled out of some city pub or nightclub and ran into Louis Dale. I knew him vaguely from the neighbourhood, and he offered me a cigarette, before suggesting we walk home together. We talked and smoked and laughed, and when he finally left me at the top of Tohunga Crescent to walk to his parents' house nearby, the sky was already getting light. This became our routine; wherever we'd been around town, sometimes miles out and in any weather, we'd walk home to the gully.

For five years, Louis was my close and only friend, and we spent all our free time together. Our haunts were the pubs and nightclubs in central Auckland, and the various flats he lived in, especially one in the Brooklyn apartments in the city.

He was a graphic designer, the elder brother of the painter Jenny Doležel (she used their real surname, which their father had Anglicised to 'Dale') and a talented artist himself. He was tall, blond, half-Czech, wildly funny, talented and beautiful. He was original and entertaining, he made me laugh, and I loved him.

Louis had a slightly deformed left hand. It was smaller than the right, with the little finger missing. He hid it, and it dominated his body language, giving him a lopsided, graceful gait. To make things harder, he was left-handed. He'd been bullied because of his hand, and because he was original and artistic in an era in New Zealand when those qualities were not prized, they were frowned upon.

At school, bullying was widespread and accepted. The teachers were rough and intolerant. There was absolutely no attention paid to 'mental health'. You got on and fitted in, or you got hell. Conformity was valued over all. We'd been hit at primary school with the leather strap and the boys were caned at the grammar schools, although not at co-ed Selwyn College, where Oliver and I both ended up.

Oliver had been bullied at Auckland Boys' Grammar, because he was small and bespectacled, and had buck teeth. He was tormented by the boys and caned by the men in charge. The schools reflected the society; they were repressive and harsh. Back then the ideal man was an All Black: gruff, butch, monosyllabic.

Louis and I were temperamentally rebels and outsiders. We were also resourceful, enterprising and energetic, which meant we were a suburban menace, our own hectic little crime wave.

One of Kay's favourite anecdotes, which I described to her in detail, was the night Louis and I blew up the phone box at the bottom of Seaview Road. We had run from the hilarious explosion and flames and hidden in Bloodworth Park from the police and dog-handlers who'd shown up. The fact that Kay seemed most to relish was that we'd hidden in a clump of fennel bushes on the edge of the estuary, meaning the police dogs were unable to track us, even though they'd got very close, because the aroma of the fennel plants had masked our scent.

I didn't fill Kay in on everything, but I told her a lot.

'Rebellion', I understood, was okay in her book, very funny, and sometimes even 'marvellous'. This took in vandalism, graffiti with spray-paint, minor arson, being arrested, expelled, revolt at school, any other mayhem we could come up with.

Louis and I were obsessed with phones. It wasn't yet the era of cell-phones, but Louis had a keen (actually prescient) sense of phones as an accessory and a desirable objet. They were an interesting collectable, because the models were always being updated. We coveted the latest, most modern style. We specialised in stealing phones from public places, with all the risk that involved. Louis, who had left school and was working as a graphic designer, would take the phones home and paint and decorate them in creative ways.

My impression was that, for Kay, our graffiti and our ongoing theft of phones was acceptable because it was pure 'rebellion', and intrinsically amusing. Louis was regularly arrested for this kind of artistic crime. Another item we prized and often stole was pot plants. I can see Louis toiling home in the early hours of the morning, bent under the weight of a giant palm or rose bush in an ornamental pot. We were always trying to outdo our last most daring exploit. Kay seemed to find our adventures funny, and they often were. I spent a lot of effort telling her about them, giving her what she called 'the blow-by-blow account', making her fall about.

I could make her laugh as easily as Karl did; it was always a genuine current between us. I knew exactly what would crack her up. She had, as one cousin put it to me, the wonderful ability to be 'absolutely pole-axed with mirth' — and I did too. Louis was a funny guy, and we both committed crime in a state of amusement; it was all about the laughs.

There was never a moment in my memory when Kay tried to slow this down, or deliver a parental warning about where the comedy could lead. It led to damage. But the odd thing was that when, later in life, I tried to tell Kay and Karl that I'd suffered, that it's not funny being on the wrong side of the law, that it becomes *very dark very quickly* (try being locked in a police cell overnight, or herded into court cells with other offenders, or strip-searched and humiliated by male officers who laugh at your body — it is not funny) they accused me of 'losing my sense of humour'.

Endless jokes, a minimum of piety.

They had never had those experiences themselves.

I remember Karl picking me up from the District Court after I'd been arrested. He commented on a duty solicitor's nice legs, and told me I'd looked 'very beautiful' in the dock.

He was kind, it was good of him to show up, but it was like being picked up by some distracted stranger (checking out the hot solicitor) who was only vaguely paying attention to the circumstances. I'd spent the night in the cells, and it was beginning to dawn on me that none of this was funny. It was grotesque. Awful shame was hanging over me in a cloud.

Rebellion, the kids' form of 'jokes and no piety', was really in full swing around that time at Tohunga Crescent. The person providing the entertainment for Kay on this front was me. But the material tells me this: she had different dimensions. I saw little Kay, doubled up with mirth at the latest blow-by-blow. She was also blameless, respectable, a good mother trying to deal with the unruliest kids in the world.

Kay once said, chuckling, of a young member of the extended family who'd fallen out with his parents: 'Of course, he spent time living under Grafton Bridge.'

If I imagined the boy living under Grafton Bridge, his misery, fear and desolation (the sense that his mind was alone), she wasn't pleased. Again, I was being humourless, critical. I was being pious.

It was when it occurred to me to question or reinterpret the rules of the literary family, to try to describe real emotional experiences — what it must have been *like* for the boy living under Grafton Bridge, what it was *like* being lost in the Pararaha Gorge — that Karl started calling me a scold and a fantasist.

He urged, 'Try to free yourself from the grip of this unreal fantasy.'

But why were we so wild?

One long-running episode that kept Louis and me and, by proxy, Kay, entertained was when Louis got behind the reception desk at the Hotel Intercontinental and stole a skeleton key that opened every room in the building. He and I spent nights amusing ourselves in empty rooms, making free with the mini-bars and stealing every phone we could find.

Karl was busy and often absent, and I didn't regale him with stories of chaos. He spent a block of time each year abroad, months at a time, writing the latest novel, conducting his affairs, and his affairs. There were academic conferences, book festivals, meetings with his UK publisher and his literary friends in London.

He wasn't particularly bothered by what I did, but, unlike Kay, he did consistently tell me to get educated. His insistence that I work hard at school was the reason I kept at it and did well. He countered Kay's take on education.

Perhaps this was the most singular mystery: that a writer, poet, literary critic, a university professor laden with degrees, was married to a woman whose approach to education was genuinely subversive.

She didn't simply accept she was the uneducated one, she pushed a reality in which she was not on a par with Karl, but not so different, because brilliance was innate; educated people could be dull and narrow, and uneducated people could be geniuses, just born that way.

All that's true in a sense, but Kay refused to acknowledge the value of formal education, the gaps it fills. When I published *Foreign City*, a novel about an artist, she said, 'I couldn't imagine where you got all that stuff. About painting. How on earth?'

'I studied art history. I've got a BA,' I said.

Always the enigma, the shapeshifter, Kay evaded rules while seeming to abide by them. Civic duty wasn't something she pushed, in my memory. She'd been the youngest in her family, had been Little Kay, and still was. I never had the feeling I was being mothered; it was more like negotiating with a contemporary. I sometimes had the odd feeling she was younger than I was.

She told me, 'My world was different from yours. Much less secure, less affluent. Immigrant parents. No sophistication, no higher education. Semi-rural Henderson, totally rural ramshackle Omokoroa.'

She spoke of Omokoroa with dread; it was the farm where she'd been regularly sent as a child, from the age of about three, to stay with alcoholic relatives who lived in squalor and chaos and didn't look after her and her sister at all. She couldn't stop it happening. Her protests were not heard. Omokoroa came to seem significant to me as a shadow, a hidden clue to our lives, and I would return to it with the idealistic aim I'd had from the beginning, to look for understanding and forgiveness, for 'truth and reconciliation'.

Now she'd left all that behind, and her lawlessness was concealed. Karl was an intellectual star, and so, as a couple, they were defined by that. She was an anarchist, enabled. An anarchist in hiding.

In my short story 'Daughters' I described lovelessness, the way a lack of empathy might be passed down. The 'daughter' of the story is approached by a man who seems to need help, and instead of responding she fends him off:

The man at the waterfront — I couldn't remember what he'd said. Something about himself. Or about his body. Had he told me he was hurt? Out in the harbour the current — smooth water crossing ripples — formed a snaky question mark. Was it possible he had asked for my help? I laughed. You came to the wrong place, mister. Sorry about that.

In the same story I wrote about committing vandalism and petty crime, the puzzle of it. What were we doing, what did we even think we were doing? The daughter of the story ends up working as a receptionist in the brothel her stepmother runs:

And the men, the clients — they reminded me of something. They reminded me of myself. Long ago, in all those back yards, the empty houses in the drifting afternoons. The breaking and entering. The searching, the rummaging. And then the emptiness of a white courtyard, ribbons of light glancing off a pool, the strewn pile of knick-knacks and trinkets. A kind of daze afterwards, a confusion in the lull. What did the men want? What did I want? What I stole I threw away. I didn't want it, not really. What was the thing we looked for and couldn't find?

Even while writing the story, I was trying to get at something without knowing what it was.

Only now is it clear to me, the thing I looked for and couldn't find.

Kay's talent for looking after children involved being patient, good company, and willing to throw herself into activities and expeditions. As she put it, it was as if she herself was one of the kids. As a grandmother, after Paul and I returned from London, and later, after Leo was born, she would play gin rummy, hang out in the bush reserve and build huts, join in imaginative games and projects. She would come back from the park with tired, happy grandchildren and report, 'We've had an *idyll*!'

She spent hours at the Army Surplus Store with Leo, which he loved. One day they bought a real sword there and carried it home on the bus. She embraced adventures. Always, there were maximum laughs.

Because of my memories of childhood anxiety and insecurity, I was vigilant with my kids; they weren't to be left alone; they were to be kept safe until they were old enough to be independent. I paid close attention, and yet, until my years of questioning, it never occurred to me to wonder about episodes like the Pararaha, or to doubt Kay's judgement. She was aware of my vigilance, though. She knew I was paying very close attention.

Childhood memories: I remember Kay giving me a jar of hot water to warm my hands in winter, and her sleeping on my bedroom floor when I had bronchitis, to make sure I was breathing. I remember taking long walks with her, a lot of intense talking, and my ability to make her laugh. She hardly ever smacked, and if her 'nerve broke', as she put it, she would only stamp and yell, which wasn't particularly alarming for kids used to Karl's rages. I remember her getting up to me in the night, and also the sense that she was in some struggling way a bit of a child herself. I have an early recollection of wanting to look after her, elaborately guiding her down the mountain track at Mt Maunganui, a fantasy in which she was helpless and dependent, and I was strong and in charge. I wrote this in *Metro:*

> *When I was a child I had disagreements with my mother, as one does. I remember sitting in the bath arguing while she toiled in the next room over some chore to do with my baby sister. There must have been one too many comebacks from me, in the echo chamber of the bathroom. She stormed in, slapped me about the shoulders and shouted, 'Animals are not as important as humans!' While capable of much storming and weeping myself, I was oddly unmoved on that occasion, calmly looking up and seeing the displaced steam, whirling and rearranging itself, sucked after her as she raced out the door again. I remember driving her mad on the subject of size. 'How can we have any real perception of size? We have no idea of scale. Because the universe is endless . . .'*

I have memories of her distress at Karl's first significant affair. I recall sitting on the windowsill aged four or five, looking out at a thrush on the wet lawn, and listening to her crying. When she went to pieces she would, as she described it, 'just lie down on the floor'. They had to hire a Karitane nurse to mind us while they packed to go to Menton, and whenever she talked about that time, of the affair and their departure for France, I was given to understand she'd spent a lot of time lying on the floor.

She was probably physically demonstrative when I was a child, but I never had the experience of being hugged by her as an adult. Once, after she'd had a minor car crash, I forgot and tried to hug her — she leapt backwards, bristling. It was a humiliating moment. I've looked at photos of her and Margaret and me; she's a small figure sitting pressed against Margaret, I'm leaning goofily towards her and she is drawing as far away from me as possible; there is space between us in every photo, created by her.

I found a late photo, Christmas 2019, of her with Oliver and Margaret on either side leaning in; such a close pose couldn't have included me.

When I turned into a teenager, I had the eerie feeling I'd lost a brother (the Oliver of my childhood) and a mother. I remember a sudden loss of control, bursting into tears and sobbing with misery, and the way Kay sat across the table from me just watching, not moving, not speaking, her eyes sharpening like a cat focusing on a mouse. Instead of expressing empathy she would adopt a stance. I remember her tone turning melodramatic, as she delivered her opinion on why I'd brought some misfortune on myself. Her rhetorical tone seemed so intense, so histrionic and weird; I've never heard it anywhere else. It was grandiose, delivered with a flourish, intensely cold.

At those moments she seemed (to me) able to radiate a complete lack of affect, an aura that made me think of her as some kind of elf or changeling, a character in a fantasy. Once I'd become a teenager she would never go near me physically at all. I remember feeling mortified when I'd bumped into her by accident: that I'd touched her.

I tried to translate the puzzle into fiction. In *Mazarine* I wrote:

One day, when I was about seven years old, she ran over a dog that lived in our street. I was in the back seat, and recall the impact, a high-pitched bark that turned into a shriek, followed by an unpromising silence.

Inez realised what she'd done and was immediately enraged. Instead of stopping to investigate, she jammed her foot on the accelerator, powering off up the road in low gear. Like so many incidents from childhood . . . it seems a baffling mystery now. Why did she not stop and check whether the dog was dead, or horribly injured and in pain? Why not look for the owners, own up to the mistake, apologise? And why the fury?

This was the question I wasn't supposed to ask: growing up and later, why was my experience of Kay different from everyone else's? What was wrong with me? She was always a lovely woman. She was warm, chatty, friendly, open-minded. People enjoyed her company and genuinely liked her — loved her. Conversations with her could be fascinating. She retained information, had huge general knowledge and was sharp and often funny.

Sometimes I had the sense of almost creative trickiness, of dark laughter offstage (of the little gypsy perhaps). One year, I referred our cleaning service to Kay, and the nice woman, having done the cleaning at Tohunga Crescent, would turn up at my house full of praise: 'Your mother,' she would marvel, 'so kind. So lovely. She always *hugs* me!'

There was such a disconnect between my own private reality and the family story, and the family line was so aggressively enforced that I seemed to live in two worlds.

I noticed too much, which in itself creates difficulty. In my novel *Soon*, I wrote:

> *Maybe the less sensitive you are to signals from the animal kingdom, the easier it is to love and be loved.*

Now I find myself searching for incidents, trying to find evidence that my impressions were real. One year in the recent past a young PhD student stayed a week at Tohunga Crescent, and they brought her to lunch at Paul's and my house. They had a connection through an overseas university where Karl had been a visiting fellow. She was beautiful and charming, and Karl was delighted by her company.

He said to me privately, 'Kay *hates* her.'

'Oh? Why?' I asked.

'Well, for one thing she's rather affectionate. Kay absolutely *loathes* her.'

I laughed. It seemed to fit.

On the last day of her visit, one of our children went on an outing with my parents and the young woman, and described an argument between the young woman and Karl about 'women in the workplace' — something to do with the difficulty of combining work and motherhood — in which Karl so comprehensively squashed the woman's ideas that she was shocked and crushed, and opted to walk home with our kid rather than return with my parents, who motored off together in a taxi.

'It started with Kay,' the kid said. 'Kay got the fight going. And Pa [Karl] took over.'

No doubt, I thought, laughing again. Kay would have needed protecting from the young woman.

But Karl had liked the young woman enormously; I'd seen that when they'd brought her to lunch. Now perhaps he wouldn't see her again. Look what Kay had made him do.

When otherwise intelligent people behave irrationally, powerful forces are at work. The way I saw it, Kay took the submissive role, but it was more complicated than that. In her own way, she was a powerful force.

This was what *she* was up against. One day when Paul and I were living in London, Karl came to lunch and told us about his recent trip, driving through the former Yugoslavia with two beautiful Croatian women, both associated with his publisher. It had been an intense experience. He showed us photos and revealed, not quite expressly but clearly, that he'd had an affair with at least one of them. For me this wasn't shocking, it was fairly standard; by that time, it seemed each new novel told the story of a new covert relationship.

Kay was back in New Zealand, and only found out about the affair later. (Even after she'd found out, he made her accept they would invite one of the Croatian women to stay with them when they were on holiday in France.)

As we were looking through the pictures of Karl and the two women on the edge of the Adriatic, the phone rang. I answered and heard Kay shouting. I made out her words, 'I've broken in!'

She was beginning, as usual, in the middle. She was agitated and distressed, but eventually I got the story. It was three in the morning in New Zealand and, acting on some instinct, she'd just spent three hours breaking into the padlocked trunk in Karl's office. When she'd finally smashed the lock open with a hammer, she'd found letters that were evidence of love affairs she hadn't known about.

Back at the table, Karl was dreamily stacking his pile of photos.

I said, 'Mum's on the phone . . .'

Over the years I'd listened as she'd agonised in great detail about his infidelity, and I'd sympathised. Margaret would run away blocking her ears, but she was excused on the grounds that she was sensitive, 'like Kay'. I said (no doubt self-righteously and unrealistically, but with her welfare in mind and wanting to be kind) that the cheating was unfair; she should put her foot down, tell him it was unacceptable. She told me I didn't understand, she couldn't live without him.

Years later, after Paul and I had split up and I was distressed that he'd cheated, Kay said to me in a dismissive, scornful tone, 'So much fuss is made about infidelity these days.'

It was such a cold-blooded piece of hypocrisy, such a pivot, that I broke out in a shameful protest. Did she not remember her own agony, how deeply she'd suffered, how I'd listened to her talk about every affair? And now to pretend I was just making a silly fuss?

I argued, went on like a lunatic, so intense was my indignation. I hadn't gone off like that since I was a teenager. We were staying at Margaret's house in London. (Fortunately, Margaret and her husband were out.) Both parents seemed astonished, as if my reasoning was beyond them, my outrage inexplicable.

Kay was adamant; her new line was that she'd been cool with Karl's infidelity all along. It couldn't be otherwise. She was scornful of my 'sensitivities' about being cheated on (and temporarily left). She had 'never' suffered trauma and depression, been overwhelmed by Karl's disengaged behaviour while she was struggling with young children, never been distraught over his continued lying. She had never 'just lain down on the floor'. She and I had not discussed the problem at length, over years. None of my memories were valid. Our shared experience, my memory of it *was not real*.

Perhaps I'd heard so much from Kay about Karl's infidelity and the details of their marriage that in the end, when she decided to alter the story, I had to be blocked out.

The following morning, I was appalled by my loss of control, at the way I'd lost my temper. Kay and Karl were due to travel to the South of France, and they motored off together in a taxi . . .

My years of questioning had started by trying to understand Kay's imposition of silence — I was no longer asked to supply the stories she wanted. This mercurial person I'd yearned to love and care for, who was, I was always told, 'so honest it was almost a flaw', so guileless she just 'came out with things' and 'couldn't lie'. She was the person to whom Margaret and I had told our stories *first;* she was the riddle at the centre of all that was unspoken, and she was, for so many reasons, mysterious. It was an almost impossible challenge, one that could only be approached, cautiously and obliquely at first, via fiction. *It's material. Go and make a story out of it*. Perhaps she was only a subject for fiction. In this, as in her whole life, she was a novelist's problem to have.

If she was the one we'd told our stories to first, I believe she also shaped and elicited the content and tone of them. Invariably, we told her what she wanted to hear. She did us the favour of listening to us, even if we were editing our narratives to please her.

I wonder if, when she was growing up, anyone ever listened to her.

I wonder if this is relevant to her understanding of the silent treatment as a devastating weapon — whether in some fundamental, instinctive way, she understood the power and significance of narrative in the orientation of self and mind.

All my life she'd maintained her marriage to a highly educated man who had a towering intellect, a raging temper, a complete lack of marital fidelity and a wildly sensitive nature. She'd kept her place and her grip during times when she'd almost lost her hold. She told me many times that his infidelity (especially when she was stressed and fragile from dealing with young children), his anger and alienation and her indignation had driven her to the edge of sanity. But they held together, depended on each other, and he would call her 'part of myself'.

I tried to make a portrait because I was trying to understand. It was their custom to evade definition. I wonder if, beneath the surface, there was a continual power struggle. He cheated on her, but he also (surprisingly often) confessed his infidelities to her, because she was the one he talked to first. His confessions caused rage and conflict. He told her off; she sulked. She matched him in conversation. He was rude to her in public; she responded reasonably, making him sound irrational. They punished each other. They fought battles, rows descending into black silences. They maintained a front, that he was 'brutally frank and honest' and she was 'so honest it was almost a flaw'. She was covertly capable of terrifying coldness while projecting an image of openness and warmth. She was capable of genuine warmth, as was he. And honesty, as was he.

They were charming and funny. They laughed at the world, they faced the world. In the evenings they lay on the sofa reading, while she stroked his head. He kept her awake in bed by making too many jokes, and sending her into hysterical mirth. His poems made her weep. She read his manuscripts and gave him a sharp critique. When he was in Auckland and not on one of his extended jaunts overseas, they went swimming and shopping, to restaurants and movies together always. She convinced him, and he convinced me, that she was weak and timid, that she needed to be protected from me. Once, after I'd had an argument with her, as they came towards me in a café he brandished a furled umbrella like a spear, its point towards me, while she tiptoed behind in a Quixotic image of the lady shielded by her knight.

She was loyally competitive on his behalf. When I told her I'd won the Montana New Zealand Book Awards Deutz Medal for fiction (I got the news in advance because I was going to be in Europe at the time of the ceremony), her face went dark. She said 'What about Karl?' and rushed off.

One day she and I met a man in the street who said to me, 'I enjoyed your novel. You're giving your father a run for his money!'

Kay was charming to him, but after he left she said, 'What a cunt.'

Her vehemence shocked me; she wouldn't normally use the word.

At her darkest, I had a sense of her looking out from behind Karl, fixing me with a black stare.

And in the end.

They love each other, they are devoted to each other. I see them in my mind's eye, down at Kohimārama Beach where they swim every day in summer. They are elderly, small; she has a bad back and he holds her hand to help her across the road.

I see them, still holding hands, walking away from me under the flowering pōhutukawa, into the sunlight.

Why write in the past tense? Because this is a story about what happened (and in the end we are all past tense). The past is fixed but the future is unknowable. Things can change. Walls can come down.

When it finally occurred to me to ask people — a cousin, a male journalist friend — whether they thought Kay was 'soft and timid', they both laughed. She was tough, they said. In control. Hard as nails. My cousin said, 'I've often been stung by her sarcasm and her sharp wit. She puts down my silly theories.'

'Sharp as a whip,' one said. 'Great to talk to. Keep your wits about you. Watch out!'

'The power behind the throne?' one suggested, although didn't sound sure. I thought about that. Not the intellectual power. But in some ways . . .

I wanted to tell the story of our family, at least to myself, in order to save myself. All my life Kay and Karl had been telling it, and now I didn't think it was accurate.

Karl was a controller by nature; he controlled the message. He wrote the story. I learned from him, and from reading: I knew how to create a composition, shape it, make it orderly and beautiful. How to push darkness outside the circle, make wrong things right, make sure no one felt a heel. (Unless they were outside the circle and, amusingly, *the shoe fitted*.)

And then I fell out of step, and started recording messy details, trying to assemble something authentic from the facts. I thought of Picasso creating a sculpture out of junk. You could make something meaningful, control the composition, without disguising its constituent parts.

To the outside world, to me in Karl's emails, Kay had to be defended as a uniquely good and innocent person, his 'first and best reader'. All of which, in many senses, she was. But he couldn't confess to any subtlety, nor concede any ambiguity.

He couldn't acknowledge any of it, the progression from his and my intense bond to my becoming an object of conflict. The warfare between them that overrode the normal ties of a family. The dynamic, the powerful forces, the damage. He was allergic to the idea of subtlety and duality, of hidden depths, unless they were outside.

One wanted to control the world . . .

I realised our realities weren't likely to converge; Karl and Kay's way of thinking would mean they would see my description (my telling the true story) as evidence of a defect in me. For them it was simple: I'd gone mad.

In the same way, they'd both interpreted the negative story about them by Janet Frame ('The Triumph of Poetry') as being motivated by Frame's 'jealousy' and 'burning envy'.

It was as if someone was telling me, the universe was telling me, these people you've loved all your life, they don't see you. You have one role. If you step out of it, they won't come looking for you.

Because if you stop, if you change, what is the point of you?

I didn't accept this. I couldn't believe they didn't see me. I kept trying to find common ground. The only way I could reply to their accusation that I was crazy for confronting any of this (that *I* was the chaos) was to raise a crude comparison: which of us fucked up (per Larkin) their children? *You two did. Not me. Not I . . .*

If I was inherently chaotic as a child (and Kay and Karl were normal), how did I create a peaceful, harmonious family once I'd got away from Tohunga Crescent?

How did the accusation that I was inherently chaotic fit with Karl's question, *Where is the girl who had such a clear sense of reality and its boundaries . . . ?*

Questioning the record, I made a discovery. My cousin Leila, the daughter of Kay's sister, confirmed to me what I'd partly, intuitively, understood as a child. She told me her mother's treatment of her had been so harsh that she still suffered from it even after her mother had died. It had driven Leila to misery, and when she had become self-destructive and self-harming as a teenager, her mother had berated her for 'causing the family embarrassment'.

That aunt of mine was famously outgoing and demonstrative, particularly known for her warmth, generosity and kindness to the young people she taught in her job. Her relationship with her daughter, the lack of empathy, was covert, hidden from view.

Leila laid it out for me, after reading *Mazarine*.

She told me that her family's verdict (including that of her siblings) had been that her memory of being singled out (the only one singled out) for that cruel treatment by her mother couldn't be correct.

They told her: what she had felt and experienced was *not real*.

I'd written a novel, *The Night Book*, which was a kind of sequel to my *Opportunity* stories. That year I'd gone from reading Dickens to reading a lot of Balzac, and now, with a growing collection of linked fiction, I'd got the idea to write my own small version of Balzac's *La Comédie Humaine*, tales of contemporary New Zealand society. *The Night Book* had been shortlisted for the New Zealand Post Book Award for fiction, and I was due to fly down to Wellington for the ceremony. I heard Kay laughingly telling a story about Leo: that he'd been heard standing on a wall at school and saying, 'I want to break the law!'

After much hesitation, just before heading off to Wellington I wrote a cautious email, tiptoeing into it, emailing because anticipating a discussion could spiral out of control: 'So, I hope you don't mind my asking and obviously tell me to fuck off and everything, but would Kay mind not encouraging Leo to rebel at school?'

The kids enjoyed school, I wrote, pressing nervously on. It was important to their welfare. They tended to take their cue from the adults. I knew from experience: telling them school was a repressive regime and the teachers were 'Nazis' would encourage them to get into trouble . . .

It did no good, all the tiptoeing. The response was a complete rejection. Once again, I was a fantasist. I sat reading the reply, pinching the bridge of my nose with my fingertips.

I didn't want to damage the kids' relationship with Kay ('we've had *an idyll*'), but I didn't want them to get into trouble. I didn't want to say anything negative to the children. In the end I would ask an expert. Why would a grandmother keep encouraging a grandchild to rebel at school?

It wasn't that I was looking for trouble. I wasn't obsessed with the kids' education; one of my few school policies was don't be pushy.

The significant phrase in my email (maybe the one that hit a nerve) was 'from experience'.

I knew from experience exactly how this could go, the damage that could be done.

How it went for me: when I started at high school, I loved it. There was the pleasure of learning, the thrill of abruptly understanding in Latin class how an inflected language works. I was part of a circle of girls and there was intense happiness in that — the joy of being part of a group. I didn't know I would lose that particular happiness and never get it back.

In the afternoons and evenings, Kay would spend long sessions with me and one of my last female friends, Jayne, questioning us about school, and working us into a state of indignation at the repressiveness, tyranny and pettiness of the teachers. Authority should be resisted, she reckoned. They shouldn't get away with what they were doing to us, was her opinion. Rules. Uniform. Conformity. The teachers were as bad as her unbearable bosses at work.

'They shouldn't be allowed to do that, I reckon. I reckon it's *wrong*.'

These sessions were mesmeric. She referred to the teachers as *Gauleiters*. These Nazis were destroying our souls with their petty regime. She painted us as fighters, free spirits, standing up to the bullying of the teachers. She focused on our youthful recklessness, stoked it, licensed it. She said nothing about the value of education, or the risk of being expelled, or the damage exclusion would cause.

I would arrive at school primed to rebel. I threw myself into it.

The school began devising sanctions, and, when the usual punishments were used up, I was demoted to a slow-learning class. Every other girl in the group was Māori or Pasifika, and we spent our days on field trips, since we were considered unable to handle academic work. While other girls were in class, we'd be up Mt St Johns 'gathering specimens' or 'sketching' (smoking, lazily bickering, gossiping) while the teacher lounged in the grass, glazed, her skirt pulled up over her knees.

In the slow-moving class I became aware of racism, the way its atmosphere touched everything we did. A memory: the class was sent on an errand to fetch chairs, and I overheard the elderly secretary, an Englishwoman, say, 'I've got some of the native girls to help. They're big and strong.' At that time the word 'native' was so racist I was stunned. 'Big and strong' carried its own implication: 'suitable for manual labour only'. The take on the word 'native' is different now I think, but back then it was unequivocally derogatory.

Back at Tohunga, discussions with Kay continued, with all the melodrama of an undercover terrorist cell. One feature of the tyranny was the school uniform. We scorned it as a symbol of repressive conformity — and Kay chuckled when we defaced our Grammar School smocks, pulling out threads, drawing on the hems, wrecking the fabric. It never occurred to me to recall my misery aged 10 at St Alban's in London, and the degree to which my suffering would have been lessened if we'd worn uniform. So many things didn't occur to me. It was a special talent of Kay's, whipping up a mood so intense, so full of laughter and collective feeling that you couldn't see your way out of the fog.

Kay was physically uncoordinated and despised sports. I'd always been good at sport, but Kay frowned on this, too, and I had confrontations with a PE teacher who wanted to teach us self-defence. This fight reflected Kay's rejection of feminism: self-defence was newly taught as part of women standing up and fighting back.

I would have liked to learn it, but there I was out in the playground protesting, making a stand against it. If only the teachers could have understood: I was desperate to please my mother. I yearned for her approval and her love. In all of my strenuous bad-girl act, I was being a really good girl.

When, inevitably, I got into serious trouble, Kay joined me in aggressive, melodramatic confrontations with the staff. During one meeting with a head teacher I turned my back on the woman, a histrionic display that makes me cringe now — and marvel. You could say it was good of Kay to back me up, but it's not the way I would ever play it with my own children. If you're acting on a person's behalf, do you barge in, tell the judge he's a jerk and the system is bullshit, and march out of the room? Not if you want to avoid a seriously destructive outcome. The disputes went on until, eventually, the teachers tired of the drama, and suggested I leave.

So there it was, I was the academically capable daughter of a writer and university professor, being encouraged by my own mother to drop out of school on the basis that education was a tyranny. The more gratuitous hell I kicked up, the more Kay praised me. At the same time, she regaled people with stories of my difficult behaviour.

It all came back to me decades later, when I sent that polite email asking Kay not to encourage my children to rebel at school. It was when I had my own kids that I started to puzzle over the way she'd cheered me on towards expulsion. I understood how vulnerable teenagers are, how vulnerable *I* was back then.

I remember the initial happiness: being part of a group of girls who were like me, and the thrill of academic interest. I kept up the drive to learn, but I never got back that sense of belonging.

There was an anti-authority flavour in the air; there had been the Bastion Point Māori land protests, marches against the Springbok Tour, and Kay was in revolt at work over the refusal to promote her. Karl had publicly objected to recent changes in the English syllabus in schools; he regarded new methods of teaching English as a significant dumbing down. He was right about this. Kay had left school at 16, so perhaps didn't have a sense of what I'd be missing if I dropped out. But even given all that, there was a strange recklessness in her campaign. The answer to the syllabus being dumbed down is surely not to reject school altogether.

At the time, I was also getting into more trouble on the streets. All the roaming at night had started to end in my being picked up by the police for petty crime, vandalism, setting fires and underage drinking. I had numerous court appearances. Kay seemed to find this as picturesque as ever, and never tried to rein in the night-time activity, even when my risk-taking increased.

I didn't have a sense of danger and would venture into hazardous places at night, hanging out with drag queens, bouncers, DJs, street kids and prostitutes, always known as parlour girls, many of whom were dully engaged in the business of self-destruction.

One regular place was a flat in Karangahape Road, where a friend lived. He was a nightclub DJ, Māori, six foot three and massive, around 130 kilos, with a shaven head, heavily tattooed. His intimidating appearance frightened people, which was useful and often funny, but from our very first meeting I'd sized him up as completely benign.

We'd become friends at a club in Fort Street. His flatmates were bouncers and parlour girls, the apartment was squalid, and the air of inertia was heavy in it, since everyone was nocturnal, and mired in stages of desuetude, addiction, struggle. I hung out there because, as Kay might have said, it was picturesque, but after a while I felt its dinginess seeping into my soul. There was a sort of lassitude among the street people, a fatalism that bothered me even as I seemed to be sinking into it. I liked the rough action on the streets, but I wasn't happy. I wanted education, intellectual stimulation, precision, clarity, beauty. I was acting against my own nature.

We spent our weekends in pubs and nightclubs, often going on to an all-night bar afterwards. I was fearless and also, increasingly, deeply ashamed. The sense of shame at being put in a cell is extreme. Appearing in court is shameful. Being continually labelled a rebel is shameful, as is school expulsion.

I had fantasies of being rescued, and, in some vague, muddled sense, getting arrested played into this. It was a yearning to come up against a limit, for someone strong and benign to be in charge. But the force I was tangling with wasn't benign, there was no rescue, there was only damage. The police were well-known for being racist, sexist and brutal.

Through all this I was serious about my schoolwork. I got good marks, I loved studying, was efficient at it, and did it well. I never turned in assignments late, never missed homework or an exam.

After I'd served my sentence in the slow-moving class, I'd arrived back in my own ('Kina' was tanned, with a Māori accent and a smoking habit) but nothing went smoothly, and I left the girls' high school for the co-ed Selwyn College.

It was a time when the nuclear ships and submarines of the American Navy were still calling into Auckland for their sailors' rest and recreation. New Zealand Prime Minister David Lange had brilliantly argued at the Oxford Union Debate that 'nuclear weapons are morally indefensible', and made his now-famous quip, 'I can smell the uranium on your breath.'

Local protests were strongly pushing for a nuclear-free Aotearoa New Zealand, and each time a US military vessel came in, protest boats would go out on the Waitematā Harbour to make it clear the ship wasn't welcome.

I and a group of kids at Selwyn decided to join the demonstration. We spent time building a raft big enough to carry five of us, and on the day we launched it down at Westhaven Marina. As we wallowed and floundered across the choppy harbour, I did perceive (abruptly, starkly) that we could be capsized, run over by a ferry, hit by the aggressively manoeuvring police launches or annihilated by the American ship itself, towards which we were paddling with suicidal determination.

But fear was lost in the exhilaration of joining the flotilla of boats bobbing around the Navy ship. Further out, Karl sailed smoothly by, one of a group of celebrities on board a yacht owned by the defence lawyer Peter Williams, QC. Karl stood at the rail looking suave, a wine glass in one hand and a protest flag in the other.

It took hours to get back to the marina, and we were pursued by police in high-powered inflatable dinghies who were as charged-up and reckless as we were. They rammed us, circled and took aim again, careering at us with jeers and insults. It was a great day, and it was satisfying that in the end the protests worked: the country was declared nuclear-free and the ships stopped coming.

At Selwyn College I earned good marks, which meant I could go on to Auckland University and complete degrees in law and arts, even though I was expelled from the school halfway through Year 13 for skipping classes. I spent the rest of that year working fulltime as a cashier in a corner shop.

I would come home at 3am after a wild night on the town and tidy my things. I've never failed an exam. I was orderly and conscientious as well as constantly in trouble.

Recently, I talked to a cousin who told me my parents used to regale the extended family with stories of my terrible behaviour.

This cousin called me Dark Charlotte. 'You were *bad*,' he said.

Good, bad? Dark? Does anyone know what they're like? No one has an outside view; even your image in the mirror is skewed. I do know this: I'm temperamentally an optimist, and I always had a sense of hope.

A memory: Paul and I and Conrad were living near Russell Square. Karl, Kay and Margaret were coming to visit London and would be staying in the house of Kay's friend in Notting Hill. I hadn't seen them for a year.

On the day of their arrival, I got Conrad ready. He was two years old, and I told him we were going to see the family. It had been so long, the day had finally come, it was very exciting. I'd made sure to get us both a haircut. I dressed him carefully, combed his hair, put on his new little jacket and shoes.

We set off walking, went down into the Tube, got on the train. Conrad was a remarkably alert and sharp toddler; he learned the names of Tube stops after one journey, and would know the order on the way back. We came up from the Underground and walked through Notting Hill. At one point we sheltered under a tree from a heavy downpour. All the way, we chattered about the family, Kay and Karl and Margaret.

When we got to the house I let him out of the stroller, took his hand and we walked up the steps. I rang the bell. Kay opened the door. I raised Conrad's hand in mine, felt my smile getting wider, more foolish. She was expressionless. She looked away and said, 'Oh, it's you.'

She turned and walked off down the hall, leaving the door open.

I picked Conrad up and held him on the doorstep. I stood there for a moment, putting my face in his hair, feeling the warmth of his little head.

Then I followed her in.

I'd got from Tohunga Crescent to where I was now without looking back, deliberately not looking back, but now I'd puzzled my way to a conclusion: all was not as it seemed. The family story was, in some fundamental way, mysterious.

There were Kay's labels, the way she decided a person's type and treated him or her accordingly. Perhaps, I thought, the labels fitted the boundaries of her reality; they were a means of divide and rule, part of a small, domestic system of power and control.

She was sensitive, clever, and she had her scars. Growing up she had, by her account, been bullied by siblings, and her mother had been teased and accused of 'pā-sneaking', having an affair with a Māori man because of the way Kay looked, especially since Kay's elder sisters were fair-skinned.

As very young children she and her sister had been repeatedly sent away from her family to stay at the farm at Omokoroa with chaotic relatives, where she wasn't protected, where the children slept five to a bed and the adults were drunk all day. Her distressed protests, her pleading for this to stop was ignored. Her mother went right on doing it.

She was tough, refined, subtle and she hung on, using every method she had to deal with the forces around her: the fiery, cheating husband, the unruly children, the world she struggled to deal with. She was prickly, dark and deceptive. She would always carry on. She had her wits about her. Watch out!

I believed everything she said until I was in my thirties, when I started to get a sense of smoke and mirrors. I decided to live with the mystery, to accommodate it, and not to question. I made this decision very consciously one day in London, when she'd come to lunch with Paul and me. I had a moment of realisation. I'd told her we were thinking of returning to New Zealand. She *so* didn't want us to, it was striking.

There wasn't anything to be done with the starkness of this revelation but to carry on with what we had. What everyone had were her undeniably great qualities . . .

Paul and I did leave London and fly back to New Zealand. When the plane landed in Auckland, I was exhausted after the 26-hour flight with small children, and worried we'd done the wrong thing. I was irrationally disappointed that the weather was indifferent, cool and cloudy. Everything seemed seedy and drab.

But it didn't take long for the mood to lift. I went for a walk and got caught in a rainstorm. It was all so fresh, the rain-scented air so soft, the storm light striking. I was exhilarated. I looked at the shafts of sunlight that Māori call the ropes of Māui playing on the choppy harbour. My senses were adjusting, recalibrating. I was home, and everywhere there was beauty: a phoenix palm against the sky, the spiky silhouettes of cabbage trees and flax, black cloud over the volcanic cones, the play of light and shade on the Waitematā.

There's sometimes a great stillness in London when the air doesn't move, and in summer I'd found this lovely, the huge oak trees, the silent, warm, walled gardens, the breathless parks. Auckland, sitting on the narrow isthmus between harbours, is hardly ever in that state of calm. It's changeable, lashed by squalls and currents, by what Katherine Mansfield called 'shipboard weather'. Nature is always breaking in, rocking the sagging fences, sweeping across the ramshackle landscape. Now I found this dynamic openness terrific, like a tonic.

We had no money, having spent it all on travel, and we rented a small, bare, basic house in Awatea Road in Parnell. There was a view over Hobson Bay, and we were back in the tūrangawaewae, the old stamping ground. After London, Auckland seemed not only beautiful but so comfortable and easy, I thought of it as Holiday-land.

Leo was born in Auckland, and three years later, Soon arrived.

'Work hard. Be good. Be Starfish!' I'd say. But Soon was the comic centre of the action.

Soon. He was tiny, but his ego was large. Small, cold, grandiose, an iconoclast, he was poignantly incompetent and frequently needed bailing out. He wasn't formally educated, but was clever and quick. Histrionic, passive-aggressive, a covert abuser, he was always ready with a secret kick, but only to creatures weaker than himself. He was jealous, competitive and sensationally malicious. He sought credit and kudos, but wouldn't do the work. When given the choice, he *always* took the low road.

He was a character . . .

and [illegible] there was beauty, a [illegible] the spiky silhouettes of cabbage trees and the [illegible] clouds [illegible] upon [illegible] the play of light and shade on the Waitakeres.

There were times [illegible] Auckland when the clouds [illegible] moved and [illegible] the huge [illegible] walled gardens and [illegible] Auckland [illegible] sitting [illegible] that [illegible] calm [illegible] by squalls [illegible] weather [illegible] always [illegible] the [illegible] landscape [illegible]

We had no money, [illegible] and we rented a small [illegible] Parnell. There was [illegible] and we [illegible] only [illegible]

Leo was born in Auckland, and three years later, Noam arrived.

We [illegible] Parnell [illegible] but soon we [illegible] centre of [illegible]

[illegible] small [illegible] and [illegible] books [illegible] being [illegible] but [illegible] was clever [illegible] with [illegible] creatures [illegible] than himself. He [illegible] and [illegible] What [illegible] beloved.

He was [illegible]

TWO

Wonderful childhood, a house full of books. But then it all began to unravel. My marriage — the base on which I'd built my happy new life, mended my tattered self-confidence and raised my children — had struck trouble. I'd been thrown into a terrifying abyss of loneliness and loss.

I'd reinvented myself once, but this time, with too many questions unanswered, I couldn't do it alone.

Karl and Kay had put off their European trip during our crisis, a decision of Karl's for which I was intensely grateful. But spending time with Kay after Paul and I split up, I'd had the sense of being shown around the Badlands; there were wafts of *Schadenfreude*: Ooh, this is what it's like, everyone's ruined down here, this'll bring you down a peg . . .

'You know he'll never be faithful.'

Paul had come back, and we were in the process of picking up the pieces. Kay and I were sitting in a café.

I sipped my flat white unhappily. 'He will.'

She sat back, lightly scoffing at my naïvety.

I wondered what signs she saw. She did have a lot of experience, it had to be said. I asked, 'You don't really know that, do you?'

She fixed me with a narrow stare and said, 'Ooh, I know all right.'

Not long after this levelling exchange, she stopped talking to me. The era of silent treatment had begun. The reason for it remained mysterious. It would extend over years, through significant dates, a health scare (mine). It was also denied. Hotly, indignantly. To mention it earned me the accusation of disloyalty and cruelty, and I knew no one would believe it. (Except psychologists. They were unsurprised. People did stuff like this.)

It was the black comedy of the literary family, the kind of detail that caused a psychologist to exclaim, 'My God, your family! What a dynamic!' Another time, she leaned back in her seat and said, 'It's Shakespearian.'

Paul and I had been in turmoil all winter; now it was spring. After another night of wild distress, I decided I needed help. I went out into the windy street and rang the office of a psychiatrist I'd googled at random: Dr Verne. I picked him because he had an office relatively close to town, in Ponsonby.

As the wind tore at my clothes and whipped the rubbish off the top of the bins, I had a premonition: something radical was going to happen. I was going somewhere new. All those years ago I'd killed off my old self; now again, something revolutionary was called for.

Much later, Dr Verne would have a word for this new stage: integration. It would be a third act; I would discover that I was not two selves, I was one, and I would be stronger when I brought my selves together.

In my meeting with Dr Verne, I ran though details about my life. I was nervous, talking so fast he held up his hand, 'Hang on, hang on.'

The room had French doors opening onto a garden. The gale was lashing the trees outside, rain ran in the guttering, there was a sudden rattling shower of spring hail. I looked out at the sodden trees in the underwater light.

I outlined the questions I wanted answered, the ones I'd had to confront when I found myself alone. My sister was able to make friends effortlessly, and was surrounded by a group of women friends while I, who had grown up in the same family, with the same parents, was so solitary I'd never had a close female friend in adulthood, and was afraid of a future in which I would become isolated and eventually die of loneliness . . .

'Hang on, hang on.'

Why were we so different? Was it genes, or some other reason?

Nature, nurture. Big question.

Dr Verne laid down his pen and considered, his fingers steepled. He said, 'You need to talk to Dr Sanders.'

'Oh, okay,' I said.

He went on, 'She's available on Thursdays—'

'Wait. *She?* She's a woman?'

'Yes, sure.'

There was a silence.

'I'd like a man. Can I have a man?'

'No. You can't,' Dr Verne said.

'But I can't talk to women,' I reminded him.

'*Precisely,*' he said.

This was the plan, as Dr Verne saw it: I would enter into a therapeutic relationship with a woman, and in the course of that we would notice what issues came up, examine difficulties, explore problems, and assess whatever it was that had separated me from female companionship. The goal was to get me to a point where I could abandon my rigid and constricting ways of behaving. I could change.

His plan sounded straightforward enough. In reality, it was a white-knuckle ride. From the very first day I came sidling into her room, I could barely deal with Dr Sanders.

I found her pretty much unmanageable.

One day, reporting to Dr Verne, I gave a summary of the difficulties I'd been having:

I didn't trust her.

I tended to interpret her every signal as negative: she was bored, she was angry, she didn't like me.

As soon as she'd established a level of trust, some small misunderstanding would cause it to vanish.

This was just the beginning. It was when I realised I quite liked her that things started to get complicated. I began to get distressed on leaving her office, as if we were parting for five years. On an emotional level I couldn't get it straight that this wasn't the case. She was so understanding and empathetic, so kind, and it was such a powerful experience to confide in someone after a whole life of not doing so, that the periods of not being able to talk seemed bleak. I sometimes had the weird sense that I was in prison, and that she would breeze in to visit every week or fortnight. I alternated between relief at seeing her — at last — and private indignation at her monstrous lack of concern that she'd kept me deprived for so long.

It was a comedy, but it was wrenching.

When we embarked on discussing traumatic experiences, I got such a sense of unreality I would be unsure afterwards whether our session had been real.

I was unable to visualise her face between meetings, and so she had a dream-like quality. Eventually she gave me a photo of her face so I would know what she looked like when she wasn't around.

Sometimes after our meeting I would know I'd met her and talked to her, but I also had the sense that I, the real me, hadn't been in the room, and I'd be distressed that I, the real me, hadn't had a chance to talk to her.

So who was this frontperson, not the real I, who'd talked to her?

Once, when we had a fraught exchange about changing her timetable, I was so upset by it I felt I'd divided into two people. I was a calm, controlled person dragging around a distraught and hysterical twin. She explained these problems in terms of dissociation. Perhaps I was occasionally dissociating around her. No big deal.

There was a small metal label on her desk that I would stare at while we were talking. This label read *Eclipse*, the name of the furniture manufacturer. I started to think of the sense of unreality, this dissociation Dr Sanders spoke of, as the Eclipse.

'Call me Marie,' she'd said early on, and I did, but in my mind she was Dr Sanders.

If it seemed I'd made her angry or even slightly irritable I would become so paralysed with despair I couldn't talk. This didn't happen to me in other contexts. I had a very high tolerance for anger, having grown up with it. (Margaret once remarked that Karl 'was angry the whole time we were growing up'.) Other people's rage didn't scare or even bother me, but Dr Sanders only had to let out a little *tsk* for me to freeze.

In general, I was easily able to make small talk in social situations, and to speak publicly at book events. My problem wasn't shyness or lack of confidence. It was an inability to get close and personal. I told Dr Sanders, It's like this: the idea of social contact seems good. But then I start worrying about how I will get away. I worry about being trapped. I remember saying to her, I feel as if I have no emotional skin. Everything burns me. I meant: You burn me.

The strangeness, the specificity of it: I loved my children and was easily able to be close to them. I loved Paul and was close to him — through all our ups and downs we always were and are best friends. We had friends we went out with, couples. I had men friends, although with them one didn't get particularly personal. I related easily with two women only, my daughter and my sister.

I prided myself on my good relationship with my kids, the care I took (driven by my determination to do better than my parents). I'd learned to operate within the limits of what I could manage, and to do well there.

But outside that, with this woman, this impossible Marie Sanders, I was lost.

It was the strangest, hardest, most fraught and disturbing experience I'd had, trying to maintain a relationship with Dr Marie Sanders. Who was, looking back on it, a fairly ordinary middle-aged Kiwi woman, of normal habits, mild-mannered, bookish, softly spoken, conventional. Not some devilish creature or witch or shapeshifter, not even remotely sinister, and yet, *honestly.* Our dealings were coloured with so much high drama (for me) I was wrung out.

I couldn't speak her language, and once I'd got close enough to want to, this was agony.

Throughout that spring and early summer, talking in her office, we were stoking my agony: this wanting to be close, this needing to get away. I experienced it as it played out. It was a brutal way to find out the extent of my deficit, to go on trying and failing at a relationship that, by now, I actually cared about. She was a friendly, warm person after all, and interesting to talk to.

The experience of trying to be near Dr Sanders, the demonstration, in real time, of how nearly impossible for me that was, led me, in some desperation, to start reading psychology texts, trying to understand.

While Margaret was a social genius, I wasn't able to compare myself with Oliver, whose behaviour seemed to me not only strange but opaque. He tended not to talk to me at all. His past and present life was one of the mysteries I'd tried to explore, but my questions were blocked and disapproved of by my literary family. If I asked, I would be given only a long list of his positive achievements. (His chant was a beautiful song.)

I made my report to Dr Verne. I described my rollercoaster ride with Dr Sanders, the yearning and the terror, the push and pull of it.

'See? I told you it wouldn't work with a woman.'

'Keep trying,' was his advice.

A character in my novel *Soon* says this: 'A house is a metaphor for the mind.' During my years of questioning I was exploring rooms in my mind that had been sealed off, opening doors, restoring light and air, tearing down unnecessary walls. I thought of it as my personal Glasnost, my Perestroika.

I could understand why this 'airing out' would induce paranoia in the family. Kay went on referring vaguely and darkly to Freud. Talking all that Freud. The way they always blame the mother.

It wasn't like that, though. If everyone is a product of their environment, every family is an explicable system. Behaviour is a matter of cause and effect; there's a place for a proper explanation.

What about fault? If fault is just a matter of cause and effect, isn't it possible to say, 'Yes it was your fault, just as some things are my fault. Sure, some things were your fault. But do you know how much I loved you anyway?'

We were told an anecdote as children: when Oliver was a baby, Karl and Kay left him at a party. They realised as they were trundling home in their car. There was the screeching U-turn, the speeding back. It was a funny story. Only now do I think about the baby left at the party. The small bassinet in a back room. The parents walking out into the night. I remember taking my first baby, Conrad, to a family gathering, and feeling exhausted and burdened. My thought was, I will never be able to relax and enjoy myself again. Because of this enormous responsibility, this weight. The thought of walking away without him is unimaginable.

I don't remember how it was between Oliver and Kay and Karl before Oliver turned rebellious at 16; I remember only the rising curve of friction and chaos. It was a wild ride and I was always waiting. The suspense itself was wearing, the cringing certainty that the next domestic spectacle was building, the stress of embarrassment as well as of the clashes and fights. One Christmas, he and Karl had a physical fight in the sitting room. I remember screaming as the two men fought each other on the floor.

Oliver and Kay had the same dark skin, dark eyes, glossy black hair, a certain way of speaking, with a rhetorical tremor. The difference was in their expressions. No matter how grand a statement Oliver came out with — and he was capable of being quite grand — his eyes gave him away. His eyes were wary.

Kay didn't have that watchful look.

She said, 'Tough love is a bad thing. You have to tell people they're doing well.' She said, 'He's achieved an enormous amount, academically, professionally. If he's ever had any problems they've been caused by his wife.'

She said, 'He would never tell a lie.'

I started to make notes on differences, similarities. I was also writing. This from *Mazarine*:

> *My family in Menton that summer, how beautiful they were! Inez with her glossy black hair, the Judge with his charisma and his clever eyes, golden little Natasha, sweet-natured, enterprising Frank, and I the different one, who loved the story they made, and would hold them there in my mind, always. Through all those years, through anniversaries, birthdays, the recurring procession of cake-and-candles, I tried to sing their tune, and couldn't. This was determined by fate; it was the story told by my DNA.*

Frances, the narrator of *Mazarine,* is adopted. I was thinking about difference. While Karl and I were simpatico, Kay always said she and I were 'different', 'too different', 'terribly different'.

All three of my own children have temperaments different from my own. I couldn't see that 'difference' was a legitimate basis for rejecting a child. Could she only tolerate a mirror image?

Or did she insist I was different because she and I looked so alike, with similar features?

Perhaps for Kay, 'too different' was code for something else. It could have meant too reminiscent (of a negative figure from her childhood), too dark-complexioned (a reminder that she and her mother had been subjected to casual racism) or, when I got older, too sharp-eyed a witness to her hidden self.

This from *Mazarine:*

> *Estrangement. Recently I was stopped at the lights in my car, and caught sight of Inez heading across the intersection. She walked slowly, owing to problems with her knee, in a kind of slow, effortful march, her fists clenched, thumbs outstretched. She didn't see me, and I sat as she crossed in front of the car, the figure I had watched and watched for all my childhood, the shape cut out of the universe and etched with precision on my brain. I watched her pass by me, not seeing.*
>
> *The tears. Who were they for? What did they signify? Do these mysteries become clear when you discuss them with a friend?*

The figure I had watched and watched for all my childhood. Every time I made a portrait of her, her shape seemed to shift.

Once, at a literary party in London, Kay walked up to the novelist Martin Amis, whom she hadn't yet met, and placed her hand flat on his back. Then she smiled and walked away. She was touching him as if he was a totem, because she admired his work.

After I got into an argument with Kay in London, I had an exchange with Karl. He said: 'This exchange is so disloyal to Kay it makes me cringe.' He said: 'You and Kay are such utterly different characters there will always be misunderstanding between you.' He said: 'She has always been undemonstrative towards you. She is incredibly tactless, but she means you no harm.'

She got things wrong. But she also got those *endless jokes*. She laughed a lot. She had close friends, and knew what to say to them.

Shown into my mother-in-law's house, Kay said to me in a whisper, 'It's simply *squalid*.' Looking around at the ordinary, tidy Mt Eden villa, I thought she must have some superior level of perception, some radar for squalor I didn't possess.

When Margaret and I were talking about a friend of Margaret's who'd just started going out with a rather vulnerable, newly divorced guy, Kay said, 'She's picked him because she can have power over him.'

I suppose it doesn't matter what conclusion I come to. Character, like a face, can be drawn over and over again. Perhaps there is no 'truth'. I could assemble enough facts for one explanation. But could I equally assemble facts to support another?

In the supermarket one day I ran into Marti Friedlander. My daughter Madeleine was mentioned, and Marti asked me, 'Is she as bad as you were? Is she as difficult? Ooh, the stories I used to hear from Kay!'

'No, she's not,' I said.

Difficult. Different. Bad. I wrote about my relationship with Madeleine in a *Sunday* magazine piece for Mother's Day:

My new baby was sensitive, given to skin flare-ups, infant fevers. She was problematic to feed, and a world champion of insomnia. I could fake vast competence all I liked, but I couldn't get her to sleep. For two years, she would scream if put to bed, and I lugged her about on my hip. In London we had no car, no money; dealing with a lively toddler and a sleepless newborn, I was a zombie, a wreck. But she grew from that restless, uncomfortable little soul into a tranquil, sunny-natured girl, generous, intelligent, competent, beautiful. And she performed a magic trick: this was a mother–daughter situation, everyone's nerves were strained to breaking, and yet I wasn't difficult. And neither was she.

I noted down this exchange on school:

Sanders: 'Your mother dropped out of school at 16. Why would she want *you* to do well? You only realised when she started doing the same thing to your kids.'

I said this couldn't be the case.

But Sanders had grown tired of my pussy-footing and prevaricating, my insistence on the lovely childhood, a house full of books. She laid down her pen and said, 'Listen. For once, let's call a spade a spade.'

I knew this was true: I'd got full marks in school rebellion (I'd really done my homework on it), because, like a lot of girls, I wanted to succeed, to please and be praised. I wanted my mother to love me, and I desperately wanted to be good.

The story I was telling had to be true. But I was telling true stories about a whole life lived in fiction.

Once upon a time when I was a child, I said something my parents thought was 'cute' and related to people as a funny story. Karl later wrote a short story in which a child said the same thing, and he gave the child a particular name.

Later, in his novel *Sister Hollywood*, he wrote a story about a male character who is 'half in love' with his elder sister. He used the same name for this fictional sister that he'd already used for the child with my characteristics, who said what I was known for having said in real life.

The use of the name in the two contexts was noted in the literary family and yet passed over in silence.

In *Sister Hollywood* the male narrator and his 'sexy' sister live in a family in which their father is, according to the sister, a 'crypto-pugilist' and their mother is 'an hysterical ghoul'. The brother has erotic dreams about the sister. The fictional mother and father fight, continually and violently, about the daughter. The mother goes in for moods, sulking, hysteria and theatrical rhetoric (shouting at her husband, 'Go on, strike me! Strike me!'). The father responds with helpless male bafflement, rage, shouting and violence.

The mother dislikes the daughter and, the father notes, has treated her as a rival. In the story the conflict is the mother's fault; she's the hysterical ghoul. What's left out is any reason why the ghoul wants to drive her child away. The daughter leaves the family, cuts off all contact and never returns.

She remains a romantic, idealised figure to the brother, who eventually goes overseas looking for her, imagining the mother must feel guilt at having driven her away. He comments that the daughter had 'become [the mother's] obsession. Either it was driving her mad, or it was the point of focus her madness had chosen.'

The daughter/sister goes away and meets a young man, who is

eventually run over by a car, and dies in front of her — a detail that, as I'll describe later, mirrored my real life.

There are elements of Karl's childhood. He told stories about his parents' volatile marriage, his father's half-suppressed violence and his mother's histrionic melodrama. And yet there's a characteristic playfulness in the description of the crypto-pugilist and the hysterical ghoul: there are echoes of himself and Kay, too.

In the narrative of a mother treating a daughter as a rival, and a character's yearning after a woman as an unattainable figure who is driven away by the intense warfare in the family there are echoes of experience denied in real life, sublimated, turned into an acceptable form — into art.

It's material, Karl would say to me. Go and write a story about it.

We all make an account of our lives by telling stories. We roll out our own narrative; it expands in the telling, and we swear we're sticking to the truth. Truth is elusive, our impressions are subjective, and everyone's take will vary. Fiction, though, is definite. Fiction is an arrangement of the facts just as the writer wanted them.

It's the world through the looking glass, strands of our own stories appearing in the fiction although they're denied in real life. A fictional mother makes a fictional daughter disappear, a real father makes a fictional version of a daughter disappear.

Occasionally, in moments of private comedy, I wonder where our selves actually reside.

'Where's all the dancing and singing?'

Our routines were verbal games. In the earliest, starting when I was four or five, he was a boy, Castle, and I was his tyrannical mother. (He'd been called Castle at primary school by kids who couldn't pronounce his real name, Karlson.) It was a scenario full of jokes and great fun. He was hopelessly dim and stupid, and I was a cruel and scathing old bag, continually beating and punishing him and telling him off for being a moron. It was all farce. I was a reasonably good mimic and I discovered early on I could make him laugh.

No one else in the family had this kind of exchange with Karl; it was uniquely ours.

He liked to sing and I liked to dance, and we both tended to exuberance. When we got older, Margaret and I would crank up the stereo and dance around the sitting room and sometimes after a few wines he would join in with full comic verve.

I used to say to him, 'Where's all the dancing and singing?' It was a catch-cry.

As I got older I read and enjoyed his novels and especially loved his poetry. He could evoke Auckland, the rain, the volcanic cones, the sky, with such clarity, beauty and precision it would bring tears, and he was witty too, funny, poignant and sharp. His prose and poetry was, to quote one of his lines, 'hard, bright, clean, particular'.

I was writing myself, trying out stories and hiding them in a drawer. He occasionally read a story or a fragment and approved. In 1984 when he published his novel *All Visitors Ashore* he gave me a copy inscribed: *To dear Charlotte — in exchange (in advance) for the one you will write. With love from Castle xx*

At some stage, much later, I made the transition from devoted literary fan to occasional critic, when I questioned, lightly and experimentally, why he seemed to pass over in silence uncomfortable details about character. I began to wonder whether the fact he was a poet first and novelist second made him squeamish about messy human reality.

I felt, for example, that his female characters, if they were intended to be sympathetic, were rather idealised, positioned as exquisitely tasteful, good-looking admirers of the male protagonist. I wished they could have some flaws. One or two bad habits perhaps? A big bum?

Could it be that the more strongly the mind recoils from messy reality, the more inclined it will be to invent a fictional scenario too smooth and perfect for plausibility? Could it be that to achieve authenticity in fiction you need to have a certain stomach for the unsavoury, ugly aspects of life?

Some sense of half-comic rebellion stirred in me, too, at the treatment of food in his novels. Positive characters had healthy appetites, were always eating with gusto, but never put on weight. This suggested a virtue: superior genes, perhaps.

The word 'good' seemed to crop up fussily and often, signalling excellent taste: a good wine, a good cheese, a good salad. A marvellous seafood pasta with a good wine. My attention to this was so specific, it must have reflected my memory of how uptight and controlling he was about food. It made me wish for the comedy of slop, grease, fat, a limp salad, just as I wished he would conjure up a woman with a few physical flaws. Enough of 'good', I thought.

In *Mazarine*, I not only made Mazarine gay, plump and poignantly unchic, but I had her so poor and thrifty she wandered through Paris looking for the cheapest café, the greasiest greasy spoon.

Karl paid me a great compliment though, after he'd read *Mazarine*: he described it as a 'beautiful love story'. He was a generous and open reader, even if there were some things he was too fastidious to write himself.

He was warm and encouraging when I started publishing fiction. He hadn't urged me to do it; he was happy enough when I did a law degree instead — but he'd always said I was the one who could.

For publishing, I changed my surname so as to be as independent as possible (even though it meant I took on grim Grimshaw), found an agent and publisher, and made my own way.

Subtleties were lost in the back and forth.

During my years of questioning, I got into arguments with Karl about what was and wasn't real. I wrote about one of those fights in a short story, 'The Black Monk'. The dispute blew up when I discovered that Karl had used my and my daughter Madeleine's matching ankle tattoos in his novel, *The Necessary Angel*.

We'd had the tattoos done together, for fun and as a symbol of our close bond. Madeleine had suggested it, and I'd gone along with the idea. I was touched she wanted to have the same tattoo as her mum. She'd chosen the owl of Minerva, a symbol she'd liked since studying classics in school. I'd written about our owls in my *Metro* column, and people knew about them. They were something we both valued, a small feature. In his novel, Karl had described characters with those exact tattoos on their ankles — a man and a woman — having sex.

When I mentioned to a cousin I was annoyed by this, he said he couldn't understand why. 'It's fiction,' he told me (pompously, I felt). But I was a fiction writer and I had children, so you could say I was in a position to know whether I was being reasonable. The idea of using one of my own children's details, for example a distinctive tattoo, in a sexual context, would seem to me perverse, an assertion, and deserving of a figurative punch in the nose. I could also say that there was something familiar and typical in it, and while I loved him and admired a lot of his work, I wanted to give him that punch in the nose, most especially because he'd gone so far as to use a detail belonging to my daughter. So I emailed him, and remonstrated.

In 'The Black Monk' I described the tension created by this:

It was a challenge hidden in plain sight, hard to confront, with family opprobrium raining down on me. The subtlety made it complicated; people wouldn't necessarily see anything wrong in what he'd done. The same tattoos? So what? It felt like a macho signal that demanded I play the submissive cypher or resist. He might call it a tribute, but it was an assertion. It neatly disrespected my bond with my daughter, which he knew I valued, and it expressed the very attitude to family relationships that had made our family chaotic. If he'd done nothing wrong, why shouldn't I write about it? Why should he have all the freedom, while I had none?

Near the end of the story the narrator considers giving up the search for answers. She has written a story called 'The Black Monk' in which she describes the dispute. She imagines she will stop arguing with her family; she will 'let go' and fall into line, will not publish the story called 'The Black Monk'.

She thinks, 'If I stopped describing what I perceived to be real, I would no longer be the black sheep.'

At this point, since the reader has just finished 'The Black Monk', he or she will understand that in the end, the narrator *didn't* let go and fall into line.

Because here is the story, published.

Kay read 'The Black Monk' and offered an opinion, using the words from the story, 'let go'. She said, 'One very old reader thinks the narrator should, must, just let go.'

I replied rather humourlessly, 'Let go of what? My mind, creative drive, ability to make fiction out of my experiences?'

I'd copied Kay into some of my exchanges with Karl about *The Necessary Angel*. He responded at first to my complaint by telling me 'the owl is a universal symbol' and that it was pure chance he'd used matching tattoos of owls on ankles. When I replied along the lines of 'Oh, come on', he changed tack and told me he'd consulted me, that I'd known and given him permission to use them. This was untrue;

what he had done a long time before was ask me how tattoos are done, about the process, just general research.

It struck me that Kay, his 'first reader,' had presumably not suggested to him he might use different tattoos, and on other parts of the body, perhaps. She was reader first, not mother and grandmother first. At no point during my dispute with Karl did she offer any empathy or understanding. They were a united front; she was silent on the subject with me, adamant in his defence.

Madeleine said to me, not infrequently, 'It's so *crazy* the way you all email each other. Why don't you just meet and talk like normal people? Or at least pick up the phone?'

She was right of course. Perhaps we were too focused on writing at the expense of talking.

It reminds me of myself shouting at Paul, who's a lawyer, 'Just talk. Stop fucking *litigating*!'

My story, 'The Black Monk': it's a case of the pot calling the kettle black.

It says: This is how it felt when Karl used my private detail in his fiction, without caring about the effect. And yet in the story I've done the same thing, although you could say that the deal was, I wasn't supposed to. That was meant to be something only he got away with.

After I published it, I was filled with guilt and sadness. I couldn't reconcile the urge to translate these family difficulties into fiction with my place in the family. All my questioning, exploring what it was about the family that was so strangely rigid, so enamelled over with denial, had made me the black sheep.

So much had been passed over in silence for so long. When I gave in to the impulse to write about it, I not only felt guilty, I had to acknowledge how slippery the idea of 'truth' is, how each of us might tell a different story about the same people and events. History is story-telling, and the search for answers only throws up a new narrative, more ironies, another twist.

Fiction, though. Sometimes it's more revealing than memoir. Fiction arranges the story exactly as the author wants it told.

The journalist Diana Wichtel once mentioned in an interview with Karl in *Newsroom* that he'd been accused of occasionally writing 'revenge fiction'. She mentioned 'The Black Monk' in that context, as if perhaps, possibly, my story could be put in that category, too. My intention was never revenge, though, and I don't think it was ever Karl's either. If you're a writer and you have a strong experience, you're going to write about it. He and I would agree that a vengeful motive will likely spoil the tone of fiction, and turn it into caricature. We both subscribed to Australian novelist Christina Stead's rule: the writer has to have a Christ-like sympathy for everyone. If you don't empathise with characters they'll be two-dimensional.

'The Black Monk' was a story first, and an attempt to explore a particular (admittedly rather unusual and niche) difficulty in a family. My overall feeling was best expressed by Madeleine whenever she and I discussed family problems, especially denial and suppression. She would say, 'Let's us not be like that.'

She meant: 'Let's be open. Let's not deny. If things have gone wrong, let's try to fix them. If we've done wrong, let's admit it.' And that's how I felt, too. I wanted to break the cycle, put space between. *Let's us not be like that*.

This was the point: a search for truth and reconciliation is the opposite of revenge. Surely the aim of it is understanding and forgiveness. When I'd had the idea initially, had joked about The New Frankness, I was thinking of the Truth and Reconciliation Commission in South Africa, held to heal the wrongs of apartheid. Victims and perpetrators told their stories. It was a process we'd followed and admired, since we'd protested against the Springbok Tour. 'Truth' was an indispensable ingredient; without openness there could be no resolution.

Only after I'd published the story did it occur to me that I'd put 'The Black Monk' out into the world without consulting Madeleine, whose tattoo, identical to mine, appeared in the story and in *The Necessary Angel*. Did this show how inescapably I was a product of the literary family, all pot and kettle, a writer who cared only about producing the fiction, and who had just engaged in the very transgression I was complaining of?

I mentioned this in an email to the writer Paula Morris, who'd read 'The Black Monk' and asked what the family had thought of it:

> *Re the story, yes, the family . . . My mother told me I should 'just let go' as the character in the story contemplates . . . and my father said the story 'puzzled' him. Still, we all get on in a civilised fashion; after all, we're so used to his outrages with fictionalising. It's sort of what we do in our family. Basically I'm the pot calling the kettle black, and vice versa.*

There's that quote of Czeslaw Milosz, *When a writer is born into a family, the family is finished.*

I found an interview in *The Irish Times*, in which the British playwright Nina Raine discusses this notion, of the family being 'finished'.

Nina Raine is the daughter of the British poet Craig Raine (a good friend of Karl's), and according to her a family of writers *can* get on. She cites a jaunty quote that possibly comes from Kingsley Amis: 'No one will ever be unflattered to appear in a piece of art, unless you suggest they're bad in bed.'

In the interview Nina Raine says, 'If you're in a family of writers there is a kind of code: you live by the sword, you die by the sword. Everything is fair game for material.'

Nina Raine is quoted as saying that after reading her latest play, which used a lot of family material, her father Craig told her, 'No, your business is not to be worrying about people's feelings. Because otherwise you will never write.'

On that principle then, it's 'never been Karl's business to worry about people's feelings, otherwise he would never write', so he was free to use my and Madeleine's tattoos in his fiction. But equally, he has to put up with my fictional response to it. I suppose it makes us even.

But the whole process was bruising and sad and hurtful. Not only for me, of course.

Stick to fiction, please!

In a joint interview he and I did with the journalist Steve Braunias at the Going West Festival, Karl read out that sentence about the family from volume two of his autobiography, *You Have a Lot to Lose*:

> *There was a minimum of piety among us, tears but not too many, shouting but not too much, some songs, some recitations from memory, and endless jokes.*

It was so blandly idealised, it set something off in me. It was part of a section of the book describing our time in the South of France, while he was still secretly conducting his love affair, and the arguing between him and Kay, as I recall it, had been bitter, stressful, extreme. He knew we had tears and shouting *way* too much. He acknowledged a bit of conflict and smoothly minimised it. He controlled the reality.

Tears, shouting. How many was too many, and how much was too much?

The 'minimum of piety' was an absolute requirement in the literary family, a standard. But what were the pieties we scorned? The definition was quite broad.

The piety of marital fidelity, clearly.

Intellectual sharpness and clarity are good. But it struck me as strange not to be able to tolerate a bit of truth-telling. Would it be the end of the world to admit the family was often in a state of emotional chaos? That life was not perfect but rough at the edges, messy, complicated?

Recently I re-read a story from an early collection of Karl's, *Five for the Symbol*. 'The Town' describes a family of five just like ours, living as we had at Garavan, in Menton. In one scene an elderly pair of locals watch at night from the olive grove as the married couple are arguing (at it again, the watchers note) and the husband punches his fist through the glass. Conflict had been allowed to find its way into the fiction.

In fiction you dare to use the real, because 'it's fiction'.

'Oh, it's just fiction,' you say, straight-faced, or with a sly wink. You're covered.

With autobiography, there must be a temptation to airbrush, to smooth over rough edges, to make yourself the good guy and right in every argument. The less able you are to tolerate the idea you've been a jerk, made mistakes, fucked up or failed, the less honest your account will be.

If you're a public figure with an eye to legacy and archiving, this curating of the boundaries of reality might extend everywhere, to personal messages even.

It can surely go wrong, though. If you go full-Trump and airbrush too much, you lose plausibility. The mask looks like a mask. People might start to doubt, object, rebel.

When I was writing *Mazarine* and 'The Black Monk', I put some real experiences into fiction. The literary family recognised the real experiences and reacted. They started telling me I was living in an 'unreal world'. If I hadn't used experiences the family recognised as real, they wouldn't have needed to question my grip on reality.

I began to wonder if the literary family were putting it about, this idea I'd gone mad. Karl was certainly suggesting it in emails, which I imagined him busily archiving. Would I now be his 'troubled daughter'? Whose worsening mental condition . . . Whose descent into insanity he struggled with forbearance to . . .

He'd been a well-known literary figure, New Zealand's 'looming cultural monument' for so long; his eye was always on the record. The older he got, the more preoccupied he was with his history and legacy. His tone in emails, as he exhorted me to get away from 'the grip of unreality,' was urbane, baffled, reasonable.

It's eerie to read an email that politely calls you a 'fantasist', to wonder if it's addressed elsewhere, to history, to the studious biographer, and to perceive that, because it's from the person you know so well, the one who could be the *favourite person in the world* (because it's from Castle), underneath his civilised tone is iron will and simmering anger.

Anger that you've stepped outside the role, broken the rules, stopped doing the job you were meant to do. Anger that you've said 'no'.

Because if you step out of line, what is the point of you?

In his novel *The Singing Whakapapa*, Karl used real letters written to him by Jenny North, with whom he had the long affair. He recorded this in his autobiography, *You Have a Lot to Lose:* 'The novel, when I came to write it, even used, with only minimal editorial improvements, her actual letters which I'd kept.'

He had adapted real letters to fit with his fiction; now I felt, as I tried to assert my sense of the truth, I was up against a master who knew how to dash off an email that plausibly created facts and denied my reality. He 'worried about my fantasising', expressed equanimity, all while establishing I was misguided, ungrateful, unworthy . . .

I began to wonder, were these letters, if they were meant to end up anywhere, really intended for Kay, who would eventually read them? Were they a message to her that said, 'Keep the faith?' I thought of his touching poem to Kay, 'You':

It's time to tell you again
How much I loved the girl
Who blushed her welcome.
Forgive my trespasses.
Stay close. Hold my hand.

Forgive my trespasses.

After these years of dispute, I would never again read a biographer's analysis of 'private letters' with the same level of confidence. I imagine the studious commentary: As the letters of 2018 show . . . As he clearly felt in his letter of . . . One can discern, from the emotion expressed in this heartfelt missive of . . .

It's unnerving that every email you now receive potentially has an ulterior purpose, one he feels is existentially important: to tell *his* story to the world.

At the height of our disputes about what was real, Karl found (it seemed to me) a way to punish me for my rebellion: he started occasionally to cut me out of things. He would give a journalist a family photo in which I was obscured by a pillar. He left out of his memoirs all mention of his and my rapport.

He also edited things he now realised I might complain about. In *You Have a Lot to Lose*, he wrote they'd always arranged a minder for us in London when we were children, and had never left us alone. (Why mention such a minor detail?) He followed this up with an email to me asserting it was the case, and went on insisting. It wasn't true.

I'd tried myself to prevent my children from knowing things I'd done. But there was a distinction between trying to lead by example and responding to an accusation. I resolved that if my kids accused me of anything, I'd be open to truth and reconciliation myself. Karl regarded this as more psychobabble and 'grotesque'.

But then, at some point in our arguing, I showed him a piece I'd written about him that was nostalgic and warm, that recalled our old closeness, and he responded, saying it was so moving it brought tears; there was a thaw; we regained our old rapport.

After this, I was in turn deeply touched when he turned up at my house and gave me a copy of *You Have a Lot to Lose* inscribed, 'Love to my special girl, Charlotte.'

Is there a difference between writing fiction about the sadness of a failed family relationship, say between a mother and daughter as in *Mazarine*, and writing fiction in which the idea of 'family' is relegated as a piety, where the only relationships really valued are romantic ones?

Answer: there are no rules.

The Singing Whakapapa, published in 1994, is a rich, vivid story, quite a triumph of novel writing, in which Karl brilliantly used his own real family history, including the lives of his grandfather, the Swedish sea captain Christian Karlson, after whom he was named, and his relative John Flatt, one of the first missionaries to settle in New Zealand.

He used the real letters of the real Jenny North, and centred the action on Hugh Grady, a man married to a wife called Hat, a judge (described in one of Hugh's girlfriend's letters as 'an old Hat') who is wonderful and competent and yet is also, we sense, unimaginative and boring as hell.

Hugh has had a passionate affair with a student, after which Hat persuades him to go with her and their kids to Europe, where he receives letters *poste restante* from the young woman who's still in love, and the affair continues, and life and family and art all merge.

Many years later, Hugh is working on his family history, assisted by an enchanting young researcher with whom he's very taken (in one scene he dreams about sex with her), and in the end he discovers she's his daughter, the product of that passionate affair involving long-distance love and *poste restante* letters . . .

What kind of a family has arguments like ours? (A family of writers.) How does it fit with our virtuous regimen of *not too many, not too much?*

All this daring and art before all, and sailing close to the wind . . . It obviously didn't occur to Karl that since one of the tattoos he described in *The Necessary Angel* belonged to my daughter, this might represent for me one liberty, one dereliction, one impiety too many. That it was, in the end, too much.

He would say that his borrowing details from life was fair game; it was fiction. That it was heavy-handed, cruel even, to complain about the use of the tattoos in a fictional story. It was savage of me. He meant no harm. He was a sensitive artist, he had made something beautiful and positive, out of affection even, and I was kicking him in the teeth; worse, I was attacking him with moral outrage, taking offence, behaving not as my old loyal self but like some hypersensitive and tyrannical 'millennial'.

But the countering voice says: have your muses and your affairs, pay your tributes and tell your stories, but treat me different. There is such a thing as family; it consists of special relationships. The role of parent, or parent figure, for example.

Call it a piety if you like, but if you scorn it you're playing with fire. Get ready for fallout. Prepare for a reaction.

In December, Karl and Kay arrived unexpectedly on my birthday. It was obvious he'd made her come along; she stayed at a distance across the room until the 10-minute visit was over, when she gave me a present: a book. It was *The Choice*, by the Holocaust survivor Edith Eger. I was so aware of Kay's reluctance I stood feeling helpless, and made some random comment to fill the silence.

A short time later Kay instructed me to 'set the family aside', despite the fact that we lived near to each other, everyone was in good health, et cetera.

She said something like, 'Remember what the old woman, Edith Eger, said in *The Choice*. You can't change the past, or the things that have been done to you, but you can take charge of it and set it aside. Set all the bad times aside, set us aside. Goodbye my darling child. Go well with your work and with your own lovely family.'

Karl's 'fantasist' emails had made me consider writing about the experience; now this directive from Kay decided it: I had to write about it, even if it was just in diary notes to myself, because it was so painful. I was getting over being told 'goodbye' by Paul, now I was being farewelled by my mother to whom, despite the inexplicable elements of our relationship, I'd remained devoted. Nothing was clear, but it seemed I had stepped too far out of line. It was devastating.

Reacting to her instruction, with its familiar, its *quintessential* ambivalence — brimming with 'emotion' (my darling child) yet starkly telling me to disappear — I sent a provocative email:

> *Yes,* The Choice. *Those bad times were set aside and folk moved on — although on the basis, of course, that first there was* Nuremberg.

I told Dr Sanders this anecdote about my birthday and the exchange — Kay's instruction and my salty email. She had got up for some reason and was standing at the window; she turned, and the look on her face was the reason why I fell for Sanders, why I had the sudden overwhelming feeling I wanted to be her friend.

She was amused, *amused* . . .

'Interesting choice of present', was all she said.

In another rare exchange, this time about 'The Black Monk', Kay wrote to me complaining that this psychologist I'd apparently consulted, whom she called The Man, would be 'acting as judge and jury', without her being able to defend herself, since all he got was my side of the story.

This was true; I could have been spinning any old line. The point of it, though, was that for the first time I had the opportunity to tell the story as I saw it.

Kay had been telling my story since I was born; I was her protagonist and she was the author. Now I'd stepped off the page and was roaming about, acting out of character and fouling up her script.

If it was Kay who'd been telling my story, given her lack of narrative organisation, was it surprising I was still lost in the maze, searching for the way, finding the thread hard to unravel?

I wrote in *The Spinoff:*

> *Recently I read a book about desire, by neuroscientist Marc Lewis. The author mentioned a study of Native communities in Western Canada. Some of the communities had high youth suicide rates, and others had a zero rate of suicide. Attempting to find out why, researchers found that youths from the high suicide communities were unable to give a coherent narrative of their lives. They had no sense of family past, of history, and no sense that they had a future. They couldn't see their lives as stories and they couldn't tell their own stories; they had none.*
>
> *The youths from low suicide communities, on the other hand, were able to narrate their own stories; they had a sense of their history and a clear concept of a future 'I'. This finding was relevant to one thesis of the book, which dealt with the idea that a facet of addiction (uncontrollable desire) is an inability to focus on the future — is the narrowing of world view down to the urgent want of the now.*
>
> *It seems fascinating to consider the idea that human beings have evolved beyond the animal to an extent where consciousness itself has 'needs' that are as crucial for survival as food and fluids. Where the brain grasps only the immediate, there is despair, where there is a sense of 'my story', where the 'I' is not lost but firmly located within a narrative context, past, present and future, then there is hope.*

It's a real-world demonstration of the idea that telling your story is existentially important. By implication, it involves a listener. A witness. Connectedness.

Being able to tell your story means you must have learned how. Someone was listening and willing to hear the truth, allowing you to grasp the concept of beginning, middle and end that would help affirm the self you see in the mirror.

Someone heard your protests, and acknowledged they were valid.

Someone helped you untangle the thread of narrative when you started a story, 'So, there was the *dog* . . .'

Every morning I walked a circuit with the dog, Philip, around the edge of Hobson Bay, across the park and home through the mangroves at the bottom of Bell Road park. In winter the cricket ground was covered in puddles, the seawater seeped onto the field and at high tide the track through the mangroves was inundated. Some days I had to wade, and would be thrilled to catch sight of eels curling ahead of me over the flooded path. The air was rich with the smell of mud and mangrove, everything drenched and intensely green after the rain.

Now the world was drying out, the incessant wind had gone, the weather had turned calm and golden, and as I sat writing *Mazarine* the sun angled in, lighting up shafts of floating dust. The garden outside my room was bright with flowers, and by afternoon I grew so glazed and distracted I would have to get up and walk fast up the steep side of Mt Hobson to clear my head.

I had needed the months of questioning, the conversations with Sanders; none of it was a waste of time. The bouts of desolation were gone; Paul and I had stopped arguing and had got very close again. I wasn't falling during disputes into that horrifying void, nothing to connect me to the world.

He and I spent time at Whatuwhiwhi at the edge of Doubtless Bay in the Far North, where Paul's English-born parents had built a bach decades ago, and had forged such a close relationship with the local Māori that when George Grimshaw died the Māori family came down to Auckland to 'take George home'. They gave him a tangi on the marae at Whatuwhiwhi and he's buried in the Māori graveyard there.

We talked obliquely, cautiously; perhaps we felt thrashing things out would be counter-productive. We didn't want to damage the peace that had broken out.

But we did a lot of remembering. Remember living in the flat in London with the kids, how hard the winters were, how Madeleine would never sleep until she turned two, and we were exhausted all the time? That harsh New Year when the streets were covered in ice and Paul was at work, and I'd bundled the toddler and baby into their ski suits and we'd walked all the way to the library, I encouraging little Conrad on through the icy cold, one foot in front of the other, just a bit further, we can get warm — and when we got there the library was closed. Our eyes stinging with cold, with dismay. The wind was blowing ice, the street was deserted, it was a long way home.

I had to say, 'Well, we're just going to have to turn around and go back again.'

The time Conrad crashed into a wall at school, cutting his head open, and I ran all the way down there with Madeleine in the stroller — no car — and when I arrived he was crying in a corner and the teacher said, 'You see, we're not allowed to touch the children.'

I took him in a taxi to be stitched up, long hours in the hospital waiting room with the drunks and crazies, another taxi home in the freezing dark. The way life with young children is so often an emergency, a crisis. The struggle back up the stairs in the apartment building (fifth floor), warming them up, making their dinner, caring for them. How we loved them, how intensely important they were; they were everything, the whole world.

The dark, the cold, the glazed hours in the frozen playground, our shabbiness and poverty: we were young immigrants living on one wage and paying high rent, and I with my scruffy stroller would be trailed by the security guards around the supermarket because I was young and they took me for one of the women who brought their babies to the Brunswick Centre to beg. I was stressed, exhausted, I had no help day-to-day with the kids. Madeleine woke repeatedly in the night; Conrad was energetic, argumentative, a little live-wire.

Was I too tense, too tired and irritable with them? I remembered endless walking with Conrad, the pale little figure in his scruffy coat, how he and I squabbled our way across London, how we struggled with the baby on the Tube, the heavy shopping bags hanging off the handles of the stroller, how their whole lives I've worried I was a bad mother, wondered how many times I got it wrong, lost my temper, lacked empathy. Whether I managed to redirect the anger I grew up with. Whether the new had exorcised the old, or would I catch sight in the mirror of some ghost self from the past? Did I cause damage as a mother, or was I *good enough?*

And the happiness: remember how Paul spent 10 years reading to them at bedtime, an hour every night, I closing the door because I couldn't stand the prose of the latest Harry Potter. (But I left the door open for the brilliant Philip Pullman.) How Paul borrowed a laptop from work so I could start writing fiction, typing on the dining table at night after we'd put the kids to bed. My prose was naïve, high-energy, charged with longing for home: the photographic clarity of the light, the bush, the surf, Tāmaki Makaurau, the beloved shanty town . . .

Paul helped me with printouts and technical hitches, and looked after the kids every Sunday, spending hours in the grim playground so I could go on with the outpouring of homesickness that became a novel, *Provocation*.

The travel, taking the kids everywhere, all the budget flights to Europe, walking with two strollers around Amsterdam, stopping to feed Madeleine who was six weeks old, the way we never stopped exploring, showing them as much of the world as we could, how we went on travelling each year, fudging it with schools if we had to (after a new headmaster ruled travel outside holidays forbidden, I rang the school each July, pretending to be 'stuck', in Israel, Russia, Portugal) because nothing was more important than the expedition. The more time the five of us spent together travelling, the closer we grew as a family. And we went right on doing it after they'd grown up, taking girlfriends and boyfriends along.

'Did we get too contented and comfortable?' I wondered. 'When we came back to New Zealand and the kids got older?' I meant: Was that why you left? When life eased up, did you find you were bored?

And did I, pre-Glasnost and -Perestroika, with my mind full of walls, keep too much to myself, was I too regimented and controlled? Had I become a regime from which my husband needed to escape?

One thing about Paul, he's a dynamic force. If something needs to change, he'll be the one to change it. But then, ever since we'd met, I'd been changing him, too.

By late summer, when I'd stopped sidling in eyeing her as if she was very dangerous, when I'd relaxed and got to know her better, I thought it was necessary to ask: Did Dr Sanders think I'd lost the boundaries of reality? Madness was her specialty, after all. She had wide experience of the paranoid, the psychotic, the deluded. I encouraged her to lay it on me, spare me nothing. If I was nuts, I needed to know.

She told me: the chant was a chant, not a beautiful song.

In the course of discussing reality and madness, we talked about magical thinking.

I told her, when I was a child I learned that to see two magpies together is good luck, to see a single magpie is bad. I assume this ancient wisdom comes from the nursery rhyme, 'One for sorrow, two for joy . . .'

Heading to a recent book event, I'd caught sight of a single magpie. It was standing on the grass, its head alertly cocked, looking at me with a round, shiny eye. I scanned the field; there was no other bird in sight. Was the book session doomed? Rationally I knew this was nonsense; irrationally I felt the sighting as a blow.

A moment later, a second magpie swooped down and joined its mate.

Relief! I gathered my papers, hurried into the auditorium and nailed it.

Dr Sanders and I were discussing irrational superstition because I wanted to ask her about my experience when Paul left. (I'd never described it to him, instead I'd tactically projected the message: busy life, people to see, none of your business what I've been up to.)

But in reality, in those first few days, I'd woken every morning with that strange, fixed idea: Paul is lost and so I must look for him. I have learned that the bereaved do this. They watch and wait. They save the loved one's clothes for when he or she returns. They search, even though the loved one will not be found.

This is magical thinking, but it's not madness. Or, if grief is a madness, it's an expected one, a temporary derangement that will usually pass.

It's necessary to exercise vigilance. The most important thing is to stick to the facts. The search has to be for what is real.

Where is the girl who had such a clear sense of reality and its boundaries and such a marvellous sense of humour — replaced by this scolding (as it seems to me) fantasist?

Perhaps the marvellous sense of humour enabled one to forego pieties, to live without inconvenient emotional needs.

Karl told me, 'Try to get outside this unreal world, in which Kay is an unloving mother and I am an indifferent narcissist carving my own memorial.'

'Those are your words!' I replied. They weren't any words I'd ever used to him, or her.

How deliberate was it, telling me I'd gone mad? Did he believe it, or was it a cynical exercise to undermine my confidence, my certainty, my sanity?

Perhaps, for him, 'reality and its boundaries' was the territory in which my function was clear: to be 'the girl', to charm, flatter, agree and exercise my marvellous sense of humour, all in the service of reality *as he saw it*. When I stopped doing that, it could only be that I had gone mad.

He could have added a word: 'my'.

Where is the girl who had such a clear sense of my *reality and its boundaries . . . ?*

I could have replied: *Where is the father who loved me, who I thought would never let me go . . . ?*

I did have a clear sense of his reality, and of Kay's, too, and I knew exactly how to operate within it, what to say, what not to say, what happened when I crossed the line.

Did they have any idea who I was? Any at all?

In an exchange with me, Karl had said, 'This exchange is so disloyal to Kay it makes me cringe.'

His loyalty is to her only. It isn't possible for him to feel loyalty to both of us, even though I'm his daughter. For both of them, it's about them. You can't get them to be reverent about 'family', just as you can't expect them to be anything but salty about dull Christmas gatherings, dutiful visits to old relatives, school events, any activity casting a shadow of tiresome convention over genius, humour, originality, irreverence.

She used to complain: some nights she couldn't get to sleep because he kept making her laugh. They laughed all the time — we all did. You can die laughing, she would say.

Perhaps Karl subscribed to the idea an artist creates his own moral universe.

I wrote to Kay, 'Our lives matter. They matter.' I meant the lives of her children. I knew that to her what mattered more was him, the two of them.

They were still the couple Janet Frame had described as being 'in the golden glow of youth and love', the pair lit with his talent and her beauty, so caught up in each other, their heads so full of poetry and laughter and literary brilliance they could forget everything, and leave their baby at a party.

I wonder what I'm doing. Perhaps, after telling my own story, that long, oral account (like the Tale of Soon and Starfish), the next logical thing was to write it down.

I wrote in *Mazarine:*

If telling the story causes harm, so does not telling it. All the time I spent with Werner, in my role as Scheherazade, I was creating a true outline of myself. I didn't believe in blame, I barely believed in free will. I believed my adoptive family and I were one entity; they were part of my self. I acted on them; they acted on me; we made our history together. All I ever wanted was not to disappear.

I woke in the night and reached for Mazarine, held onto her. Dear Life.

I picture Dr Sanders, looking out at the garden in the rain. Behind the streaming glass the pōhutukawa are drenched, the whole world in tears. On the table she has laid her pens in rows.

The sign on the back of the desk reads *Eclipse*.

She says, 'I know you love your father. Those "fantasist" emails. It's sad he threw you to the wolves.'

Throughout the year I was telling my story and I was thinking in terms of fiction. Once I realised I liked Sanders, I worried she would terminate our relationship, 'termination' being psychology's brutal term for the end of therapy.

I only had to google articles on termination to feel anxious and bereft. It seemed a disingenuous and creepy way of dressing up a horrifying betrayal. Articles about closure and 'good endings' made me furious: psychologists, those assholes. They get you to care about them, then they kick you out *for your own good*.

I needed to keep Sanders entertained, and so would spend time before each meeting deciding on pacey narratives and choice anecdotes. They were all true; I didn't lie or make things up. But I was terrified of boring her, and she only had to yawn or fidget to set me nervously ramping up my performance. I wanted to leave her wanting more. I was Scheherazade in *One Thousand and One Nights*, leaving the narrative incomplete each time, so she would never close the file.

Telling my tales to avoid the axe.

While spinning my stories and writing fiction I was also writing about fiction, especially the fashion for the autobiographical. I reviewed Elena Ferrante's *Neapolitan Quartet,* and was struck by her use of fictional selves.

> *In her Neapolitan quartet, Ferrante has created such a large cast that each book begins with a list of characters for readers' reference. In her portrayal of this diverse group, she manages brilliantly to play with notions of 'self' — with I and I and I — particularly in the characters of Elena and Lila, the two women whose friendship is at the heart of the novels.*
>
> *The books are narrated by Elena, whose companion Lila is her brilliant friend. These are wonderful, highly individual characters. And yet the reader is constantly given the sense, deliberately as it were, that the author is both Elena and Lila (as of course in a sense she must be) and that this fraying of the surface of the fiction is methodical, allowing us to glimpse, even if only at moments, the artist at work.*
>
> *Lila and Elena represent the working of a fictional device, one that's executed so brilliantly that you're left with an exhilarating sense of multiplicity: on the one hand, Ferrante has played with ideas of self, has demonstrated ways in which aspects of her own 'I and I', her own 'selves', can be depicted fictionally — dispersed between characters — and at the same time she has created two characters who are so real and so 'separated' from their creator that you feel they could emerge from the book and walk away. This ability to operate on a number of levels, from the purely dramatic to the meta-fictional, seems to me to represent a kind of virtuosity that transcends (not that comparisons are necessary or useful, but still) even Knausgaard's boldness, originality and in-your-face treatment of 'self' . . .*

I was fascinated by Ferrante's *Neapolitan Quartet* because the novels are an intense account of female friendship.

One day in mid-summer, when the lawn outside the office had turned dry and cracked and the sky was a bright hard blue, I started telling the story of Louis Dale, my own brilliant friend.

I was nineteen. We'd been to a comic French movie, *Les Ripoux*, and then to a café. We still spent nights ranging long distances around the city, and now, as usual, we were walking home. I loved wandering through the streets in the soft dark, in the Auckland rain.

We were crossing Quay Street, which was deserted in the late hour. There was the sound of a car coming fast, and I speeded up. I was ahead of Louis and had reached the kerb when he was struck.

The impact threw him onto the bonnet, and the car kept going with him lying halfway through the smashed windscreen, before the driver swerved to propel him off into the gutter. There was silence. I was aware of glittering glass strewn along the road like a galaxy, the asphalt black and shining with rain. Then the whine of the engine, the car backing up, tyres smoking, the roar as it accelerated away.

When I ran to him, he was silent, eyes closed, his shoulders trembling and twitching, his face covered in a lattice of blood. His hair was slick and in his scalp I could see grey fragments, shards.

I looked at the vulnerable hand he always hid; it lay uncovered, exposed.

I was outside myself and I was running into a gas station, shouting for help. Two men crossed the forecourt and jogged along the pavement. They tugged on Louis' body, turning him. His limbs bent like broken sticks. Around the streetlights there were haloes of orange light with raindrops swirling in them. Time stopped and jerked forward.

The street turned into a mass of vehicles and cordons and flashing lights, an ambulance, a fire engine, police cars, police running tape around the scene.

I looked at their broad backs as they crouched over him. They rocked backwards, stood up, conferring, not hurrying anymore.

They covered him with a white waterproof sheet. I knelt down and pulled the sheet off his face. A policeman stood over me for a moment and then said, 'Come on. Let's go.' When I didn't move, he took my arm and pulled me up.

I looked at Louis' shoe, lying on the road beyond the sheet. His foot in a blue sock showed under the edge of the sheet.

'Come on. He's dead. *Get in the car.*'

I was the sole witness, the only person who could identify the car. Two detectives drove me to Auckland Central police station. They asked me if there was someone I wanted to call, to come to the station. The idea was: emotional support. Karl was in America, Kay was at home in Parnell. I couldn't imagine Kay there, so I said no. I wouldn't have summoned Karl either, if he'd been around; I had no sense there was a role they could have played. The police seemed surprised I asked for no one and I felt ashamed. I thought they looked at me sideways, suspiciously.

I was questioned by the homicide squad for hours, and, because I'd called no one, I was left alone for periods throughout the night. They would all leave, then crowd back in again. They seemed, like time, to rush forward and go still, as if the night was a defective tape running through a spool, speeding up, slowing down.

The team leader was an abrasive senior detective who led a kind of surreal tutorial, bouncing around ideas about what had happened. He kept breaking off to ask if I was drunk.

'So, tell me again . . . By the way, you drunk?'

'No.'

'Stoned?' He mimed smoking a joint.

'No.'

After a while he said, 'You're not drunk.'

At one point in the questioning I laughed out loud. They stared at me and I fell silent, trying to read their deadpan faces. I went over and over my account, drew diagrams on the bits of paper they gave me. Louis was a stick figure, lying amid road markings. I was sure there'd been more than one person in the car. How did I know? I didn't — I just felt it. The car had changed direction, had swerved towards him, suggesting a deliberate action. No, I had no idea why anyone would do this. I gave a definite description of the car, colour, shape, possible model, asserting all this with confidence, yet in a detached part of my mind I wasn't sure if I was describing a memory or constructing it. Already I was separated from the memory by a wall of numbness — I couldn't connect the experience to myself.

They all rushed out again. A phone on a desk rang and rang. I sat alone in the room and watched a neon sign blinking on the horizon. There was a bank of black cloud in the east and behind it the sky was growing light. Just before dawn I was driven across town to sign a death certificate and a statement that I'd identified the body. This was so his family didn't have to go to the morgue and see him badly injured.

A suburban house, a narrow street. The Justice of the Peace opened the door wearing a dressing gown. He fanned out the forms on his dining table. There was silence. He handed me a pen. Outside I could see a drenched garden, grey dawn light.

When the detectives dropped me at Tohunga Crescent, I was wordless and numb, and at the same time, on a level I was aware of but couldn't feel, distraught. I was maddened by the numbness. I paced, trying to articulate it, the horror of feeling nothing. Kay had got up when I came in, but after a while said we needed to sleep, because she had to go to work that day. She gave me a pill and I went to bed.

Kay had told me that when her father died when she was 18, she wasn't allowed to see the body and it meant she'd had trouble accepting he was dead. Because of this, she'd made sure to take us to see Karl's mother's body in the funeral parlour, and she and I had gone to see her mother when she'd died. She believed in the idea of a viewing.

The next morning, tortured by numbness, I rang up Auckland Central Police and asked if I could see Louis' body. I was passed from one person to another. There was wariness, suspicion. Who was this person who wanted to see the body? This was a homicide investigation. The body was in the *morgue*. No, I couldn't *see* it. What's your angle? Oh, you were present at the *death*?

I persisted, hanging on to the idea, convinced it would give me relief. Eventually a voice came on the line and told me there would be plenty of time for that kind of thing at the *funeral parlour*.

I hung up, cringing. I imagined the murder squad thinking me weird and suspicious, wondering what I was up to.

A week later, I did get to see Louis in the funeral parlour. A wound on his face had been covered with pastel-covered paste, and his scalp and hands were covered. He wore a jacket and tie. He smelled of chemicals. I felt nothing.

Out in the street I looked at birds on the powerlines, the white sky.

Some terrible damage was being done to me. I knew it was happening, but I couldn't feel it, the knife gouging my heart to shreds.

My brain played weird tricks. I would catch sight of Louis on the street. Magical thinking. The thought ran on a loop, Louis was killed but *he's all right*. I waited for him to come back. I stored up things to tell him. I caught sight of him in passing cars, in crowds.

The words played in my head: Louis is dead *but he's all right*. He got hit very hard *but he's all right*. It must be the same thought process that allows a grief-stricken parent to say, 'My child is safe in Heaven.'

Safe.

I pretended to cry, because I knew I should. He was lost: I walked the city streets alone at night, looking for him. In a place outside myself emotion was waiting, but my nerves couldn't connect.

Someone, his mother probably, gave me his jacket. I had mix tapes he'd made, labelled with his handwriting in scrawled black marker. With its jagged, slanting style, his handwriting was reminiscent of his sister's drawings and paintings. In Jenny's compositions you could see the personality, the style of the Dale/Doležel family. Her paintings and prints had Louis' and Jenny's sharp features and expressions, their eyes and teeth and body language, their authentic style and their rollicking, rebellious humour.

I wondered if Jenny felt it consciously when she was painting, that she was making a visual representation of her very self. A true artist's every expression is idiosyncratic, distinct, characteristic. Among my possessions after Louis died was a map Jenny had sketched for us: directions to a party. The scrawl of sketches and handwriting was in every sense 'a Doležel'.

I hung Louis' jacket in a wardrobe. I was keeping it for him, the mirror-world logic behind that was: he would want it. I had a small pile of Polaroid photos, Louis and me in a Fort Street nightclub, a picture of us drinking wine on the patio outside his room, surrounded by stolen pot plants. The best, most characteristic photo is of Louis sitting on a rock somewhere in the bush. It's raining and there are big grey stones strewn about, perhaps he's beside a stream. It's cold; he's pulling his oilskin coat around himself. His face is pale and tranquil, his expression is thoughtful, he's looking at the white sky, at the rain.

Karl wrote me a letter. I don't remember speaking to him on the phone. He was on an extended trip overseas, and had been in California watching the Kentucky Derby on TV when he got the news, he told me in his letter. It had made him weep, thinking of Louis and me, getting ready together to go out on the town as we always did.

There was no Victim Support service back then, no system of offering information or help. I didn't seek advice or counselling (no sessions with sinister frauds or creeps), and no one suggested I should.

I watched a lot of TV, late into the night. B-grade films, cop dramas. I recall a lot of *Hawaii Five-O*. I didn't read; I couldn't read. I was blank, calm, silent. I didn't eat. I roamed around alone, often at night, covering miles. I walked so often at night in the city that the police stopped me and asked what I was doing, didn't I realise it wasn't safe to be out so late alone? I ignored them.

One evening at Tohunga Crescent I turned off the TV and it came to me: I'd seen his broken skull, his dead face. He had been violently injured. He was not all right, he was dead. I was flooded with horror, but in a case of terribly unlucky timing Kay, who must have taken offence earlier at something I'd done, appeared at the top of the stairs and struck a rhetorical tone. She said, 'Please do not be nasty to me.'

She swept off downstairs, and I was alone. I went numb again.

I thought afterwards that if I'd been able to hold that feeling of horror and to experience it, especially alongside another person, I would have done better in the following years.

> *An adverse event becomes traumatic in its aftermath when it is accompanied by a sense that one is not accompanied — that one's mental experience is not shared and the 'mind is alone.'*

It occurs to me, the bereaved are powerful. We tiptoe around them, terrified of getting things wrong and causing offence; we have to pay court, to acknowledge their awful plight. Perhaps Kay, who was acutely attuned to power in all its forms, recognised bereavement as a force.

She dwelt on the story — it was another example of the worldview she generated and managed subtly to enforce — that his friends had become hysterical with mirth at Louis' funeral because the vicar his mother had insisted on using was a bore and a drone who'd had the surreal notion that Louis had been a Christian (of all things — this was indeed tragically wide of the mark). In Kay's funny story it had to be that we were 'in hysterics' at the funeral, because it couldn't be that we were grief-stricken, that this was a calamity and a horror.

Kay's and Karl's resistance to piety: like so much in the literary family it was comedic — funerals can be funny. Perhaps it involved a lack of emotional engagement; if you're at a certain remove, a lot of life must veer between boring and hilarious.

A memory: my aunt and uncle had been married for around 60 years when my aunt died. After her funeral, Karl said to me, 'You know what I saw in his [my uncle's] face today?'

'No, what?'

'Triumph!'

When my kids' much-loved young teacher and his wife were killed in a car accident and the school laid on grief counselling, I asked Karl and Kay to tell the kids they were sorry, to acknowledge how awful it was. (To observe the pieties.) They were puzzled (Seriously? Why would a kid care about a teacher?), reluctant and foot-dragging, and finally resolved their unwillingness by drawing the kids into mocking the grief counselling: how corny and meaningless it was, just an excuse for some time off, how it involved a bogus ritual of Milo and a biscuit, how ineffably silly. They did get the kids laughing, it has to be said.

The people who killed Louis were never caught. They swerved, sent his body rolling off the bonnet, and drove away at speed. They were out there somewhere, killers, disposing of evidence, fixing their smashed windscreen, washing off the blood, painting or hiding the car. There was never a moment I felt safe. I jumped at loud noises; I was on edge all the time. I could barely stand being a passenger in a car.

Someone left flowers in the letterbox at Tohunga Crescent anonymously, with no note. I thought it possible this was the killers. They knew where I lived. The world seemed terrifying. A person you loved could be there one second, vital, warm, laughing, and the next a bloody mess in front of you, *just like that*. It could happen to anyone. Fear was everywhere.

I was lonely. Louis had been my closest and only companion; now I had no one. I was overwhelmed with shame. Shame coloured everything, it followed me, twisting my insides every time I had to explain what had happened. I would blush, laugh, shrug. Shame sweated out of me. I surprised people by smiling, or by not crying; they would frown, look surprised, glance away, compounding my shame, making me writhe with it. I had to ask for extensions for university essays. I explained using air quotes, it was because of 'a bereavement'. I laughed carelessly, as if I knew it was a lame excuse, and died of shame at the lecturer's wary, puzzled expression. I was reduced, weirdly blank, crazed with numbness. I spent weeks and months talking to no one, getting no help, turning it all inward, trying to bury it, day after day, dying of shame.

I kept walking around the city late at night, going nowhere, covering miles, just walking. Looking for him. Louis has died *but he's all right*.

It didn't occur to anyone, including me, that I needed any advice. I just needed to keep going. Karl and Kay seemed to have a somewhat impenetrable notion of grief. (Karl told me that when he was a boy and was told his childhood friend had died he got an adrenaline rush and felt exhilarated; he didn't describe a more nuanced experience after that.)

There were no hugs; we didn't do that.

On the night Louis was killed, after the police questioning and the signing of the death certificate, it was dawn by the time I was dropped at Tohunga Crescent. I was numb, and at the same time I was distressed that I couldn't feel anything. It was like being dead and knowing I was dead.

After a while, because she wanted to go to bed, Kay gave me the pill that sent me to sleep. I dreamed I was flying away over an empty red desert, further and further from civilisation. When I woke up, I remembered how far away I'd flown, and I felt as if the red desert separated me from the world. In all the time that followed, I tried to find my way back and couldn't. I'd been knocked out of the world, into a parallel universe. The red desert was a powerful image. It was vast; I was on one side of it, and everyone else was on the other.

Louis' sister told me that when the police came to let them know he'd been killed, his mother sank down on the floor, and eventually his sisters and father sat down on the floor with her, and they stayed there for hours, awake, huddled close together.

We're all animals. I wanted to be part of the human pack. I was intensely lonely, yearning for love and warmth, but I'd crossed the red desert and I couldn't find my way back.

I did find my way to love eventually, but I achieved that by feeling I'd killed off, or detached from, my former self. This was magical thinking, but the perception was a useful kind of reality.

It's not clear to me why a personal disaster can generate an overwhelming tsunami of shame.

Ashamed, terrified, lonely, craving affection, very soon after Louis' death, with no idea what I was doing, I fell in love. I was not only smitten, I moved in with a man 18 years older, a smooth operator, confirmed bachelor, charming tyrant. Call him Alex.

I met Alex at the Auckland District Court. Just before Louis was killed I'd been caught (again) drinking in a bar, and when told by police to leave had gone around the block and re-entered through a different door. The legal drinking age back then was 20, and I was just under. For this piece of silly defiance, I was summoned to court, and was introduced to Alex by the duty solicitor.

(But my life of crime was over. It would be my last court appearance. After Louis died I never broke the law again, not a speeding ticket, barely even a parking ticket.)

The court summons had arrived not long after Louis' funeral. I was in a raw state, still jumping at shadows, dying of shame.

Alex deftly got me off the charge and then, outside the court, looked me over, leaned in, made a few darkly funny remarks about the judge and invited me out for a meal.

He was tall and thin, dressed in an elegant suit. Like Louis he was blond and blue-eyed with a thin face and a long, straight nose, and like Louis he had the body language of a left-hander, the slight awkwardness needed to adjust to a right-handed world. The similarities touched me; it seemed uncanny that the universe had produced, so soon after Louis' death, someone whose way of holding a pen or using a phone could deliver a pang of recognition, a sharp in-drawing of breath.

He occupied my mind; at moments he'd say something abrasive and I'd go off him, feeling I didn't like him, but I thought about him with an intensity that was thrilling. We began talking on the phone. He would ring and just stay on the line. After an hour I'd go to hang up and he'd say, plaintive, 'Where are you going? Don't go!'

Soon after we'd had dinner together he confessed: he was lonely, there was 'something about me', he wished he could be with me all the time. He was impulsive, generous, adoring, fun.

It didn't occur to me to worry about his previous relationships, the line-up of hot-shot lawyers and 'blondes' whose photos were scattered around his house. I was dazzled by him, overwhelmed, flattered. He told me I was the first woman he'd wanted to live with since his early marriage, from which he'd escaped and fled to Auckland about a decade before.

Alex was a successful criminal lawyer. His life was expensive and flashy. He set a lot of store by appearances, he was extravagant and generous with money, and he wanted to be leading a glamorous life. He had a terrific supply of work stories and could be charming and witty. Since I was a law student by then, I could help him with his cases. I was more interested in criminal law than anything else, and I was thrilled to be able to help with serious High Court trial work. Again it was as if the universe had produced him for me, his speciality the subject I was most fascinated by.

He asked me to move into his house. He talked impulsively about marriage. I moved in and he overwhelmed me with love and affection. I was enchanted. I'd been starved of love and companionship, was craving human warmth and touch. The physical and verbal affection was extraordinarily moving to me. I was accepted. I had a companion, someone to love, I'd found happiness and safety.

I would have done anything to regain that joy when it was taken away.

I don't recall how long the initial happiness lasted. Things slowly started to go wrong; specifically, I started to fail at things. I wondered why I kept getting it wrong, why he was growing critical, cold, disappointed. I would do something for him, expecting him to be pleased, and would instead be stunned by his furious dissatisfaction. I couldn't understand it; he'd previously been delighted by the same thing. It was disorientating.

It was gradual. His displeasure became a constant, alleviated by the odd reward when I tried extra hard to please him. I was confused, desperate to get back the love I was losing because of my shortcomings.

I scurried around trying to win him back. I'd succeed, there'd be relief, happiness, and then I'd disappoint him again.

His line when exasperated became, 'You're useless. Useless.' He was overworked and stressed, and I was burdening him with my mistakes.

He would mention he wanted something and fly into a rage when I returned, saying I'd bought the wrong thing. Once he wanted oysters. When I came back with Pacific rather than Bluff oysters, he was furious. I had no idea what the difference was.

I tried harder to get things right, to do a good job. I was dying for affection and love, and I was a perfectionist. I'd get it right then I'd get it wrong, and be furious with myself. I was 20 years old and failing at something I'd been so moved to have achieved, a relationship with a highly intelligent man who loved me.

I had no one to advise or help me. I felt Karl and Kay would have been embarrassed if I'd told them what was going on; they certainly wouldn't have wanted to 'interfere'.

He was high-powered, charming, a big personality. I'd grown up with the idea that a domineering man was to be placated, that his rage was somehow sacred, evidence not of bad behaviour, but of his righteousness and intellectual rigour. I'd been trained for the man I was now living with.

The dynamic between us was powerful. I was intellectually a match for him, but emotionally vulnerable, naïve and completely outfoxed.

He had an array of tricks that made ordinary bullying seem homely and straightforward. I had never met a more manipulative, subtle and cunning person — nor have I since. There was a kind of grace and allure about him — when he was affectionate he was utterly charming — yet his behaviour was compulsively destructive. So much of his power and talent went into hurting and controlling people that probably, ultimately, he hurt himself, too. He always ended up alone. He'd had a lot of suffering and perversity in his early life.

I watched him, and living with him was a kind of master class.

He sharpened me up, berating me for my shyness and lack of assertiveness, for traits he saw as youthfully slack and lazy. He made me politer, a better speaker. He improved my clothes, my grooming and posture. He wouldn't tolerate dreaminess, lack of efficiency or lying around. He showed me I could work much harder than I'd thought, that I should put more energy into everything.

Watching him I learned how not to accept no for an answer, how to push for what I wanted, how to ignore opposition and get things done. I saw him manipulate, I watched him charm, behave with sweetness, be verbally ingratiating; I watched him intimidate and bully.

In court I saw the way he could win over a jury, appeal to them, draw them in, make them feel as if they and he were on the same side. He could make jurors love him. He knew how to turn 'I' into 'we'.

He surprised people with big, generous gestures, and others with acts of gratuitous cruelty. A small trick was to return photos. I saw how disconcerted a friend would be when a sheaf of photos, the ones featuring the friend only, was extracted from a pile and unexpectedly handed over after a cull. The handing over was friendly, as if it were a present — look what I've got for you! — but the subtle message was 'I don't want a record of you. Your memory is cancelled.' The friend would thank him for the pictures, looking confused, not quite able to identify the source of the sting.

He hid aggression in a show of warmth. He used anger, either cold or explosive, and unexpected moves: sudden passivity, charm, abrupt fury.

Long after I'd parted from him I would hear myself coming out with some phrase of his, or a tactic or tone of voice — doing evil in return. I knew first-hand the psychological effect of his moves.

But while I was living with him I was always bewildered, struggling to keep up.

I had Kay's submissiveness as a model, but I wasn't temperamentally like that; I'd been the arguing one in the family, the one who'd challenged Karl. Although I blamed myself for the fights with Alex, I couldn't easily submit, and the relationship grew increasingly volatile, distressing and violent.

He was wrong, I felt. His behaviour was wrong. But I kept trying to please him. It just about killed me, standing up to him.

He had a large base of clients charged with serious offences, including murder, manslaughter and rape. We studied forensic photos of crime scenes and postmortems, and read statements about attacks and deaths. I found this fascinating and yet, immersing myself in the details of violent crime, I was growing, on some dissociated level, more and more afraid, looking at pictures of autopsies and horrific injuries, and reading statements detailing extreme violence.

I began to have the sense that in order to express an emotion I had to act it out, put it on, fake it.

'It's just a bit of rain . . .'

It was summer, the time just after Christmas, long hot empty days, the city shut down and the streets empty. Alex's house faced the harbour, and I woke to find the sea had changed colour. A tropical cyclone had blown down from the Pacific Islands. The water was turquoise, flecked with white, and the sky above it was dense, dark grey, shading to black.

Downstairs I found Alex in overdrive, bustling about, packing. I paused on the step. 'We can't—'

'It's a bit of rain,' he said.

'It's a cyclone. It's got a name. It's dangerous.'

He went on packing.

We drove across the Harbour Bridge, heading for Whangaparāoa. Alex had borrowed a yacht and we were going to sail it to Kawau Island. No cyclone was going to mess with his plans.

'Look at the sky'. I pointed.

There was an intense turquoise haze on the horizon. The sea was navy blue and broken up by choppy waves. Over Rangitoto Island there was a strange configuration of clouds, like great rags hanging in the pearly-blue glare. Below it the colour of the sea had intensified, as if there was a disturbance spreading across the water.

Sudden changes in the light. The wind buffeting the car on the bridge.

'Good sailing weather,' he said.

This was from *Opportunity*, a story called 'Storms'.

No one else was out on the water. Launching into the harbour we immediately lost our dinghy and had to go round and round trying to catch it. I had never sailed on a yacht before. Out in the gulf the sea was wild, the wind screamed, rain lashed my face and I was violently seasick. The yacht pitched and rolled and plunged through the huge swells, Alex grappling with ropes and the sail, while I lay clinging to a thin wire and throwing up over the side.

Those childhood experiences of near-drowning came back to me.

I thought we would die, but after a long time we made it to Kawau Island, and sailed into the shelter of the horseshoe-shaped harbour, surrounded on all sides with pine forest.

The next morning we woke on the boat to find that the engine had leaked fuel all over the floor of the cabin. It was uninhabitable.

Alex stormed off, up into the pine forest, and when he came back he said, 'I've found a place.'

He led me through the trees to an empty wooden bach. He forced a window and broke in. We lived there for five days until the storm died down. There was little chance of being discovered, since the storm had kept people away from the island. We hauled our supplies up there from the yacht, foraged for bedding in the bach's dank linen cupboard, listened for days to the howling wind, the rain drumming on the iron roof at night.

His stubbornness got us into that fix, and his lawlessness got us out of it. He always had an outlaw quality. Once, for example, we got it on together in the library of the High Court. Once he turned up to visit me riding a motorbike given to him by a criminal client. His clients, because of their nefarious activities, dealt mostly in cash. They would pay him in cash which he would secrete around the house. In my first novel, *Provocation*, I wrote about sofas crackling with banknotes, wads cascading out when a cupboard was opened.

He empathised with his clients, was good to them.

'There but for the grace of God,' he would say.

Most of the clients loved him, but if he got them acquitted and they weren't on legal aid, it was hard to get them to honour their bills. Their reasoning was, I was innocent all along, so why should I pay? The rule with non-legal aid clients was payment upfront. In cash if the client insisted.

There was always the risk a criminal client would fly into a rage. One of Alex's colleagues had his life threatened, his garage burned down.

But Alex was a diplomat and a charmer, when he needed to be.

Each day we stayed in that empty bach on Kawau Island I worried the owner would turn up and discover us, but I believed, too, that Alex would make it all right, because he always had an angle, always knew the right thing to say.

He had his insecurities. His deepest was imagining I was flirting with other men. One night he lost control, accused me of cheating on him, and punched me repeatedly in the face.

After that I stayed inside for days. My face was swollen and black with bruises. One night I woke up to find him sitting by the bed, watching me. I couldn't appeal to my parents, and I had no one else to ask for help, and nowhere to go. I was so frightened and lonely and hurt, I felt I was losing myself completely.

In the period afterwards, he behaved with great sweetness. He agonised over this 'fight' we'd had. How could we have been so crazy? We must love each other so terribly, so passionately. He and I were lost, he said. It was the two of us against the world. Only I understood him; I was the only woman he'd met who was tough and original enough to be with him. We would get through this together.

'You look so pretty,' he said.

I had moments when I couldn't breathe. I couldn't lie straight in bed; I had to sleep curled up in a ball. I felt that knives were going to come up through the mattress. I was deeply ashamed. My facial injuries were so bad that the tutor in my legal professional class rang to ask if I was all right. I said I'd been injured in a car crash, knowing he didn't believe me. I was fine, I told him, *dying of shame*.

Not long after the bruises had faded, Alex was blaming me for what he'd done. I was a flirt and a cheat and useless, and I had provoked him.

One morning I was walking up the street, heading for a lecture, when my head began lifting off my body. I was rising while my body kept walking, I was above myself looking down.

Going to pieces, coming apart, falling apart — these idioms describe a psychological state. I had the actual sensation of disintegrating. But I kept going. I'd always liked studying, and got good marks. I went to lectures and courses, I passed exams. When the time came for graduate interviews, I got a job straight away, in a large commercial law firm, Simpson Grierson.

Something stubborn and orderly in me kept going, despite the fact that I'd fallen apart.

In my novel *Provocation* I wrote about a violent relationship between an older man and a young woman. In the scene where the man attacks the woman, I had her participate in the fight by kicking him, cutting his forehead with her high-heeled shoe. In reality, Alex's worst attack so took me by surprise I didn't defend myself. I could tell he had lost all control; I could feel how seriously he was injuring me, and I was sure I was going to die.

I didn't describe or discuss this experience with a single person until, years later, I sketched it out rapidly in Dr Verne's office.

'By the way, is this relevant to anything?' I asked him, offhand (*dying of shame*).

I told him about expecting to be killed. I mentioned walking up the street and suddenly rising so far above my body that I was looking down on myself. I mentioned permanent fear, jumping at noises like a cat, being so afraid I couldn't lie straight in bed.

I remember this comment: 'When he lost control and attacked you, you thought you were going to die.'

And, 'You went on living with him after that?'

The question made me wonder. I tried to recall. What is it like to go on living with someone after an experience where you were sure, you knew, he was going to kill you?

It's complicated. There's relief.

Relief?

Relief that he didn't. That initially, he's sorry. He's tiptoeing around, remorseful, he asks himself aloud how he could have done such a thing to a person he loves, such a beautiful woman; he says how beautiful you are, how special, the most lovely and clever woman he's ever lived with; you're fiery, sure, maybe you're a bit loose with your attentions, with the good-looking guys — he pauses, steadies himself — no, no, you're lovely, *how* could he have lost his temper so badly?

He says you and he are trapped in this intense, passionate love that's driving you both crazy, the only way to figure it out is together. No one else will understand. It's our secret. He makes you love him, turns 'I' into 'we'.

Not long after, once the drama and the injuries are fading, his temper flares again, because look what you've done, the stress is killing him, he has to do everything while everyone around him is *useless*, and now he's telling you no wonder he did it because no one, *no one* is as useless, or so much of a flirt and a cheat . . .

And by the way, as soon as the evidence has faded, he didn't do it at all. You're making it up. Violence, what violence?

Your memory of what happened *is not real*.

There must be fear, living with a person who could have killed you if, while falling, you'd smacked your head on the concrete, or your neck had fractured, or he'd squeezed your throat too hard. The greater the fear, the harder the mind works to cordon it off, keep it separate.

The fear will evaporate. A sense of security will return. Why? Because you surfaced. Because you survived.

Alex and I both knew, from our work together, the extent to which chance plays a part in violent crime. The difference between assault, manslaughter and murder often comes down to dumb luck. We knew this as we frowned over our files and inspected our gory photo books, as we fought it out on hot Friday nights when I still, despite everything, couldn't submit, couldn't stop fighting him verbally even though I blamed myself every time, even though I knew he could snap again and beat me to death.

One thing about violent crime: up close, it loses its aura of horror. The word 'murder' creates a shiver, but, up close, most violence is straightforward, squalid, messy, not intrinsically frightening on inspection, after the fact. 'Murder' became ordinary in that sense, but on another level I was drowning in fear, because I felt the nearness of violence, felt its threat, as past experience and a possible future. I'd moved into Alex's house only months after seeing Louis killed. I remember infuriating Alex by crying at night, being unable to stop, because the world was so bleak and frightening. I was desolate, but I had nowhere to go.

I thought about my relationship with violence. When I eventually had my own children, I made a rule: smacking wasn't allowed. I vowed to do everything I could to restrain myself. Parenting is stressful and I made lots of mistakes, especially early on, but the rule stood. If I lost my temper and broke it, it was my fault.

Smacking proved completely unnecessary, as I'd suspected it

would. It's easy to bring up kids without hitting them. You don't really need to 'punish' kids either, if you're getting it right. Looking back I'd say, if you've got to the stage of punishing them you've probably lost your way, and something needs to change about you.

Paul wasn't smacked as a child, not even once; it never even occurred to him to hit anyone.

Could I say that all my intense combat with Karl primed me for that violent relationship with Alex? Conflict, loss of temper and 'lashing out' (even though Karl only slapped) wasn't unfamiliar, or an outrage.

The old question: why don't women just walk out the door? Why stick around? I always knew the answer to that. I knew the paralysis, confusion and grief that keep you hanging in there, the bargaining, the hopeful belief in one last chance, the exhausted submission to mind games and threats. The optimism. And the perfectionism — wanting to succeed, to get it right. The shame and guilt. The love.

I blamed myself for every fight. I tried and tried, and could not please him.

Alex was an unusually fascinating person. He was talented, clever, original, charming. He was stylish, elegant and attractive. He could be poignant and funny and very often made me laugh. His childhood had been tough; he told me about his father running off, his mother's breakdown, how he'd had to study for exams out on the steps of his grandmother's state house. About visiting his mother in the mental hospital.

He said to me, 'You're the one who knows me best', and I felt this was true, that I'd engaged with him on some deep, imaginative level, so much so that I used elements of his character in my first novel, *Provocation*, and again in my portrayal of a New Zealand prime minister in later novels, *The Night Book* and *Soon*.

Readers thought I was writing about Prime Minister John Key, but the main aspect of Key I focused on was his wealth, and the way voters were (wrongly, I thought) persuaded by the idea that a successful businessman would be good at running a country.

I was interested in Key's poor upbringing and that he'd spent his life distancing himself from it (he went from childhood in a state house to building himself a mansion in Parnell that was so large as to be absurd). The early deprivation seemed to have made him intolerant, perhaps not an uncommon reaction to adversity, I thought. His government had worked to reduce state housing: hard work, not handouts. Having climbed up the social-welfare ladder he was busy kicking it away from those below. I could understand it; it seemed a kind of revulsion, one he ought to have resisted. It reminded me of Paul's mother, a British immigrant who forged such strong links with Māori that she and her husband ended up with the honour of being buried in a Māori graveyard in the Far North, but who was also capable of being a xenophobe: 'I didn't *come all this way* to have a horde of *foreigners* crowding me out.'

The fact I was interested in Key's personal details and his position didn't mean I admired him as a politician. Nor that Alex resembled him: unlike Key, Alex was genuinely charismatic. As prime minster, Key was highly popular, goofy, approachable, perceived to be a nice guy, but as a politician he was shallow, often cringeworthy, and none of his policies appealed to me. The whole point of the prime minister character in my novels was that he wasn't one I would have voted for myself.

In the novels, the traits I gave my Prime Minister David Hallwright were Alex's: the skill at power games, the attractiveness, the elegance, the charming menace. I toned Hallwright down, though; I didn't want him to be violent or abusive.

I had Balzac's *La Comédie Humaine* in mind: David Hallwright was loosely a representative of society in all its corruption, and my main character, Simon Lampton, was the Rastignac figure, the man whom you expect, at the end of *Père Goriot*, to renounce society after experiencing its corruption and venality, but who instead throws himself into it, embraces it, says, 'Here I am, I'm ready for you.'

I preferred Balzac's salty representation of what *is* to a Dickensian happy ending signalling what *ought to be*.

I *ought* to have walked out the door. But while I was living with Alex, I believed the conflict was my fault, and I kept trying to make it better. I had no one else to love, no one to confide in, and nowhere to go. I not only didn't leave, I wanted to hang onto him. I was a perfectionist. I wanted to succeed.

I also kept standing up to him; I never stopped.

It all ended with Alex after a fight, I can't remember which. There was one where he threw a jumbo bucket of KFC coleslaw at my head. There was another where I ran along the road and he ran after me, and I fell and banged my head on the pavement.

Blaming myself, dying of shame, reaching out into the void and catching nothing, I left for the last time and didn't know where to go.

I hung onto my job. At the law firm, I was criticised for reading the paper rather than chatting during breaks — I was not a team player. Morning tea was an ordeal; I was nervous and my hands shook. Stuck behind a wall, I struggled to know what to say, and I was regarded as standoffish and cold.

I needed to move into a nice flat with some young women, to retreat into the embrace of friends who would, in the way of chick lit and corny movies, help me get over my heartbreak in marathon sessions of weeping, hilarity, ice cream, wine . . .

But that would have involved admitting things had gone wrong. It would have required membership of the human pack.

I blamed myself; if I'd been in some way better, I could have got on with Alex. I could have managed it all, succeeded in the relationship.

No one could know any of it. I was still paralysed with shame.

A man I'd known at law school, Sean, offered me a room in his flat. I went to have a look at it. It was an apartment built on the flat roof of a nine-storey office block, the CML Building, in Queen Street. The building was scheduled for demolition, and all eight floors below the flat were empty. To get to it we entered the mall at street level, and unlocked a door at the back of the mall that led to a lift. We rode up eight floors and got out on the landing, after which we walked the final flight of stairs to the flat, a single-storey concrete structure, its ranch sliders opening onto a large roof terrace, with a view over the buildings of Queen Street.

I looked around carelessly, glancing into the bedroom, which was sunny and spacious, the windows open onto the roof area. I checked the small, dingy kitchen and the terrace outside, where Sean's flatmate Karl was lying on the concrete, sunbathing and reading a book. Karl was a policeman, relaxing before his shift at Auckland Central. He was friendly. I noticed his book, a serious novel (how surprising, how ingratiating), also that he was unusually handsome.

On the way back down, Sean showed me some of the empty floors. The furniture and partitions had been cleared; shafts of light through the dirty windows lit up cobwebs and dust. On one level a huge metal safe stood in the middle of a wide stretch of carpet. It looked stark, sinister. I felt frightened just looking at it.

But down in the bright, busy mall, amid the shoppers and with a view of the sunny street, I shook off the feeling of apprehension, and said I would take the room.

The rent was cheap because the block was due for demolition, and the location was perfect. It would take me five minutes to get to work. Each morning I exited the building, crossed the street, nipped up a back alley, took the elevator and I was in the foyer of the law firm. From the roof of the CML I had a view across the rooftops to my boss's office, so I could see when he'd arrived at work in the morning.

The first Gulf War had started, and I'd got addicted to CNN. Some lunchtimes I would sneak back to the flat so I could catch the latest on the war, which had its own logo, theme music and cast of characters: the ghastly Saddam Hussein, his degenerate sons Uday and Qusay, the Scud missiles he ineffectually lobbed into Israel, the American president whom I took for a fraud and a dissembler, not knowing what worse crooks and liars were to come.

(It was my intense, lonely surveillance of the first Gulf War that allowed me to dismiss early on and with complete confidence the big lie about Saddam having weapons of mass destruction. If you'd paid attention at all, if you'd watched his gimcrack Scuds damaging a letterbox in Tel Aviv, you knew it just couldn't be so.)

I made my new bedroom as comfortable as possible. The flat was shabby and stark, and my flatmates were messy, careless guys. The place was all very manly and butch, with Sean's collection of Marlboro cigarette packets, his guns (he owned a .303 with a telescopic sight that we messed around with on the roof; I don't know how we avoided an Armed Offenders callout), and Karl's weights, buckets of protein powder and workout gear. Also Karl's books. Karl actually read proper literature; moreover, his name was absolutely improbable: Read. Constable Karl Read. Every time a letter came for him, I'd think it must be for my father.

On the subject of Karl's books: Constable Read read more than I did. In my last years at law school and while I lived with Alex, my reading had dwindled to a halt. Alex, whose idea of great literature was a fat paperback by Robert Ludlum, and whose notion of fine writing was hilariously wide of the mark — browsing through the *Herald* he would pause, hold up a solemn hand and read out in a reverent voice some passage, often of sports writing, that he found especially powerful, and I would press my lips together at how bad, how very bad, enough to make you scream with laughter, but I would feel a tenderness, too, because one of the most touching things about him was the quaint purpleness of his speech, and I thought of it as the only thing about him that was innocent. During that time, something had gone wrong with my reading. It slowed, dwindled and limped along until, having grown up in the house full of books and having judged *reading* as the other necessary thing along with *roaming around*, I'd stopped completely.

I read legal cases and texts, but no fiction. There was something very wrong with this, I knew. It represented a kind of depression, a mental paralysis. Looking back, it seems the most telling symptom of struggle and despair. I would glance at the improbable Karl, sunbathing and sipping his protein shake; I would marvel at his tan and his muscles and his good looks, but even more at the well-thumbed copy of *Catch-22* on his knee.

The way out of my current struggle would eventually involve fiction. Reading was part of the salvation and the cure. Even though I'd made my way through an arts degree as well as the law, had spent years at university grappling with Chaucer and Katherine Mansfield and Henry James, it took me a decade of reading the classics to recover from the state I'd got into, to catch up and reach a point where I felt qualified to review books.

Now, on the roof of the CML Building, I gazed at Constable Read with the numb respect of an illiterate.

At first it all went smoothly. Karl spent long shifts at Central police station. Sean (slow-speaking, humourless, gun-toting Sean) was either at work or crouched in his room on the phone, chain-smoking Marlboros and trying to get women to go out with him.

There were problems living on top of a dead building. It wasn't easy to get rid of the rubbish, so it tended to mount up and stink before we got around to lugging it downstairs. Pretty soon I couldn't bear going into the squalid kitchen and so didn't cook, but lived on takeaways and snacks.

I was still reeling from my troubles with Alex. I was mostly at work and wasn't focusing on the flat. But the summer break came, work finished for two weeks, and Karl and Sean went out of town on holiday. Now I was completely alone.

On the last day of work I stayed late for the drinks in the boardroom. I emerged from the law firm and bought myself a takeaway. On Queen Street, using my first key, I unlocked the glass doors of the closed, silent mall. I walked past the empty shops, and used the second key to enter the second door. Now I was by myself in the huge building, with eight floors of vacant space above me.

It all crowded in on me.

I'd been desperate for a room and a solution after Alex, and I hadn't thought about it properly until now. Until I was alone. If people, rough sleepers or God knows who, had got into the vacant space during the day, they could still be in here. No one would hear me call for help.

I stepped into the lift. What would happen if I got stuck between floors? Would anyone answer the call button of a lift in an unoccupied building?

The building was a trap.

I stepped out on the eighth floor and listened. From somewhere below I heard a metal clang. I ran up the stairs and locked myself into the flat. I dragged a deckchair out onto the roof and started to eat my takeaway, but I couldn't taste it. I listened and listened. Every sound made me freeze. The noise of the street floated up from below; all around me were high-rise buildings. I could see people in lighted windows, but I was alone.

I was locked in. It was fine.

But a new thought came to me. I got up and inspected the ranch slider doors. They led to the sitting room, and now I saw they didn't lock properly. I couldn't get the latch to work. There was an extra access point behind the flat that would allow people to get to the roof during a fire. I realised if a person got into the building and accessed the roof, they would be able to enter the flat through the defective sliding doors.

I thought of the empty floors below. All that enclosed space, set apart from the street, was its own lawless territory, and I couldn't shut myself off from it. I couldn't protect myself. If anything happened I wouldn't be able to get out, and way up here, no one would hear me scream.

I was so frightened I lay in the deckchair staring up at the black sky, and I didn't know what to do. I couldn't go back to Tohunga Crescent. I had no friend I could call on, nowhere else to stay until my flatmates returned. I'd been sad to be alone on a summer night after the work drinks, I'd felt lonely and ashamed of being lonely, but now I was terrified. I thought of leaving the building, but I was too afraid; it would mean braving the stairs, the lift, the vacant floors, the mall.

In the days that followed I spent long, desolate hours walking around the city. I went to the beach by myself, to movies. I sat in the park, thinking about Alex and Louis. I made sure I got home before dark, but once I was in, the night was the enemy and the ordeal. I sat on the deckchair out on the roof, paralysed with fear. I drank wine and smoked cigarettes, staying outside on the roof until I was so exhausted I would creep into my room and sleep, waking with nightmares, praying for the dawn. Only light would bring relief, but even during the daytime I was afraid, especially getting in and out of the building.

I yearned for safety, for human warmth and touch, and I didn't know where or how to find it. Along with the terror was helpless amazement, that I'd got myself into this bizarre situation, marooned on top of a pile of condemned concrete, above a labyrinth of dead rooms, with no sure way to shut myself off, to be safe. But this is how it goes; when things go wrong it's a cascade. One disaster leads to another. Once you're vulnerable, circumstances get crueller. If you have no support, defences start to crumble, choices narrow, the choices you make are hurried and increasingly unwise, the worse things get the more you lose your way.

Lying on the deckchair on the roof, I wondered at what point my story had gone so wrong. Was it when Louis died, or was it decided earlier? Was it when I learned to stand up to Karl who shouted, 'Don't you *ever* say "no" to me. *Ever.*'? Perhaps that early combat had made me insensitive to risk, not wary enough of Alex, too willing to blame myself when it went wrong. Was it because I was, as Kay said, 'too different', because I had 'something bad' in myself? And if so, how did *that* happen? Was it genes, an unlucky star, a curse, a single magpie at the window when I was born?

Looking up at the lighted windows, I felt like the last person left in the dead city. I was utterly alone.

Desperate, dying of shame, I went out and drank solo in a pub in Queen Street. It was a vicious circle; loneliness was so humiliating it couldn't be admitted, and the shame made me avoid contact.

Standing at the glass doors on Queen Street that night after the pub, I was too afraid to go in, but I had nowhere else to go. I stood out in the street while it grew emptier and the feeling of danger increased; now there was no one in the heart of the city except drunks, street kids, the homeless, the people I feared could get into the building during the day when the mall was open, who could be anywhere on the empty floors, moving quietly upwards, towards the roof.

I watched a drunk lurching along the street trying the doors of cars. It started to rain. I turned the key and opened the glass door. I locked it behind me, forcing myself to walk to the far end of the silent mall. I unlocked the wooden door, closed it behind me and now I was alone in the dead building. In the lift I was so frightened I stepped outside myself. I had the stunned, reeling sense of unreality — the eclipse — that accompanies bad news.

Running up the stairs I made it into the flat, barricaded myself in and began another night of terror, another vigil.

There's that soft question asked in magazine interviews: What advice would you give your young self? Here, it would obviously be: Get out of there. Pack your bags, check into a motel and never go back.

I knew I had to get out. The detail, the timing, of my escape from the CML Building isn't clear now, perhaps a reflection of how desperate I was. It's a blur. I do know this: the gun-toting Sean sent me on my way. Specifically, he decided I'd been rude to two of his friends, and he asked me to leave. I suspect my bags were already packed.

I definitely *was* rude. Sean must have come back from his summer holiday, perhaps with his friends in tow, a couple. I'd remembered details he'd told me about the man: that he was a devout Christian and that once on his farm he'd tied a disobedient sheepdog to a fence and beaten it to death, just hit it and hit it until it died. Sean seemed to think this was evidence of his friend's 'toughness' and 'resolve'.

I was disgusted by the story, and repelled by the sanctimonious bore and creep now parked in our sitting room. With my nerves shot and my bags packed, and after probably a few hundred glasses of wine, I burst out in a stream of rudeness about Christianity, God, hypocrisy and cruelty to animals. It was received largely in silence, but the next morning I found Sean had pinned an 'eviction notice' (written in felt pen on A4 paper) to my bedroom door. There was a line I remember about his friends' Christianity being 'as much a part of them as the food they eat'.

Right, I thought. I'm having a nervous breakdown. Nothing matters anymore.

There was ill will. I left, having lightly vandalised a few things. (That's for the dog, I thought, putting my foot through something or other of Sean's.)

I went to work, where my days in the office had taken on a surreal, lightly garish quality. I was managing (trying) to keep up a front while everything was unravelling. I drifted and dreamed through the hours. I'd done detailed legal research for the partner that he'd praised; now he'd given me a more complicated project, a step up and a reward, and some days I felt I was on top of it, but on others I couldn't focus at all. Now, on a cold, clear day I gazed out of my high-rise office onto the rooftops, watching the city silently moving below, and desolation and weariness filled my mind.

I answered an ad for a flatmate in Gibraltar Crescent, in Parnell. Again I had to move fast, and again the choice was bad. I moved in with three strangers who were orderly for the first few days, but soon took to rollicking home at 3am and going right on partying. They did this any night of the week. Again I couldn't find peace or space or get any sleep. One day I was sent by the partner to appear in the High Court on some minor matter, and found I was so exhausted I could barely speak.

It was an era in Auckland when there were so many armed bank robberies the *Herald* had started publishing a sarcastic daily column to goad and reproach the police, who were failing to solve the crimes. The column was called *Today's Armed Robbery*.

It would transpire, after the police finally roused themselves to arrest her, that a frequent visitor to the house at Gibraltar Crescent, the best friend of one of my flatmates, was the blonde girl getaway driver of the gang that was pulling off 'today's armed robbery'. High on adrenaline post-heist, she would bang on our door at 3am, shouting for drinks.

All I knew was that I never got any sleep, and it was getting harder to go to work.

One night another of the flatmates tiptoed into my room and asked if he could join me in bed. When I said no, he wouldn't leave.

The next morning instead of going to work I sat on my bed and imagined hitting myself repeatedly in the face. I didn't know why, whether it was an expression of despair or a way of forcing myself to keep going. I was so stressed, so cornered and desperate, the only thing left was to imagine turning on myself. After that, I knew I would have to move again. Only this time, I would get lucky.

I had a friend at work, Eugene, a lawyer I'd known since school. It turned out he was looking for a place, and he and I found a tiny two-bedroom house, an old railway workers' cottage, in Avon Street in Parnell. We had a bedroom each, a little sitting room, a spacious back garden with a lemon tree.

Eugene was clever, civilised, funny, even a good cook. In the mornings he ironed his shirt, took a taxi to work and covered for me (I drifted and dreamed and often struggled in late) by turning on the light in my office and putting a cup of coffee on my desk so the boss thought I'd arrived. Eugene was a great guy, a real friend. For the first time, I'd found a place I felt safe.

My new flatmate did another great thing: he decided to invite Paul Grimshaw to dinner at Avon Street. Paul worked upstairs at the law firm, and I only knew him by sight. I picture him in our tiny sitting room that evening, jigging his leg restlessly, making the floor shake and looking unconvinced, as if wondering what he was doing there. Eugene had pinned up a lot of press photographs he'd collected when he'd worked as a journalist for the *Auckland Star*, and each time Paul shifted and fidgeted another photo fell off the wall and hit him on the head.

Eugene made a pudding that involved pears. The pears were undercooked and kept shooting off the plates, like those long-ago rock-hard kūmara at Tolaga Bay, and amid the comedy of the flying fruit Paul and I discovered we liked each other.

Shame had kept me lonely and apart, and prevented me from seeking help. Shame was the red desert that cut me off from the human pack. But there was this to be said for shame: it stopped me falling completely to pieces. If no one could know, there was nothing else for it, I had to soldier on and pretend all was well.

Shame was the scaffolding that kept me upright.

Once, in desperation, when I was living with Alex, I made a booking at the student psychological service. I should have said, 'I'm stuck in a violent relationship, I'm terrified, I saw my friend killed, I need help.' Instead, having been blind-sided in the waiting room by a searing attack of (what else?) shame, I told the psychologist an elaborate, stylised story. I remember it revolved around the theme of 'three blond men', all of whom were left-handed. They were a boy called Julian I'd been fond of at Selwyn College (one of those with whom I'd built the raft and sailed out to protest against the American nuclear ship) and Louis and Alex. These three men *were* all blond and left-handed, but why I decided to tell this story I have no idea. I set it out, with its fatuous symmetry, as if desperately pulling my tattered dignity around me. It was a spontaneous derangement, brought about by shame.

It's material. Make a story out of it.

The psychologist to whom I was telling the story sat very still, perhaps concealing his bafflement, waiting and watching, trying to figure out what on earth I thought I was doing.

I remember he suggested I come back, but I swept from the room with a mad, careless laugh.

'Why would I come back? I've told you the story. The Three Blond Men. That's it!'

Perhaps I'd dimly grasped that the way out of the maze involved narrative. But my literary upbringing had taken over and I'd started to compose.

I hadn't realised the way to save your life is to tell the story that's true.

One summer day after we'd been talking, Dr Marie Sanders got the idea we should drive over to Alex's house and park outside for a moment. She had a theory that returning to the scene after all these years would help to resolve the trauma.

As soon as she'd parked her dusty Corolla in the street, I was struck with a sense of exquisite comedy (What were we *doing,* and what if he came out? The idea of louche, disgraceful Alex confronting sensible, good Marie Sanders in her big jeans and woven shoes was too hilarious) before my mirth turned to tears. As we debriefed afterwards, as she helped me to limp through the rain in a nearby park, she spoke of relief, of letting the trauma go.

But secretly, I was crying for Alex. His lawlessness, his dark laughter, his wildness. Our field trip had brought it all back, and it came back to me again not so long ago, when I heard that Alex had been ill for six months and had died. What a terrible person he was, how I'd loved him.

We all have a secret history.

This was what I knew from experience: when things go wrong there's a cascade effect, life narrows, you start making the wrong choices, you lessen the ability to look after yourself, and without support the choices you make are increasingly bad. The worse shape you're in, the crueller the world becomes.

None of this could be admitted; the old self's story could not be told.

I remember writing a story in which a woman said she felt like she'd surfed down a giant wave and hadn't fallen, that she'd walked away upright. This was important: to keep walking upright.

The new self was polite, economical with words, formal, perhaps even a little chilly. A cool customer. The new self did not admit an intimate acquaintance with life outside the ivory tower. Sensibly, steadily, the new self set about creating a new life. Found a nice partner, adopted his surname (Mrs Grimshaw!), had three children, began a career.

I started writing novels and short stories. I wanted to review contemporary fiction, but I knew my grip on literature had loosened, so I gave myself a task: 10 years of reading the classics to get back in shape. After that I got a job writing fiction reviews. I was a swot. A swot with a secret: I wasn't the person I used to be. I was someone completely new.

Occasionally it bothered me, the inability to share. It came to me forcefully at IFOA, the International Festival of Authors in Toronto, where I'd gone with my novel *Soon*. Throughout the Canadian tour, at the Calgary, Vancouver and Banff festivals and now in Toronto, writers had been thrown in together and constantly talked about themselves, sharing stories and details. My default response was to evade and deflect.

A British woman writer abruptly gave up asking me about myself and said, 'You're a strange one, aren't you?'

I realised what a barrier I was putting up, how it blocked and prevented friendship.

Invited to confide, the new self would evade, glaze over, refocus and begin to talk about *you*. The new self asked the questions around here; the traffic was all one-way. Women who tried to invite the new self for coffee would suddenly find themselves alone . . .

Everything depended on that original soul murder: making sure the old self was dead.

I wonder about Kay. Was she a reinvention? Were there parts of herself that she left behind in rural Henderson where she grew up, or in wild, lawless Omokoroa?

That morning in the flat in Gibraltar Crescent, after I'd struggled to get rid of the flatmate who'd crept into my room, I felt so lonely and distressed and defeated I sat on the bed and imagined beating my own face.

I didn't know why I was doing it, except that it expressed the way I felt. For years, until I exorcised the habit by describing it (by the way, is *this* relevant?), I mentally beat my face — did it in my imagination — either as a result of shame or embarrassment or some other distress, or just as often to urge myself on after a setback, when I needed to keep going.

It was the new self beating the old one to death. It was a way of driving myself forward that worked, but was, according to psychology, unnecessarily punitive. There were kinder ways of motivating myself, it was suggested to me.

'Don't beat yourself up,' I was told. 'Treat yourself kindly.'

When I described a woman beating her own face in *Mazarine*, my editor Harriet Allan at Penguin Random House suggested I change it. It was too extreme, she felt. The reader would lose sympathy with the narrator if she seemed too crazy.

I saw her point, and instead had my character break a mirror 'symbolically' by throwing it across the room.

We weren't a normal family, were we? Why was that?

Were we just intense?

I was used to studying up on a subject, going to the books. As the summer days got hotter and the city emptied out, as I went on seeing Sanders once a fortnight, I put aside my novels and started reading books and articles on psychology. It was kind of a layman's binge, a venture into concepts I'd had no idea existed.

I read that when psychology students are learning about mental illness they start to diagnose themselves and those around them. Suddenly they've all got personality disorders or depression or PTSD. This makes sense. Reading about some neuroticism or mental condition, it's possible to recognise a kernel of it in yourself. Obsessive compulsive disorder, say. Haven't we all, when anxious, repeatedly checked that the door is locked, or cleaned too thoroughly, or failed to turn off our mind when it's spinning on repeat?

I wanted to understand, I wanted to learn, and as I ranged through psychological articles online, the journal studies and websites dedicated to particular mental illnesses and syndromes, I too began to diagnose myself and those around me. Soon I had a lurid array of mental conditions, and so did most of the people I knew. Here a sociopath, there a psychopath . . .

A little bit of knowledge is a dangerous thing.

By chance, while immersed in all of this, I was offered a new volume of Sylvia Plath's collected letters to review for *The Spinoff*. Sylvia Plath possibly (or likely, depending on what you read) had borderline personality disorder, which led to her admission to McLean Hospital, and later her suicide.

This had me reaching for the psychology texts.

A recent theory on borderline personality disorder (I read) is that it involves a failure to mentalise. Mentalisation is described in Anthony Bateman and Peter Fonagy's *Psychology for Borderline Personality Disorder: Mentalization-Based Treatment* as 'the mental process by which an individual implicitly and explicitly interprets the actions of self and others as meaningful on the basis of intentional mental states such as personal desires, needs, feelings, beliefs, and reasons'.

Reading people, in other words?

I knew I could read people. I was intensely observant. Writing fiction wouldn't be possible otherwise. I could read the mind in the eyes, I was acute at reading people, including women, except in one context: socially, with women. When I was required to move from my usual position, standing to one side and watching, this was when my mind went blank.

Mentalisation can go offline in some contexts, I read.

Was this just a fancy way of describing shyness?

Personality disorders, I read on (busily diagnosing this one and that one), are formed when you're young, and can persist over a lifetime. Borderline personality disorder is caused by an invalidating environment, one where the child's internal experience is not named or acknowledged, where the child's emotions are rejected, not recognised, suppressed.

I frowned over the texts. One theory: the problem starts with a failure of epistemic trust, the mechanism by which humans learn to appraise social situations. This failure is adaptive, and not irrational but rational; trust fails to develop in environments where trust would expose the child to danger. It's a mistrust that makes sense in response to frightening or dysfunctional caregivers. If trust isn't established, social learning is impeded. The individual is left with an inability to mentalise, to understand the mind of others.

Borderline personality disorder used to fill medical professionals with dread because it was thought to be incurable, and because patients with the condition can be a nightmare to treat: suicidal, dramatic, demanding. These days it's considered treatable and finite; people often lose the symptoms as they age. They grow out of it.

In my *Spinoff* review of *The Letters of Sylvia Plath Volume 1, 1940 to 1956*, I wrote about Plath's intense relationship with her mother, Aurelia.

> *There was something rotten in the relationship, completely masked in Plath's letters and brooded over in her journals, in which she grapples with the terrible anger of the unloved. You could attribute Plath's rage*

to an 'unbalanced mind', but the imbalance had to come from somewhere. People who are loved know that they are; when there's doubt about love, it's a reliable indication it wasn't there.

Plath was explicit in her secret complaint: being unloved by her mother had a life-long, destructive effect. A secure self can't develop on its own; it can only be formed by relating, and Aurelia had reflected a void back at her. In her journals, Plath accused her mother of 'vampirism', or effectively of what Henrik Ibsen called 'soul murder': a withholding of love that had deformed her.

Her fury at the fundamental wound is compounded by what she sees as the lying forces of the 'powers-that-be'. What maddens her is her mother's falseness. In the journals she rails against the familial charade that conceals her mother's 'deadliness', even as she participates in it in the letters, and reinforces it herself. The more she conforms and behaves like a loved daughter, the angrier she becomes, until finally she takes out her rage — on herself.

Ploughing through the newly published first volume of Plath's letters (it's around 1300 pages long) I compared the letters with the entries in her private journals. In the letters, she plays the part of the loving, dutiful daughter, *Dear Mum, Dearest Mummy, Dearest, Most Revered, Twice-Honoured Mater*, straining for a gushing, affectionate tone. But in the private journals she lets rip with her true perceptions, and her rage.

I wrote in the *Spinoff* piece:

After her suicide attempt, when her psychiatrist Dr Ruth Beuscher gave her 'permission to hate her mother', Plath unleashed fury on Aurelia in a series of private journal entries:

'I don't imagine time will make me love her. I can pity her: she's had a lousy life; she doesn't know she's a walking vampire. But that is only pity, not love. On top she is all smarmy nice . . .'

'I feel her apprehension, her anger, her jealousy, her hatred. I feel no love, only the Idea of Love, and that she thinks she loves me like she should . . .'

'I feel cheated: I wasn't loved but all the signs said I was loved: the world said I was loved: the powers-that-were said I was loved . . .'

'She's a killer. Watch out. She's deadly as a cobra under that shiny greengold hood . . .'

In 1958, Plath wrote in her journal,

I am experiencing a grief reaction for something I have only just begun to admit isn't there: a mother's love. Nothing I do (marrying, saying 'I have a husband so I really didn't want yours', writing, 'here is a book for you, it is yours, like my toidy [sic] products and you can praise and love me now') can change her way of being with me, which I experience as a total absence of love.

There's an eerie disconnect between the gushing self of Plath's letters home, and the furious truth-telling self in the journals. In my review, trying to get at the disconnect, I wrote about the 'many layers of Sylvia', by which I meant her selves.

She calls Aurelia a 'killer' in the journals, and writes, oddly and disturbingly since her father was long dead, 'I have a husband so I really didn't want yours'.

Like most first-time readers of the journals, I'd been struck by Plath's unbridled ferocity as she blazed into the territory of the unsayable. Motherhood is a sacred concept. It is unacceptable to suggest a mother could be loveless. When you start reading psychology texts, though, suddenly nothing is sacred. It's a bluntly recorded fact: mother–child relationships are complex, a minefield. I began to see the journals in a different light. They seemed less outlandish and more believable. The vehemence of Sylvia's assertions was a kind of proof in itself. If all was normal, where did that rage come from?

People who are loved know that they are; when there's doubt about love, it's a reliable indication it wasn't there.

So how did she express the 'lack of love'? Famously, she used images of the Holocaust.

In her book on Plath and Ted Hughes, *The Silent Woman*, the writer Janet Malcolm noted Plath is reported to have said to the Scottish poet George Macbeth, 'I see you have a concentration camp in your mind, too.'

The Silent Woman discusses the criticism Plath attracted for using images of the Holocaust in 'Daddy' and other of her *Ariel* poems. Malcolm wrote:

> *The connection that art draws between collective and individual suffering is drawn by Plath's art in a way that not every reader has found convincing.*

She cites Irving Howe, who wrote in his book *The Critical Point* (1973):

> *What illumination — moral, psychological, social — can be provided of either [extreme situations] or the general human condition by a writer so deeply rooted in the extremity of her plight?*

Elsewhere Malcolm quotes George Steiner in the *Cambridge Review*:

> *What extra territorial right had Sylvia Plath — she was a child, plump and golden in America, when the trains actually went — to draw on the reserves of animate horror in the ash and the children's shoes?*

Janet Malcolm writes:

> *To say that Plath did not earn her right to invoke the names of Dachau, Auschwitz, Belsen is off the mark. It is we who stand accused, who fall short, who have not accepted the wager of imagining the unimaginable, of cracking Plath's code of atrocity.*
>
> *In* The Bell Jar *Plath conveys what it is like to go mad. In the* Ariel *poems she gives us what could be called the waste products of her madness . . .*

In this, Malcolm defines the hell Plath is evoking in her poems as the hell of 'madness'.

Asking questions, reading up on the material, ploughing through the giant volume of Plath letters, I had got interested myself in defining the hell that Janet Malcolm called 'madness'.

Define 'madness.'

What was the madness? As Marie Sanders might have drily put it, the Plath family had a few problems. What about the poem 'Daddy'? It's about the most baleful thing you've ever read. In it, Plath used images from the Holocaust. Was this 'wrong' of her? And what was she trying to do?

Plath kills her father (and probably Ted Hughes) in 'Daddy'; she annihilates him, pushes a stake into his heart. I thought about my own father, the poet. What had I accused my poor daddy of lately? Not violence or vampirism but airbrushing, smoothing over. Rendering us unreal. Fictionalising us to death.

But for Plath to use the Holocaust? I spent time thinking about this; it seemed relevant to that line formed by psychology, from one human mind to the collective madness of millions. And the 'connection that art draws between the collective and individual suffering'.

It's obvious to place genocide above murder on a scale of evil, even though every murder of an individual is an atrocity. The Holocaust was the greatest of crimes because of its scale, and it was also 6 million cases of individual suffering, 6 million murders. It was cultural murder, too, the individual equivalent of which is perhaps what Ibsen called 'soul murder'.

Appearing, in 'Daddy', to equate her own suffering with the Holocaust earned Plath the accusation of outrageous solipsism. How could she — the child 'plump and golden in America, when the trains actually went' — dare to place herself in that context?

In art, any treatment of the Holocaust that doesn't place it at the absolute centre, the ground zero of consideration, is often an outrage. A 'take' on the Holocaust is dangerous territory. It's ersatz, wrong. Because how dare you insert anything else? How can there *be* anything else?

Judging art, we tend to value the big-picture focus, the grand scale and historical over the minute and interior (or Hysterical Realism over a 'women's book'). Plath was accused of thinking within the parameters of her own little world, of trivialising. But perhaps she wasn't so much equating the significance and magnitude of the Holocaust with her own suffering (which would be absurd) as evoking the abyss that each individual mind must have confronted. Her offence or daring was to take a vast horror and scale it down to one mind — to the human.

Despite her 'plump and golden' existence, her own abyss was that much of a horror and an existential threat to her that in the end she killed herself with gas.

Dr Sanders had told me about her work in a forensic facility. The inmates described to her lives damaged by abuse, neglect and lack of love. These were people who, in some cases, had survived their parents' genuine desire — and attempts — to kill them.

She once said, randomly, out of the blue, 'Some of my clients have been through their own individual Holocausts.'

Their own 'Hell'.

With my head full of Sylvia Plath, I said to her: 'I can imagine that kind of fear. You're young and frightened and confused. You have this instinctive understanding: the person who wants you to disappear is not a murderer, or the people in the next village, or "the Nazis", it's the person on whom you most depend, who reflects your self back at you, who tells you who you are, who's supposed to keep you safe and protect you. A person so close, there is nothing between you. What if *that* person wants you to disappear?'

There is nothing between us.

She's a killer. Watch out. She's deadly as a cobra . . .

I went on (Dr Sanders neutral, her head on one side, listening), 'In that case you'd be on your own. The "powers-that-be" deny there's anything wrong. You are crazy, an hysteric, to suggest such a thing. What you're seeing and experiencing is *not real.*'

'It's a horror,' Dr Sanders said. She added, 'As horror goes, it's right up there.'

Perhaps it wasn't the hell of 'madness', as Janet Malcolm put it — some illness that has inexplicably struck — that Plath was evoking with her Holocaust imagery, but the abyss: the existential terror of the individual whose sense of connectedness and safety is fundamentally threatened, who experiences the terror that the 'mind is alone'.

I see you have a concentration camp in your mind, too.

What if you grew up with an absence of maternal love, as Plath described it in her journals?

It would not only be shameful, it would be definitive: you are unlovable. Your mother has the ultimate riposte: if you'd been lovable, she would have loved you. She knows you're unlovable because she has shaped you; your interactions with her have created your self. (But you could put it the other way: if your mother had loved you, you could have been lovable.)

It has to be *your* fault, because the world knows she's capable of love: she loves others. Other children, other people.

Perhaps outright maternal hostility would add fear to the shame. On some level, when you're young and defenceless, you know instinctively that your dependence on your mother is total, that if she wanted to, by act or omission, she could kill you. Things would be more complicated, more destabilising again, if the threat were hidden.

If you were a writer grappling with these questions, would you write about them? Would it be morally wrong to put them on the page?

There's that quote of Janet Malcolm, 'This is what it is the business of the artist to do. Art is theft, art is armed robbery, art is not pleasing your mother.'

A mother, displeased by art, can reach for another riposte. She can say 'this is our life through the looking glass'. She can say 'this is fantasy'. She can say 'blame my daughter's upbringing; it's what she does because she's *just like him*. She's spent her life in fiction — a whole lifetime of making it up.'

Karl's take on children: they would pretty much bring up themselves, and would turn out the way the genes dictated.

In *You Have a Lot to Lose* he wrote:

> *What struck me often, observing our children on these trips, was how much that was in each character sprang from the particular mix of elements from the gene pool. So long as each received basic nurturing and security, the character formed itself on its own terms and each was unique.*

He goes on to say how nice his children were and how much they were loved, but it's rather robust and impersonal; 'the character formed itself on its own terms and each was unique'. It sounds as if we were plants. Add the right potting mix, water, leave to develop. It doesn't linger sentimentally on the human interaction. There's a dusting off of the hands and a hurrying away, perhaps a sense of the poet's ungovernable spirit; on the surface so domesticated and orderly and yet always escaping the domesticity, paying it a quick lip service before making off, fast-walking into the distance.

The dog might come to heel, but his dog spirit is not tamed.

Where was Quesada whose grapes fattened uneaten at his door
Whose fields were ripe, whose mill wheels were always turning?
He was beyond the horizon, riding against the sunspears

The character formed itself on its own terms, *nothing to do with me*.

A parent could not be responsible for the way the cards fell: a wayward son, a daughter who was difficult (and who lost the boundaries of reality), a golden and sanguine youngest. It was the luck of the genetic draw. If everything was down to genes, there was no responsibility for the way people turned out, nor was there any point in enquiring how someone's personality had been formed. And no need for shrinks, obviously.

He did briskly mention 'basic nurturing and security', whatever his notion of that was.

What is 'basic nurturing'? Food, clothes, a roof. School.

Define 'security'. Is it waiting to see if they surface, if they survive?

On some level, obviously a naïve and obtuse one, it surprised me that the literary family blocked out the information I was trying to understand. How we turn out the way we do: surely it was the kind of thing you'd want to know if you were interested in poetry and literature? As Socrates said, 'The unexamined life is not worth living.'

I went on ploughing through articles, trying to puzzle it out. Perhaps Kay's labelling of my children as types was one kind of failure to mentalise, since she wasn't paying attention to what their minds were like. She wasn't empathising and she wasn't really observing.

I wrote in *Mazarine:*

The surface had enabled me to get on with Inez. Complicated mental tricks were called for; none of it came naturally. It must have been hard for her, too. The faint uneasiness: you're just too different. What if the mask should slip, and her eyes reflect a void back at you? Imagine the sly wink, the secret elusive channel, all darkness. No one else sees. You are bad in your self. There is no love, only quicksand. I would like you to disappear . . . Soon . . .

All is material and all is connected.

Where would Sylvia Plath's art be without the sinister Aurelia, without Daddy?

How could I publicly disagree with Karl, write stories about troubled families like 'The Black Monk' and novels like *Mazarine,* without being a bad, disloyal daughter? Dark Charlotte.

Only an unnatural daughter would look her mother in the face and name what she saw there, what Sylvia Plath called 'a total absence of love'. Only a crazy daughter.

But I'd been trained: It's material. Go away and write about it. Karl had written three volumes of autobiography; he'd layered the ingredients of our lives into his poems and novels and memoirs. He had used the material of our lives his whole writing life.

Could I question the family fictions, and tell the story I called real, while keeping faith with my basic belief? There is very little free will. There is no place for blame. We are all the sum total of our experiences; we all manage as best we can.

I thought about this fact: Leo and I *loved* Soon. Starfish was good; Starfish was nice, but Soon was the star of the show.

In my years of questioning, everything in the literary family changed. But when I looked back I realised things had been shifting and altering for some time.

In 2013, when the writer Hilary Mantel had been publicly critical of the fact that (as she saw it) the Duchess of Cambridge was forced by social pressure to be unnaturally thin and plastic-looking, Karl responded in a poem called '2013 New Year Cartoons'. The cartoon verse for Hilary Mantel made the savage little point that while the Duchess' body may have looked, according to Mantel, as if it had been designed by a committee, Mantel's own body certainly couldn't have been. But her novels on the other hand, could.

It's clever as a deadly little skewering of the novels, but to me it seemed illogical and offensive to respond to Mantel's comment on the body issue by making a derogatory comment about her body. It rather proved Mantel's point.

At a launch in a bookshop, Kay turned a line of Mantel's books to the wall, saying Mantel had been 'cruel to the little girl', meaning the Duchess. I remember arguing briefly and then giving up. It was too irrational.

I took Mantel to have meant that the Duchess (like the plastic and dead-eyed Ivanka Trump) was forced by social pressure to appear thin, mindless and flawless. Mantel was critical of that pressure. Karl's response seemed sexist and wrong, and I argued with him about it. Disputes like this started to blow up more often. Looking back, it was unavoidable. In order to prevent conflict, I would have had to leave my mind at the door.

Now I was re-examining everything. I'd written in *Metro* magazine about the jury trials in which Louise Nicholas had accused New Zealand policemen of historical rape. The men had been acquitted, which had caused outrage, and, despite no one having been convicted, Nicholas was always described as a rape victim.

Looking at what I'd written, I thought I'd been right on the law, and right that the cases had been weak on evidence. A week after my article on the Nicholas case was published in *Metro* I was out walking with Leo when a black car stopped just ahead and a man got out and began hurrying towards us. I recognised John Haigh QC, a criminal lawyer who'd defended one of the police in the Nicholas case. I'd never met him, but he was clearly about to speak to me.

I winced, expecting a rebuke, delivering it to myself; how had I dared to write about his case, what effrontery, I was an idiot, everything I'd written was wrong. But he shook my hand, was effusive and warmly appreciative, and told me it was an 'excellent piece of writing on reasonable doubt'. Then he bustled back to his car, leaving me slumped with relief. It was like a wishful fantasy: the perfect expert emerges from the universe to tell you, *you got it right*.

A few days later, my old criminal law professor Bernard Brown popped out of the supermarket queue and also told me I'd got it right.

So there was that, but what about the social implications of the case? Now I wondered whether I'd been stuck in a rigid worldview. It was one of those landmark trials that create change; it had transformed the way police dealt with the public, and that was a good thing. Had I been open enough to that?

I started arguing with Karl and Kay about other high-profile sex cases. When we had these disagreements about men and women, sex and power, we were arguing about more than just the facts. In some fundamental way, we were realigning. I was throwing off a way of thinking I'd absorbed, and was now rejecting.

Kay had said, 'I hate the Me Too movement.'

Karl said, 'Me Too is the "yes people" of now.' And, 'Their icon should be Miss Havisham.'

He had written in his autobiography *You Have a Lot to Lose* that his long-ago affair with Jenny North, when he was an academic and she was a student, didn't amount to the kind of power imbalance the Me Too movement was addressing. He was intransigent on the point and I recognised it would have been pointless to argue, nor did I want to, really.

Karl and Kay's dispute was with the mob rule of social fashion, the howl of the *vox populi*. They objected to the tyranny of wokeness and purity tests, to the fact that reasoned argument was met with irrational outrage.

This seemed reasonable, up to a point.

Kay said, frowning and high-minded, 'Harvey Weinstein. The poor man. I'd like to know about his background.'

I thought about this. I'm sympathetic to criminals in the sense that we're all victims of circumstance. There's very little free will.

And in these times, in our Time, when Trump has been undermining institutions, when democracy and journalism and the rule of law have been under attack from a corrupt demagogue, everyone does need to be an institutionalist.

In his book *On Tyranny*, Timothy Snyder wrote:

> *The European history of the 20th Century shows us that societies can break, democracies can fall, ethics can collapse and ordinary men can find themselves standing over death pits with guns in our hands. We might be tempted to think that our democratic heritage automatically protects us from such threats. This is a misguided reflex.*

Snyder sets out rules to defend democracy, the second of which is: *Defend institutions. It is institutions that help us preserve decency.*

I agreed: institutions should be defended. Mob rule should be resisted, and accusations should be tested in court, as per the rules of evidence. Trial by media and public opinion is wrong; rule of law is paramount. In 2018 I objected to a media campaign in *The Spinoff*, publicly accusing a man of sexual harassment. My take was, if there's been a crime, call the police, put it before a court.

But in the literary family, the take on high-profile sex cases didn't direct itself to specific circumstances, and it was only humane about the accused. In this, it seemed reactionary. The accusations were rejected as feminist and fashion-crazed. There was no empathy for alleged women victims — none.

At a dinner party at our house with family, Kay said the young British backpacker Grace Millane had been 'guilty of contributory negligence' in her own death. She'd been murdered in 2019 while on a Tinder date, her body stuffed in a suitcase and buried in the Waitākeres. I might once have accepted Kay's take as 'bracing' or 'daring', but now I found it so lacking in empathy for the shining, innocent young victim, it seemed chilling. It made no sense. It had no legal basis. Also, it was strange. I felt sure that if Grace Millane and her Tinder date had fought and she'd hit him with some object and killed him, Kay's sympathy would have stayed with the young man — as victim. It was a consistent bias, one I couldn't fathom. I wondered if it was a kind of misogyny; if so, it bordered on seeming masochistic.

We argued about the Roast Busters case, the young Auckland men who'd caused a scandal by bragging on Facebook about having sex with underage girls who were too drunk to consent.

When Karl wrote a letter to *The New Zealand Herald* calling the uproar over the Roast Busters case a 'moral panic', I typed a short post on a blog, wanting publicly to disagree with him. As I saw it, the outrage wasn't about 'teenagers having sex', it was about sex without consent. I wrote: 'Sex without consent is rape.'

Eleanor Catton weighed in too, saying on Twitter he was trying to shut down discussion about rape.

I knew that in the family I'd lost my charm. Where was the good sport, the girl with the marvellous sense of humour, who dared to question the fashionable line? In a restaurant after a book launch, when the complainants in the Roast Busters case were mentioned, Karl leaned into my face and said with maximum scorn, 'They weren't raped.' But how did he know? For him it was just teenagers messing around; if some girls felt they'd got raped (and had the fact broadcast online to humiliate them), too bad. Experimentally (and wanting to fight with him), I said, 'Imagine if the complainants were male.'

Kay said, 'If they were boys they would be more upset. Because the assaults would be gay.' This implied, presumably, that a gay assault would be more upsetting because 'unnatural'; conversely, that a heterosexual assault was more 'natural' (a bit of messing around) and therefore tolerable.

We went around and around it, and it was no use arguing.

In an online interview, Karl referred to my publicly disagreeing with him over the Roast Busters as a 'reproach'.

'A reproach sounds emotional,' I said coldly. 'What I did was point out you were legally incorrect.'

He wouldn't call a man reproachful or scolding. I could see how far outside the boundaries of his reality I had gone.

He told me in one of our email exchanges that he'd grown up with a set of expectations: that he would have to go to war and his sister wouldn't (i.e. men had it tough too, or tougher), that women were weaker so men must defend and protect them, and that men were 'more important'. He agreed all this was outdated; things had needed to change on this front.

In his 1997 novel *Villa Vittoria*, which is a page-turner, almost a thriller and a genuinely pacey read, there's a sex scene where a woman says 'no' at the last minute:

> *She knew that if he had forced himself on her at that moment she would have felt she had no right to complain. She might even have been glad to have the pleasure without the responsibility.*

The man gives vent to disappointed rage. He paces and rails at her:

> *She was adolescent, weak, afraid of life. Rape was what she was asking for and what she deserved.*

His rage is described as 'ridiculous'. She responds, 'Lie down, Fido.' (Again, the image of the dog coming to heel.)

This idea of a woman being 'glad', if he'd forced her, to have the 'pleasure without the responsibility' appears as an aside in another of Karl's novel too, *The Secret History of Modernism*. It seems to me a (male) fallacy that a woman could experience 'pleasure' even if forced. As a matter of physiological and psychological fact I would have thought a woman needs to be 'actively participating' to experience pleasure.

It seems strange too, to describe a refusal to have sex as 'weak and adolescent' — as in shirking adult female duty perhaps? The little rant — 'no right to complain', 'rape was what she was asking for and what she deserved' — is consciously provocative. It's not naïve, it's full-on gadfly.

Elsewhere in the novel, feminists are (again) making trouble at a university, wanting to ban Henry James' *The Bostonians* for its negative portrayal of 'the groaning sisterhood'.

In *The Necessary Angel,* which is set in France, there's an exchange between characters about Valérie Trierweiler, President François Hollande's ex-partner, who wrote an unflattering portrait of his infidelity. Trierweiler is described in Karl's novel as 'an angry woman'. She's 'an angry woman', presumably, because she complained. A nice woman doesn't do that.

It's easy to cover this objectively: attitudes evolve, mores change.

Perhaps Karl, a man of his time, would look back and concede he was too slow to adapt, too inflexible. (Or perhaps not.)

At the height of these battles, he loved to mock the groaning sisterhood. While he always pleaded 'rationality', his resistance to change began to seem tinged with misogyny, at least a distaste for the kind of woman (too solid, too bossy, too powerful) who would want to bring him to heel. (Lie down, Fido.) For such a political man, why so resistant in this sphere only?

Misogyny, to my mind, is not rational. It's emotional. It's probably all about being scared of your mum. Dr Sanders once told me, men who've been hurt or humiliated by their mothers will do anything to avoid that pain. They will only tolerate women they feel they can control.

So we argued, which is standard: nothing startling about finding your parents too conservative. Unless I'd been afflicted with infantilism, or simply accepted everything Karl said in a spirit of bland diplomacy, conflict was inevitable.

It wasn't startling and should have been merely abstract, but there was something problematically personal in it. Questioning Karl's stance felt like an evolution of roles: from nice cheerleader to outsider, enemy even. Did it mean our rapport could only survive if I played a certain type?

We would end up arguing about Woody Allen and Ronan Farrow too, who I thought were a Greek tragedy of our time, the brilliant father and the son who took issue with the self-indulgence, amorality and bad behaviour of the father. It was a generational and a temperamental clash. The father's pursuit of artistic and social freedom, his marvellous comedy, his profound insight, his narcissistic insistence he could do whatever he liked with people close to him — the relationship with Mia Farrow's daughter Soon-Yi — with no consequences. The son's pursuit of equality and justice.

(I'm referring, for argument's sake, only to the established allegations against Woody Allen, not the unproven ones — blame my legal training for this.)

Woody Allen seemed to want to create his own moral universe. It reminded me of disputes with Karl over *The Necessary Angel*, in which I imagined the countering voice:

> *Have your muses and your affairs, pay your tributes and tell your stories, but treat me different. There is such a thing as family; it consists of special relationships. The role of parent, or parent figure, for example.*
>
> *Call it a piety if you like, but if you scorn it you're playing with fire. Get ready for fallout. Prepare for a reaction.*

There was the fact that Ronan Farrow had whipped up a protest in 2019 that caused his father's memoir to be pulped by a publisher; the chill of that, the image of Farrow as tormentor of an old man, as ideologue, as *book-burner*.

But perhaps Farrow felt Woody Allen had been utterly indifferent to him and his siblings; this would explain Farrow's own lack of mercy.

Karl described Ronan Farrow as 'super creepy, alien, pitch-dark matter'.

I agreed on this point: you couldn't 'cancel' an artist because of his personal life. To require an artist to be a good citizen, to refuse to read Dickens ever again because he was cruel to his wife — that was perverse, wrong. It had to be about the art. Two facts could be true at the same time: Woody Allen had done things that made him at least a jerk (the proven actions) and many of his films are brilliant. Movies like *Crimes and Misdemeanors* are not only funny, they're profound. They're about the struggle for meaning in a godless, morally neutral universe. *Bullets Over Broadway* is hilarious but also poses a serious question. It's asked early on: 'Who would you save from a burning building if you could save only one: an anonymous human being, or the only remaining copy of the complete works of William Shakespeare?'

The exploration of the artist's will to create and to accept no compromise plays out comically between the film's central characters: one a failed playwright and the other a gangster who turns out to be a real artist, and who demonstrates it by being ruthless in pursuit of art, shooting the terrible actress who's ruining the play. The failed artist lacks this merciless focus, and slopes off into obscurity.

Woody Allen, whose art was about the amoral universe, had let himself off various societal and family norms, the lawless father alienating and outraging the righteous son. It was a Woody Allen movie in itself.

For Karl it was black and white, or at least that's how it sounded to me: Woody Allen good (the artist), Ronan Farrow bad (pious little creep). I thought that was simplistic.

In our arguments, Karl and I were sometimes skirting around outright hostility. He was reminding me of the boundaries of his reality, and I was driving right through them. At moments I felt I, too, became alien to him, pitch-dark matter.

We would make it up again — we always made it up. There would be an email or a phone call about something unrelated, and we'd end up reconnecting. At a dinner or a book launch we'd quickly regain our old easiness. But in some sense now, always, we were arguing about ourselves.

In June 2020, Karl published his memoir *You Have a Lot to Lose*. He was interviewed on RNZ by the broadcaster Kim Hill, who asked him about his affair with Jenny North. He'd written that even though she'd been a student and he was a lecturer 18 years older, it was not a Me Too situation. Kim Hill's questioning was predictably, albeit mildly, challenging and needling, and at one point she'd said, 'Your wife must be a saint.'

That evening Steve Braunias had a birthday party at the Cordis hotel in Auckland, and I ran into my parents there. I went over to Kay, wanting to say something kind and encouraging about the interview, which listeners had emailed in to describe as being a bit tough on Kim Hill's part.

Kay was furious about the 'saint' comment and the fact Kim Hill had asked about the affair rather than focusing on 'what's on the page', and when I rashly said Karl could have left it out if he didn't want people to ask about it (I thought he was being treated quite leniently overall, and of course people would zero in on it) she began to berate me about the affair, fortunately not audibly since we were in a big crowd. She seemed to think I'd criticised him for it, which I hadn't, that I represented the enemy (pious creeps, feminists), and as her voice rose I listened to her saying, of the affair, 'It wasn't a power thing. They were just two souls. Jenny was so clever, the things she wrote. Two souls . . .'

It began to seem surreal, being shouted at by my mother at a party because she thought I'd criticised Karl's affair; it *was* surreal, as well as a blast of cold rhetoric and hostility, and I thought about what she'd thrown away in order to get to this point. She was Karl's first and best reader, and that was it.

Though tempted, I didn't make a crack about her drinking the Kool-Aid. I only said, 'It wasn't *me* who interviewed him this morning.'

It kept coming back to me after the party. Being berated by my mother as she defended Karl's affair. 'Two souls . . .'

We didn't believe in conventional family connections. This seemed to have become the prevailing family ethos. We were literary, and the most important thing was the art, what was on the page. Kay wanted to embrace this, to prevail, and even, to use Karl's word, to 'triumph'. And on her terms, she was doing just that.

She had used silence as a weapon, because she understood its power. She knew a mind not listened to is a mind cancelled. The response to that lay within the family ethos: to write about it, and this she would also understand.

I wanted to write about all of it. I wanted to write about family and free will, to give Kay her due on her terms, and I had the words of my daughter Madeleine in mind, too, about breaking the cycle, not doing the same in return, words for us, the next generations.

Let's us not be like that.

Two days after the party, Karl sent me a draft of volume three of his memoirs. It included a passage about the novel I'd been annoyed by, *The Necessary Angel,* and a description of an episode of depression, when he came back from Europe and attended the Marlborough book festival. He stayed at a winery called Dog Point and suffered terrible jet lag — so bad that reading final proofs of *The Necessary Angel* he decided it was a disaster that should never be published. He wrote that it was only Kay's strength of mind when he got back to Auckland that saved him from withdrawing it. While in this depressed state at Dog Point he wrote a poem, and it helped to pull him towards recovery.

After a day of frost and sunshine
in the valley of winter vineyards and winding streams
that teach the far brown hills by definition
and the farther mountains by peaks and caps of snow
Dog Point at 4 a.m.
showed me the night of another world
created by gods and peopled by their children
each one distinct, a point of brilliant light
each family a constellation
and needing all together
a name to match and affirm their magnitude —
'the Heavens' for example or 'the canopy of the stars'.

There is a dream of love
so far from the avidities of lust
and dramas of fidelity and possession
it is like that southern sky at night
burned across by a single shooting star.

It's a beautiful, striking poem, a knockout poem; it evokes the universe: cold, brilliant, mysterious, blazing. There's a ringing note of hysteria, grandiosity, some icy-fiery Nordic or Teutonic madness. The love 'far from the avidities of lust and dramas of fidelity and possession'; why is that love a dream? Why is it glimpsed as another world, peopled by gods, far away among the stars? Isn't that kind of love (love far from romance and lust) available close by, on Earth? Love for children, friends, family?

Or is there some other kind of love again, out there in the morally neutral universe, some Wagnerian dream-love, not subject to Earthly rules, reserved for gods and their children?

At the end of the chapter on this episode, he records the approving verdict of the first and best reader on *The Necessary Angel* and its characters:

> *Kay re-read it recently and said it was* le vrai *C.K. — with Sylvie the dream, Louise the reality (and wife) and Helen the writer's ur-self.*

There is a dream of love . . . .

It was the exchange at Steve Braunias' party that made me see that in our literary family writing was the correct, the acceptable response. If, as Kay would now have it, Karl and Jenny North were 'just two souls', and if Kay's distress over Karl's affairs and her confiding in me about it, and my years of listening to her and empathising; if, now, that memory of mine was not real, and if in our family we believed so firmly in a minimum of piety that she and I were ourselves not mother and daughter, but just another 'two souls' (and Karl and I the same), and the only thing that mattered was, as she would put it, 'what's on the page', then I didn't think she would object to my putting us there.

She wanted to triumph and she did not want to disappear, and so I would honour that, by taking out the diary pieces I'd worked on, recording fragments of our lives. I would put them together, finish them, and name my account for her enigmatic image, the ghost self from long ago, lit by winter sun, framed in a blue-and-gold mirror.

'All teenagers are a bit borderline,' Dr Sanders had said. She'd waved her hand, dismissive.

It was autumn and the streets were strewn with leaves, rain falling straight down in the windless air, a softness and silence over the city. I looked out at the rain, at a thrush hopping on the wet grass. I'd walked through the mangroves with the dog, Philip; now I was at my desk, the manuscript of *Mazarine* in front of me.

Sanders had talked about complex trauma. Complex PTSD.

'You had terrifying and violent experiences . . .'

She had given me a book, *Trauma and Recovery* by Judith Herman. I skimmed bits of it, horrified by the case studies. I stuffed the book under the bedside table and didn't read anymore. Our weekly cleaning person kept sucking it out with her hoover and placing it on the bed. I'd come home to find it there, and wince with guilt.

After I'd been seeing her for six months, Sanders had pressed another book into my hands. While she didn't believe too much in diagnostic labels, she felt it might be 'useful for its general ideas'. It was about the lifelong effect created by growing up with a certain kind of parents. Cue case notes of hair-raising parental behaviour, and poignant accounts of emotional deprivation.

I wedged it under the table next to Judith Herman's. After a while the cleaning service got the idea, and stopped pulling them out. They lay under there gathering dust.

I couldn't bring myself to throw the books away. They stayed there, evidence of my disloyalty and badness, my crime.

My desk was piled on one side with the year's books: Knausgaard, Ferrante, Plath (journals, letters, poetry, *The Bell Jar*), Janet Malcolm's *The Silent Woman*, the *Letters of Frank Sargeson*, C.K. Stead's *Collected Poems*, and, in their own heaped and teetering pile, biographies, scandalised accounts and scathing takedowns of President Donald Trump.

On the other side were the psychology books, a full range from academic to self-help. Online, I'd found hundreds of scientific studies, which I enjoyed reading and trying to decipher, skipping through the incomprehensible statistics and going straight to the discussion at the end.

Popular psychology was all about healing. Wholeness. Wellness. The ubiquitous mindfulness. Psychology lite emphasised an idea I hadn't seriously entertained before: you have to take care of yourself. It went further: you have to *love yourself* in order to be able to love others. I rejected this as bullshit (how was it even conceptually possible?), but I thought about it. My modus operandi, with the children and family in particular, was that I had to look after others only. I more or less didn't exist. This whole idea of self-care, while atrociously corny and new age and verbally unaesthetic, was also potentially appealing. Instead of beating myself to death all the time, could I treat myself kindly? A new way of living . . .

Was it possible?

That all this would be mocked by the literary family for the therapeutic language, for the 'acceptance of conventional wisdom' and the 'pieties', made it seem a marvellous indulgence and vice.

The studies were investigations of human behaviour. It was all about cause and effect; Freud featured as a historical figure only. I was looking at something more like the study of animal behaviour: if you inflict this on a person, the resulting effect is likely this.

Despite Kay's dark predictions, the only time I heard a psychologist refer to Freud was one who said, 'You know, as Freud once said, "Sometimes a cigar is just a cigar."'

I pushed on with the novel. This was one thing I wanted to know: writing in *Mazarine* about a mother–daughter relationship, was I describing a character who'd once lived on the borderline?

Which character?

Was the past a ghost reflected in a blue-and-gold mirror?

After Plath's letters and journals, I'd re-read *The Bell Jar*, her record of meltdown, and enjoyed its youthful tone, sardonic jauntiness and black humour. The novel and Plath's letters had coincided with my other reading, focused as it was on forbidden territory: the through-the-looking-glass world of family dynamics.

'Forbidden' in the literary family, that is. We Steads were that rugged band of troopers, with our *endless jokes, songs, a minimum of piety.* We certainly didn't have deep, dark reserves of furious emotional weirdness.

Reading about borderline personality disorder, I was (like the first-year psychology students) making an imaginative leap that was part invention, part genuine memory of emotional experience. The frantic sense of isolation, of spinning without connection, that seemed to be the experience of a borderline mind; it was a description of a mind that had not been heard or listened to or understood. A mind cancelled.

It was as if I'd opened a window and caught a glimpse of some city that was foreign and yet eerily familiar. The foreign city. Those streets, those dreaming towers.

Had I been there many years ago, or had I read about it in a book?

I'd recreationally diagnosed various people. I'd decided a wildly unstable and uninhibited journalist I knew was borderline, and in fact just after that I noticed she'd described herself on Facebook as 'borderline borderline'. It seemed to have become almost fashionable to have a disorder like PTSD, depersonalisation or anxiety, although it was perhaps not yet entirely cool to be schizophrenic or bipolar.

This round of secret diagnosing on my part made me recall the wry scepticism of Australian writer Helen Garner, who, in her brilliant account of a murder trial, *Joe Cinque's Consolation*, described watching clinical psychologists give evidence that borderline personality disorder was the cause of the accused young woman's irrational behaviour:

> *In the lobby at lunchtime I stood about with the two journalists. They giggled and glanced this way and that, comparing notes in whispers on how many of Dr Byrne's categories and symptoms seemed to apply to them. A problem in establishing a solid sense of* Who am I? *Definitely. Mood swings. Absolutely. Significant impulsivity? Of course. Fear of abandonment?* Totally. *Easily angered? I mean,* hellooow?

Our laughter was slightly shrill. No one said it but we were all thinking, Call that mental illness? She's exactly like me.

The young woman on trial had committed a serious crime, and in her account Garner was preoccupied with notions of evil and free will. Her questioning reflected her horror at the crime (was this 'mental illness' defence believable, and if so, was it a sufficient excuse?), but it also elucidated the fact that all mental abnormality must exist on a spectrum. She and her journalist friends could see themselves in the description of borderline disorder, just as one can see one's own minor compulsions in a portrayal of full-blown obsessive compulsive disorder.

Yet the young woman in question must be so much *further* along the spectrum — she was on trial for murder, after all.

According to my reading, complex trauma can also cause some of the traits that Helen Garner referred to: unstable and intense interpersonal relationships, unstable self-image or sense of self, impulsivity, instability of mood, intense anger, dissociative symptoms. The difference was: people with borderline disorder had trouble being alone. If they found themselves alone, they felt annihilated. Hence the frantic efforts to avoid abandonment.

Only connect. Somewhere in here was a clue, I thought, to the sense of being lost in the void, of feeling there's nothing to hold you to the Earth. The despair, the desolation. It's not so much about physical proximity, but the feeling that can't be borne, that the mind is alone.

The mind is alone. What does that mean? The mind can be alone in a crowd, in a family, in a marriage. For the mind *not* to be alone it has to be understood, empathised with, heard.

I was just fine on my own and always had been. I loved setting off for a foreign city by myself, and while writing I liked to spend the day solo. I preferred it. Still, solitude is a different thing from not being heard.

But I thought about my youth, all that risk-taking, getting arrested, vandalism, roaming around at night. The silence, the sense I was disappearing. Was that 'inherent', or was I mirroring someone else's self? Is there a difference? Perhaps there is, if later you are able to change. If you leave that old image behind. I left Tohunga Crescent and went towards chaos, but when I finally found what I wanted with Paul, the chaos fell away.

Perhaps *all* young people are a bit like that. But I wasn't so sure. I had my own children to compare, and I knew they didn't come close. They didn't tick any of the boxes. They didn't get in trouble. They were strong-willed and definite personalities, but they were sanguine and easy to deal with. They were particularly remarkable for rarely being angry, or even 'moody'. We had none of the screaming rows, the drama, the day-long fights, the sulking and silences, the slamming doors, of my literary family.

'*You* were the chaos,' Karl said. In an interview in *Sunday* magazine he dismissed my veiled public comment about growing up in a wild household. He said:

> *You'd have to ask Charlotte what it's about, because it's very internal to her. It's not apparent to me. I was certainly not a very authoritarian father. I don't think any of my kids would say I was very authoritarian. One of them — not Charlotte — has said we were too libertarian, that we didn't impose enough order or discipline on them. So she might have meant that.*

The idea was 'very internal to' me, meaning, presumably, in my head, invented.

(In a later interview in *Sunday* magazine Karl said, of Janet Frame's cruel story about him and Kay: 'Janet's story was a strange act of malice for which the motive had come *from within herself*, not from anything I or Kay had done to her.' My italics.)

Of his children, he said it was all in the genes. Upbringing was nothing to do with it. He said Tohunga Crescent had been orderly, and that he'd found loving letters from me to Kay, written when I was 10.

There must have been many loving letters from me. (I loved her.) But was the complexity simply beyond him? It seems unlikely.

The journalist Diana Wichtel recorded this exchange about me with Karl in her interview in *Newsroom*:

> *'She said family life was chaos and I said, "You were the chaos" and that went on record.' She has written of failed attempts to communicate with parents and siblings 'in a spirit of truth and reconciliation'. He says, 'Yes, well, I think her memory of her childhood and my memory of her childhood are somewhat at odds.' People can have completely different experiences of being in the same family. Has his grim prognosis made him more open to understanding hers? 'The answer to that could be very complicated. I don't know if you saw a piece Charlotte wrote when I was made poet laureate.' Yes. Terrific, honest writing. 'That's such a beautiful lyrical piece and I think that really represents the kind of feeling that exists between Charlotte and me. But there are these other things that seem to be surfacing in which, as far as I can see, she's revising her view of her childhood. Well, she just has to get on with that and when I'm dead write her version.' Does the thought of that worry him? 'Not at all.'*

I thought about his comment, 'And when I'm dead, write her version.' But there's no prospect of reconciliation, no dream of a happy ending with the dead.

In an email to me he said, of the second and third volumes of his memoirs, that he would never write anything negative about any of us — he couldn't do it — it would seem disloyal and improper. He did say that he supposed what he was writing could be seen as a denial of whatever I might write, although only indirectly, but he would never engage with what I wrote about the family and contradict it. He went on to say he didn't see why two versions shouldn't be true — just two versions of the truth.

I decided not to reply saying I thought his 'two versions of the truth' sounded positively Trumpian, like Trump adviser Kellyanne Conway's infamous 'alternative facts'.

He told me he could never do a Knausgaard, because one would have to feel better about oneself than he did to do that.

I was the chaos. And yet there was that other self, who came home and tidied the bedroom with obsessive neatness, and studied, and passed exams — and didn't pass chaos on to my kids.

I was 'revising my view'. This was 'internal to me.' I was remembering a lot of *too many* and *too much*.

Calling a spade a spade: Oliver's behaviour in the family home was beyond unruly, too. There was a high level of anger at Tohunga Crescent, and, amid the tidiness and cleanliness, disorder. The parental control exercised by Karl was furious and repressive, yet oddly ineffective in relation to the big issues, perhaps because he was so often elsewhere. He was working, he was writing, he was in London or France for months at a time. He liked to be away, seeing his London literary contacts, conducting his business. There were academic conferences and writers' festivals and extended fellowships. There were the love affairs that fuelled the fiction; a new relationship would get the next book going. He did love to escape, understandably. Kay exerted no control at all. She set the tone: varying levels of hysteria (from hilarity to angry shrieking), and we children followed suit.

Karl, in a manly way, did either funny jokes or towering rage.

One day, by Karl's own account, when he came home and found Oliver, aged 16, upstairs with his friend paralytic and drinking whisky, he walked away, saying nothing. He said later he hadn't really understood about alcohol, and he'd been embarrassed. He acknowledged he should have done something.

He may well have been embarrassed, but he knew all about alcohol abuse, having noted it among friends like Maurice Duggan and Barry Humphries. He'd heard Kay's stories of being sent to stay with the drunks at Omokoroa. Alcohol was everywhere.

For whatever reason, he walked away.

I read: the family is an interdependent system.

There is nothing between us. There is nothing between us.

Chaos doesn't exist in a vacuum. Kay's stories of her childhood involved suffering, particularly from being sent away with her sister, aged three onwards, to stay with the rural relatives in Omokoroa, who were rough, negligent and chronically drunk. She was open with us about how harsh this was.

I don't like to think of my mother, a tiny, sensitive child, trying to cope in an environment that was frightening, squalid and chaotic. It was rough old times. Her distress and protests were not heard by her own mother, who went on sending her away every year, letting her know that what she was feeling either wasn't valid, or didn't matter.

Karl's parents regularly clashed; he described family life as fraught, filled with shouting, drama and fighting, and his mother as tyrannical, histrionic and possibly rather cold. He was a dreamy child and his mother thought he was unintelligent. His father made him a woodwork table so he could work with his hands. Neither parent was seeing him clearly, or with sensitivity or attention. (We made much use of this in our games when I was a child: dim-witted Castle was always being packed off by me to do his woodwork.)

When Karl started to succeed academically his mother told people he'd worked hard, overcoming his slowness. I remember one of his anecdotes of childhood: when he broke his arm, his mother was so furious she hit him.

Wouldn't a brilliant, sensitive boy in such a family recoil from harshness, turn away from ugliness and make his own beautiful reality?

That rainy autumn, Paul and I were walking along Karekare Beach with the dog. I looked out at the rolling surf and said, 'Is nearly drowning just part of growing up in New Zealand? A rite of passage in an island nation?'

'I'm not sure . . .'

'Did *you* nearly drown as a child?'

'I don't think so.'

'Did anyone you know?'

'No. Why?'

I'd been thinking about the stories, how I'd flipped upside down in the rubber ring when I was two, how Oliver had jumped off a wharf aged one. Each time, it was Karl's sprint that saved us. He'd gone tearing down the beach, he'd run along the bank; he'd reached down and scooped the baby up.

He didn't wait, he ran. The times we were drowning when we were children, it was Karl who pulled us out and saved our lives. When he was around, that is.

I didn't tell anyone I'd been poring over psychology texts. I tried covertly to understand in light of what I'd been reading, hoping to discern a theoretical basis for my questions.

Offhand, I made suggestions to Sanders: 'I don't know anything, but it sounds to me as if . . . Do people sometimes . . . ?' 'By the way, is this relevant . . . ?'

Progressing in my reading down the personality disorders, I stopped at narcissism, and the behavioural traits of President Trump. I read about the ways a narcissist will control a relationship. The tactics, the reign of confusion and division. Black-and-white thinking, entitlement, grandiosity, lack of empathy, gaslighting. Scapegoats and favourites.

President Trump greatly interests psychologists, I read, because he's flamboyantly pathological. His narcissism is so textbook, so classic, that at the time of writing Harvard academics are recording it for their students in real time. His madness is a reality TV phenomenon, playing 24/7. We keep wondering, how much more destructive will the orange buffoon turn out to be? Will he win a second term or, if he loses the election, will he refuse to leave the White House?

In a time of global pandemic, as his fellow Americans are dying, when the health system is under pressure and he has no coherent plan, the President describes his own performance: tremendous, perfect, beautiful, great job, 10 out of 10.

When challenged with facts he calls reporters nasty, disgraceful, fake news, liars. He can only hear praise, criticism isn't allowed; anyone who questions him is bad. He controls his reality. This keeps him happy, as the country's death toll grows. He doesn't face the problem, he walks away. It's catastrophic for his people; it's not great for him either.

What caused his madness?

According to accounts, Trump's parents were grim, cold and controlling. His niece, the clinical psychologist Mary L. Trump, in her book, *Too Much and Never Enough*, describes the President's upbringing as abusive. Personality is formed when a person is very young, and Donald Trump was damaged by his mother's emotional unavailability and the fact his father was, Mary Trump says, a sociopath. Trump's crimes, his imprisonment and separation of children from their parents at the US southern border for example, are the result of his inability to empathise.

The President can't deal with the pandemic, she says, because that would involve him admitting a fault: that he was wrong in underestimating its seriousness. He expresses what she calls 'toxic positivity': he can't admit anything. Everything is beautiful, his chant is a beautiful song.

Trump went on to license a familiar type of narcissism in his followers: folks who feel knowledge is innate, who don't believe they need formal education, who say, on climate, on a pandemic, 'No pointy-headed scientist, no "expert" is gonna tell me what to do!' President Trump himself scorns education and expertise: he relies on his own very stable genius.

Are all tyrants and despots narcissists? The emotionally abusive parent, the man who hits his partner, the leader who murders millions. Their lack is empathy — 'the lack is the human'. If so, how did it begin? Not in the genes, but in the lived experience. Right at the beginning, in the formation of a mind.

Way back in smallness and mundanity, in the pages of a women's book.

It had been the line between the individual and the collective that I was interested in as I'd gone on writing *Mazarine*, the transmission of 'madness' from the mind of one to the mind of a group. From individual narcissism to the collective narcissism that is nationalism. Or family pride, family front and face.

I kept coming across this fact: a narcissist requires praise. The whole world is a mirror; he can only see himself. As long as you admire and flatter you will enjoy his favour, but if you stop praising, if you question, you will injure his ego.

It will dawn on you that your purpose is to provide praise. Once you've stepped outside that role, you don't exist. You will be exiled to the outer.

If the whole world is a mirror . . . Could he or she love you for your own sake, despite the fact you stopped cooperating? Would he or she go looking for you, try to find you? Could he or she love you as you walked away?

I'd started to notice a change in my meetings with Dr Sanders: there was less of the eclipse. Misunderstandings still paralysed me, but mostly I felt at ease. The conversation ran smoothly; we had plenty of laughs. It's a striking experience to have your perception altered. For the first time in my life I was actually seeing women, and many looked attractive, friendly and heart-warming. I felt like going towards them rather than avoiding them.

I went on writing *Mazarine*:

> *It struck me again: I had changed. I saw women everywhere, elegant commuters, tourists, shop assistants, old ladies towing little dogs, and it seemed that a filter had been removed, there was no barrier, I felt open, free, benign. It struck me, that I could be altered in this way. Instead of remote and separated, I felt part of something. Instead of not seeing, I was clear-eyed, in touch, connected.*
>
> *'You've changed my brain,' I said.*

The change was radical. After a whole adult life, *instead of remote and separated, I felt part of something.*

Every day I worked on *Mazarine,* and every fortnight I put aside the fiction, opened the mirror book and told the story that was true. The true story had to be good, meaning well-told: Scheherazade was still afraid of termination, of the axe.

Now the routine was set; I would walk through the city while running through the story, shaping it, reminding myself of details. The easier it was to talk, the further I got from Tohunga Crescent, and the closer I came to it, too.

One day walking home I took a detour through the marina;

walking alongside the yachts with their masts clinking and jinking in the wind, the rain falling on the water. I remembered the trip out to Kawau Island with Alex, the way the horizon pulsed with black cloud, the flashes of sheet lightning, the plunge and heave of the green waves. I remembered thinking I was going to drown. I felt myself sinking under the boiling waves, pulled by currents, down into the calm deeps, the underwater silence.

There was the sentence that had caused so much trouble: 'Telling your story is existentially important.'

I saw now why it was existentially important. My reading about psychological syndromes and disorders, all the studies and articles and textbooks, had led me on a path from the Trumps to Knausgaard to Janet Malcolm to Sylvia Plath, but none of that reading had achieved as much as relating the true story to another person had done.

Telling the true story had changed my brain.

Where the brain grasps only the immediate, there is despair, where there is a sense of 'my story', where the 'I' is not lost but firmly located within a narrative context, past, present and future, then there is hope.

This is what is existentially important: to be heard and understood, to have a listener affirm it, to know the mind is not alone. You are not an idealised character in someone's fiction, you are real. Your literary family is not a work of fiction, they are real. What you have seen and heard and experienced is real. Your protests are valid. In every story about a dog, there is a beginning, a middle and an end. The chant is a chant, not a beautiful song. The thread that will lead you out of the maze is the thread of narrative.

But I can't talk to women, I'd said.

Exactly.

You had to learn it was possible. In real time.

Marie Sanders, she was so quick. She was Ariadne, whose thread led me out of the maze. As soon as I tried to turn a thought into clumsy words, she understood. Sometimes it struck me, though. What I'd lost. What I'd loved, and what was lost in the telling.

There was her exquisite understanding, and there was always a space between us, because how much will be left out in the slow unravelling of a story full of troubles, a whole life: the summer weeks in the bush at Karekare, the surf beating on the black sand beach, the rain in Tohunga Crescent, Menton in the South of France where the sea and sky were so beautiful they made me euphoric, the olive grove in a thunderstorm, the camping trips and travelling and adventures, the canoe Karl bought us, the high-jump set he built for us in the back yard at Tohunga, the sound of my parents laughing in their room at night, the beauty of my father's poetry, his jokes, the way he might, after a few wines, turn antic and comic and balance the wire from a champagne cork on his nose, his brilliance and intellectual courage, his brave iconoclasm, his optimism when he finished a book: *this* will work, *this* will succeed; the things he built and planned and created, his hopeful anxiety in the camping ground at Calais in the rain ('You'll get used to this. You'll love it, kids, I promise!'); his physical recklessness, his sensitivity, his kindness to animals, so kind he would even befriend possums in the bush at Karekare; his affection, his nicknames, his memory of himself as a boy, listening to the *huge rain* on the iron roof, the jokes, the novels and stories and poems, the games, what I would sometimes tell him when I was a child: *You are my favourite person in the world.*

I'd spent a long time thinking about family and place, place and family. When Paul's elderly mother Audrey died during the 2020 coronavirus pandemic, it so happened I'd just been asked by the *Sunday Star-Times* to write a very short story (maximum 600 words) imagining the end of New Zealand's level four lockdown.

Even though the space allowed was so tiny, it was an opportunity to write a tribute to Audrey, and I grabbed it:

AFTER LOCKDOWN

When George and Audrey talked about emigrating, he wanted to become a farmer. He'd signed up for the War underage and had been at the liberation of Changi. He'd travelled and got a taste for it, and while Audrey barely knew how to read a map and hadn't been anywhere, she trusted his ideas, so they left grim post-war Manchester and sailed to New Zealand.

After that George said, 'I'm never going home.'

They found work, and started exploring the country, venturing further until, one summer, they made their way to a rural settlement in the Far North. They kept going, past beaches and a marae, where the road came to a dead end. Here at the edge of Doubtless Bay was a small wooden house.

It was getting dark. Audrey was doubtful but George said, 'Look, the gate's open.'

He knocked and asked if they could camp on the land.

The house belonged to Biff (Pawhau) and Roma Rupapera, and that summer began a friendship that lasted the rest of their lives. They camped at the Rupaperas every holiday, until they could build a bach nearby.

George and Biff fished together. Audrey and Roma sat talking under the pōhutukawa at Whatuwhiwhi Beach. They called this 'putting the world to rights'.

Over the years the families grew close. The children all played together. Roma was a respected kuia, mother of nine; she and Audrey were both churchgoers, upright, community-minded. You would see them, under the tree beside Aunty Song's bach (a house no bigger than a large packing crate) airing their opinions on the world, Audrey solemn, her back straight, talking in her thick Mancunian accent, Roma grand and slyly humorous in her leopard-print hat.

When George died, the Rupaperas came to Auckland. Roma told Audrey, 'We've come to take George home.'

After his tangi on the marae, George was buried in the Māori graveyard on the hill at Whatuwhiwhi. From there you can watch the currents sweeping across the water, the gannets diving like missiles into the sea.

Audrey lived on in Auckland. She spent time with her devoted daughter Jane, with her grandchildren. She went faithfully to St Barnabas Church in Mt Eden. She knew all the church controversies, the scandals. Asked to comment she'd turn discreet, priestly. On rare occasions she'd cut loose, revealing a sense of humour so rich you marvelled at the self-control it must take to conceal it.

She started to struggle and grew frail. She passed out and was rescued by her neighbour. In hospital she said, 'See that bed over there? There's been a fire burning on it all day!' She moved to a rest-home.

Two days into the Level Four lockdown, Audrey had a turn. A doctor came. It was best, he said, that she stay where she was. It would not be long.

Level Four imposed its rules: one visitor at a time. Only fifteen minutes at a time. Only her children could visit. No grandchildren. No touching. Stay two metres away.

As she lay dying, first her son then her daughter spoke to her across the room. Her elder son, a paramedic, was in lockdown in the Far North. Her children couldn't gather at the bedside, couldn't meet after she died. There could be no last visit at the funeral parlour, no funeral.

There was only this promise: after lockdown.

After lockdown, she will be farewelled at St Barnabas. After lockdown she will travel North one last time, to join George on the hill at Whatuwhiwhi, in sight of Doubtless Bay. After lockdown the gate is open, and Audrey Grimshaw will go home.

Re-reading this short piece about Audrey, I wonder: is it sentimental to believe in the idea of family? Is 'family' a piety? Are we all just unconnected 'souls'? The memory I'd had, that could have been a recollection of existential terror — of the mind being alone — was it a glimpse of a world stripped of sheltering threads, where 'family' is relegated below the ego and the universe it creates? The threads are stories, about why we matter to each other, why love exists. They are our cover, our skin.

Without them we burn. Without them, everything burns us.

Leila and I were the daughters of two sisters, first cousins, girls together at Tolaga Bay and at Rotokauri. We were scruffy tomboys dressed in shorts and sneakers, at our happiest outside. We liked physical action: climbing trees, exploring, swimming, roaming around. We both had a problem with faces. I couldn't see a face in my mind's eye, even those of my family, and her grasp was so shaky she sometimes didn't recognise herself in the mirror.

She inflicted on me what her mother unloaded on her, tirades against ingratitude. Her mother said: 'You're so lucky. Imagine if you had Sarah's mother. Imagine if you had Jane's mother.' And Leila would think, '*If only . . .*'

As a teenager she took to burning herself with cigarettes, incurring her mother's wrath: she had embarrassed the family.

Leila's mother was famous for her warmth and tolerance, particularly towards young people. The family told Leila her experience of her mother's coldness wasn't real. There was no evidence of it. In fact, all evidence was to the contrary. She'd been a tremendous mother, a perfect mother, 100 per cent the best . . .

I took it all in, noted it down, I relished the detail and found it darkly funny, and knew I would make a story of it, even while I was crying with fear and writhing with nerves, even as I was *winding down the car window* in the morning and *winding it up* at night. I took it all down because I recognised Leila's silent language, as if I'd seen a familiar gesture in a mirror, or read her story in a book.

We both loved our mothers, and we wanted to be good. We jumped through hoops, went to the *n*th degree, *strove* to be good. We didn't know why one mother's enigmatic quality mirrored the other's. We didn't know why we'd disappointed them, or understand how we'd got them so wrong.

They never let us in on any secrets, never told us if they'd left part of themselves behind, in rural Omokoroa perhaps, where anything could have happened, where all was chaos and no one was in charge. Where they were sent despite pleading and protests and tears. Perhaps any darkness had to be pushed away, outside themselves. Perhaps their own effort to be good was so hard-fought there had to be one place in their lives, just one, where they put Omokoroa, fastened its darkness.

So my cousin and I grew up and performed a trick. We disappeared. I killed my old self and emerged completely new. I hid the old self for decades, secretly put it away, until everything fell apart. I started telling the story, and everything changed again.

But Leila's trick beat mine. Not surprisingly, she aced me. Leila walked right through the looking glass and into another world. Now, when she looks in the mirror she doesn't see a strange woman. He sees a strange man.

She didn't act until her mother had died. She waited, and then she embarked on her change. She had the surgeries, took the hormones, and slowly she was transformed.

'Who's that guy?' someone might ask. 'Have I met him before? How do I know that face?'

That guy — solid, rugged, bearded — is my cousin Leila. And now his name is Luke.

She walked through her reflection and disappeared; now he says, 'Leila's gone. I'm happier this way.'

Luke's brothers made a few objections at first. One said, 'Why do this? You're lovely as you are.'

But why would she believe him? That same brother had told Leila her experiences were *not real*.

Only connect. Amid the piles of articles on my desk I found this, on contingent mirroring: a mother mirrors a baby's emotions, showing understanding but stylising the imitation, exaggerating (oh no, you feel so sad, so hungry!) so the baby knows the mother is not feeling the emotion herself, but is conveying, through the pantomime, that she understands. In this way a baby learns her mind is understood by another mind, one separate from the baby's own. It's a lesson in separateness, and also connectedness. You are separate (the mother's experience is different) but you are safely connected, because you're understood.

But what if the mother doesn't do this? If she lacks the instinct, say, or perhaps in some abstract sense she wears a mask. What if she reflects a void at the child? Or what if she exactly mirrors the child, meeting rage with rage, fear with fear? The child never learns to be separate, and isn't sure its mind can connect. Is haunted by the threat of abandonment. Never learns to look in the mirror and see the solid outline of a self.

The ability to cause trauma in subtle and undramatic ways. The ability to shape or distort a self. The ability to create or do damage. This is the power of motherhood.

The human mind is highly resilient, though. It can withstand all sorts of problems and setbacks. The studies show this: in order not to cause damage you don't have to be a perfect parent, or even a good one. You just have to be *good enough*.

Luke looks in the mirror and sees a guy. He has made a new self. There's no going back to Leila, the ungrateful girl he left behind. Leila the girl, storming along the riverbank, running up from the lake. Leila with her death stares and her tellings-off and her tangle of curly hair. Leila is gone. When he looks in the mirror, does he catch a familiar gesture? Does he have a distant memory of her face?

I look in the mirror less and less. After my years on the outer, after arguments and disputes, all the questioning and all I left behind, my face is older. I even had to walk away from Marie Sanders. She was a woman I would have liked as a friend. But she finally did it, that consummate professional. Winter came, my story ran out and Sanders gave Scheherazade the axe.

But I'm happier, for all that — for so many reasons. This for example: even though I don't see her these days, I know what Marie Sanders looks like. My mind's eye has opened, and I can visualise her face.

He sat in our living room jigging his knee, making the wooden floor of the old cottage shake. Eugene's *Star* photos peeled off the wall and rained down around his head. For days afterwards we would be picking up drawing pins. We ate amid the comedy of the flying pears, and we discovered that we liked each other.

He was large, loud and popular. He drove an antique car, an enormous old Daimler with high seats and an ancient gear system. One night I was walking in the evening up Parnell Road when he drove past me, music blaring out of the open windows, the car crammed with people he'd gathered up for a night on the town. I watched it disappear over the hill, the music and voices and shouts of laughter fading.

Once he was getting changed in the carpark of a nightclub while I looked on, I can't remember why, perhaps there'd been a deluge of rain, and he stood shirtless and recited the whole of Portia's speech from *The Merchant of Venice*. 'The quality of mercy is not strained . . .'

He was benign, good-humoured, tough, clever, solid; he was formidable, and fun to be around. There was always an aura of comedy, but with a difference I had a craving for: it wasn't dark. It was sunny.

I left the law firm. I'd spent too much time glazed and staring out the window, too many days grappling with my disasters ever to regain the ground I'd lost. I didn't enjoy the view of the CML Building where I'd spent those terrifying nights (sometimes I'd catch sight of Sean on the roof terrace, moodily smoking a Marlboro), and I'd never warmed to commercial law.

I found a job with a criminal barrister and soon I was back to extreme violence: we were working on a murder trial. A woman who'd locked her husband out of the house after an argument had discovered him climbing in the kitchen window. She'd seized a knife and threatened him with it as he came in over the benchtop. Their luck was bad; the knife only penetrated half an inch, but it touched his heart and he died.

She'd been an orderly citizen and wife; I recall the judge describing her as 'house-proud'. In a moment, with one impulsive move, two lives (and the lives of the children) were blasted. The jury believed she hadn't meant to kill him. They convicted her of manslaughter.

She'd tried frantically to revive him as he lay on the kitchen floor.

Paul owned a flat in Owens Road in Epsom. There was one upstairs bedroom, a small sitting room and kitchen. It was down a long right-of-way, quiet and surrounded by trees, and there was a sunny fenced front garden.

I moved in with him, we were happy together, and at 5.12am on a morning in early summer, in the year after we'd met amid the comedy of the flying pears, our son Conrad was born.

After the birth everyone allowed some respectful hours to pass so I could recover, and at long last, when Karl finally walked into the hospital room to see his grandson for the first time, I said to him, 'Where's all the dancing and singing?'

My baby son was so lovely, I was so happy and elated, I felt there should have been a carnival in the streets.

That summer I left violent crime behind. I left shame and fear behind, too, buried with the old dead self. I sat out in the garden at Owens Road with Conrad in the pram beside me. He was a tranquil baby, a good sleeper, lively when awake, with a beautiful face and a smooth little head of white-blond hair.

It was warm in the square of sun, the trees were full of squabbling birds, a ginger cat stalked along the top of the fence. Through the gate the driveway curved away under the pōhutukawa trees to the road. It was bright and peaceful and safe, and I had begun my project, working my way through the classics.

I had a new idea, too: I was going to write a novel.

Afternoon at Owens Road. The sun has gone and we've moved inside; I've fed the baby and laid him in the cot in the bedroom so I can go and look for a book; now I'm standing on a chair reaching up to a top shelf. Stretching, I nearly overbalance. I find what I'm looking for, but I hear from upstairs a sharp, high-pitched wail, a cry so unusual it sends me jumping off the chair, dropping the book and flying up the stairs to the cot, where I lean over in alarm: what's gone wrong, why is he squalling that way?

He's wriggled free of his bedding, he has his hands up to his head and now I see, a button on his sleeve has caught in strands of his hair, a little clump that's got matted. His forehead is sweaty, his tiny fingers are white, his fists clenched. He's pulling his own hair and screaming.

I understand. I make faces, ham it up. Pulling your own hair, ouch, it hurts! Oh, my funny little boy! I pick him up, he stops crying straight away, as I lay my hand on his forehead. I find a soft brush, sit down on the bed and start to brush his hair.

It's late afternoon now and the sun is going down behind the trees. I can see myself reflected in the window, leaning over the small blond head, gently untangling the strands. Beyond us, the long shadows of the trees stretch away, and the volcanic cone of Maungawhau rises above the rooftops. We sit together in the warm silence as I smooth the baby's head, as the shadows lengthen and the lights come on in the wooden houses.

Soon Paul will ring. We will talk, I will tell him about our afternoon, and he will say, as he always did:

I'm coming home.

Charlotte Grimshaw
July 2020

WORKS CITED

'Spectacular Blossom' by Allen Curnow. First published by Mermaid Press, 1957.

'At Dog Point' by C.K. Stead, accessed online at http://www.poetlaureate.org.nz/2017/08/last-last-cks-signs-off-as-laureate.html.

'Quesada' from *C.K. Stead: Collected Poems*. Published by Auckland University Press, 2008.

'You' from *The Red Tram* by C.K. Stead. Published by Auckland University Press, 2004.

You Have A Lot To Lose: A Memoir, 1956–1986 by C.K. Stead. Published by Auckland University Press, 2020.

BY CHARLOTTE GRIMSHAW

The Bad Seed, published 2019, a compilation of *The Night Book* and *Soon*
Mazarine, published 2018
Starlight Peninsula, published 2015
Soon, published 2013
The Olive Grove, published 2013
The Night Book, published 2010
Singularity, published 2009
Opportunity, published 2007
Foreign City, published 2005
Guilt, published 2000
Provocation, published 1999

'Grimshaw's descriptions . . . are a joy.' — *Times Literary Supplement*

'She is a master with mystery, very contemporary and astute. Her language is relaxed, spare and perfect.' — Jane Campion, *The Guardian*

'There is no denying that Charlotte Grimshaw deserves her place amongst the top New Zealand writers of fiction. Her writing is sparse: words are not wasted. Characters are deftly penned and well-defined: each one can be imagined, liked or disliked. Settings are vividly described often in poetic imagery.'
—*The Reader*, Booksellers New Zealand

'Grimshaw's novels always deliver tension, intrigue, drama. Her stories are contemporary, usually vividly set in Auckland or thereabouts and packed with plot. Serious doesn't mean po-faced, though. The book bristles with life and is full of sensations, humour, rippling interchanges and sudden poetry.' — *NZ Listener*

'Reading Charlotte Grimshaw is always a huge delight, sinking as she does into a place of implication, indirectness and suggestions of the sinister.' — *Otago Daily Times*

'The other thrill of these books, and *Starlight Peninsula* in particular, is the craft of storytelling . . . some of the most thrilling and nail-biting reading I've done.' — Pip Adam, *Metro*

'This stunning novel not only brings an authentic conclusion to the knotted lives of its knotted characters, but also continues to provide the "star spangled Kiwi metropolis" slant Grimshaw brings to the epic contemporary serial. Whether Grimshaw is writing about Parnell or Mount Eden, her prose sparkles.'
— *Dominion Post Weekend* on *Starlight Peninsula*

'. . . people seeking a tightly plotted, incisive depiction of the corrosive effects of power will find time spent reading this novel well invested.'
— *Publishers Weekly* on *Soon*

'This is a truly riveting novel.' — *The Globe and Mail* on *Soon*

'Finally, there is the stunning achievement of *Soon* . . . Grimshaw brilliantly demonstrates how far the boundaries of the crime genre can now be expanded. On one level, *Soon* is an often satirical view of insider politics in a sister Commonwealth country. It is also an absorbing study in personal relationships . . . Crimes here are subtle — political, corporate and moral — but they fuel an accelerating crisis. And, suddenly, you realize you're enmeshed in an unconventional thriller that will carry you along to a smash climax.' — *The Vancouver Sun*

'I was left marvelling, not only at Grimshaw's ferocious talent, but at her gall, her audaciousness, her mischievous ability to play with a reader's expectations of fiction . . . This is an intensely readable, indeed engrossing, very filmic novel.' — *Landfall* on *Mazarine*